Own Your Story

Empower. Connect. Create Change.

Baltimore, MD

Own Your Story

Empower. Connect. Create Change.

EDITED BY:
Susan Freeman
Lesley Marlin
Jennifer Thibodaux

FOREWORD BY:
Eugina Jordan
Author of *Unlimited*

AUTHORS:
Cheryl Aufdemberge
Rebecca Baumgartner
Natalie A. Borneo
Michelle M. Bufano
Sara Burke
Tiffany Castagno
Gena Cox
Marcie Dickson
Jan Anne Dubin
Daphne Turpin Forbes
Susan E. Frankel
Anne Stark Gallagher
Alexis Gladstone
Lindsay Griffiths
Judy Hoberman
Homeira Izadi
Nori Jabba
April Joy
Drew Isserlis Kramer
Caroline Markel
Lesley Marlin
Serena Mastin
Sheila Murphy
Jenn Ocken
Sameena Safdar
Nita Sanger
Lauren A. Tetenbaum
Jennifer Thibodaux
Courtney Thomas
Jing Wang
Becky Whatley
Michelle Wimes

Ramses House Publishing LLC
Baltimore, MD

Freeman Means Business LLC
2552 Sunset Drive
Riverside, CA 92506
www.freemanmeansbusiness.com

Ordering Information: Special discounts are available on quantity purchases by corporations, associations, and others.

Book Layout ©2013 BookDesignTemplates.com
Cover image: Shutterstock

Own Your Story: Empower. Connect. Create Change./ Editors: Susan Freeman, Lesley Marlin, Jennifer Thibodaux -- 1st ed.
ISBN 979-8-9904289-0-4 print; 979-8-9904289-1-1 ePub

Published by Ramses House Publishing LLC, Baltimore, MD
www.publishingforlawyers.com
First Printing, 2024
Printed and Bound in the United States

Table of contents

About the Authors

Feel free to follow and connect with the authors on LinkedIn

CHERYL AUFDEMBERGE is a registered citizen of the Cherokee Nation and the founder and CEO of Big Red Tech Works, a digital marketing company. Cheryl has more than 15 years of experience in the digital and legal marketing fields where she utilizes her passion for social media and in helping clients grow their online presence. She is a Workhuman* Certified Professional with two associate degrees, a digital marketing certificate, and various professional certifications.

Cheryl has been a passionate committee member of the Freeman Means Business #EmpoweredWomen annual storytelling event since 2020. She is active in her professional association, the Legal Marketing Association (LMA), and has served in various local, regional, and international leadership roles. Recently, Cheryl served as Sponsorship Liaison for the 2023 LMA Midwest Conference. She is currently leading an LMA Midwest Learning Lab group, serves on the LMA International Well-Being Committee social media subgroup, and manages its online Resource Center.

Cheryl is serving as a member of the LMA Kansas City Steering Committee. She has been chosen as chair for the 2024 LMA Kansas City Steering Committee. Cheryl is based in the Kansas City, MO, metropolitan area. She can be reached via email at cheryl.aufdemberge@gmail.com.

REBECCA BAUMGARTNER brings almost 20 years of experience in leadership, operations, human resources (HR), and diversity, equity, inclusion, and belonging. From her role as a change agent to her ability to engage and develop team members, Rebecca works with businesses, leaders, and teams to leverage people resources to achieve business outcomes.

In her current role as Senior Vice President of People and Operations for a large nonprofit, Rebecca is responsible for leading overall human resources strategy including talent acquisition and retention, organizational design and cultural development, employee relations, strategic planning, and overall operations for the organization. Rebecca works across all departments and functions to build and manage an HR organization that reflects and supports the organization's dynamic needs. In previous roles, Rebecca led global human resources and diversity, equity, and inclusion initiatives and programs for AM Law 100 law firms.

Rebecca is a Certified Diversity Executive, ICF Certified Executive Coach, and a SHRM-certified Senior Human Resources Professional. She is a proud member of Chief, an invite-only network focused on connecting and supporting women executive Leaders and serves on the board of several nonprofit organizations. Most importantly, Rebecca is the mother of two amazing sons. She lives with her boys, her husband, and their dog, Charlie, in Kansas City, MO.

NATALIE A. BORNEO is a charismatic values-based leader, innovator and change agent who spends her workday collaborating with sponsors and experts to create workforce development opportunities for women across the globe. She serves her community and champions humanity focused causes as a member of nonprofit and service organizations, including The Long Island (NY) Chapter, The Links, Incorporated, The National Coalition of 100 Black Women, and a member at large on the board for the Girl Scouts of Nassau County. When she isn't working or serving in organizations, Natalie squawks for the Freeman Means Business Wonder Women in Business Podcast amplifying the stories of women and their journeys.

Natalie established her leadership training consultancy in 2022 NB Consulting, LLC, and teaches development workshops for women, students, and organizations. She is a certified John Maxwell Leadership Trainer, a scholar in Leading Change Management from E-Cornell, a graduate of the Institute for Nonprofit Practice's Core Leadership and Management Program and earned a certificate of completion for Managing Emotions in Times of Uncertainty and Stress from Yale Center for Emotional Intelligence University.

Natalie is a graduate of both Fordham and Howard Universities. She has two wonderful children and resides in West Hempstead, NY, with her husband, Henry.

MICHELLE M. BUFANO is the founder and CEO of Michelle Bufano Business Consulting, LLC, where she leverages her legal background to help female entrepreneurs navigate risk and thrive in business. She is also the founding partner of the Law Offices of Michelle M. Bufano, LLC, a small practice dedicated to providing legal services to female founders.

In addition to assisting women in fulfilling their entrepreneurial dreams, Michelle is the founder of and primary contributor to The Midpoint Blog, as well as a coach, author, professional speaker, and discussion facilitator through her company, MMB

Media, LLC d/b/a as HerPoint. Her first book, *Views from the Midpoint*, is expected to be released in early 2025.

SARA BURKE holds a master's degree in Urban Affairs and an undergraduate degree in English, Theatre and Dance from Saint Louis University. She has a minor in French.

Sara Burke was the founder of The City Studio Dance Center in St. Louis, MO, which she founded in 1986. Sara is a choreographer, dancer, dance instructor, photographer, painter, author, and arts diversity consultant. Sara consults for local dance companies and works with young dancers helping them start companies.

Sara relishes her role as "mentor." One of her most important and impactful accomplishments was to learn Dunham Technique from the legendary Katherine Dunham. She studied with Miss Dunham in East St. Louis in the 1970s and danced with the Dunham Company. Sara's experiences studying and dancing the Dunham Technique changed her life and she has been committed to promoting diversity through the Arts ever since. Her experience was life changing.

Combining the arts with her business has been a challenging and rewarding experience. Sara received both a Mayoral Proclamation and an Aldermanic Proclamation for her contributions to the life of the arts in the city of St. Louis. Sara additionally received the prestigious Links Award for her "Outstanding Leadership in Culture and Arts" for the betterment of St. Louis. Sara also received the 2012 Grand Center Visionary Award for outstanding arts professional. Sara received the rare and prestigious award from the Urban League of Saint Louis for her cultural and diversity leadership. She also received the prestigious Woman of Achievement Award.

Sara is a co-founder of "Calling All Dancers," a regional consortium of dancers and dance organizations designed to foster cooperation and support to enhance the visibility and viability of the local dance community. As an advisor to the "One River Mississippi Project," Sara was instrumental in including dancers from the East St. Louis dance community and including master teachers and dancers from the SIUE Katherine Dunham Performing Arts Training Center.

Her enthusiasm and passion extend to her commitment to diversity in the arts. Sara is chairwoman of the SIU East St. Louis Center for the Performing Arts Advisory Council, which is committed to preserving the legacy of Katherine Dunham. Sara was chair of the Diversity Initiative Committee for the Regional Arts Commission and was instrumental in the development of RAC's Diversity and Access Policy.

TIFFANY CASTAGNO is CEO and founder of CEPHR, LLC, a human resources consulting firm based in Pittsburgh, PA, that supports small to mid-sized businesses across the United States and across industries to build strong infrastructures, employer brands, and cultures. She is passionate about creating equitable workplaces and communities.

Tiffany's "Why" is supporting others to reach their top potential and she enjoys sharing her knowledge, heart, mind, and a conversation to make sure others don't feel excluded or have to struggle if she can share her time or resources to make it easier for them.

Tiffany is co-author of a children's book, *Can a Zebra Change Its Stripes?*, that teaches children about embracing difference and uncovers the importance of acceptance and what it means to make diversity our strength.

Tiffany was recently presented with a Jefferson Award for her volunteerism, leadership, and service to community.

GENA COX, founder of Feels Human, LLC, is an organizational psychologist, who works as an executive strategic advisor, coach, and speaker. As an executive coach, she helps high-performing leaders optimize their impact and influence as they move toward the C-suite or boardroom. As an advisor, she helps leaders build inclusive Respect2LeadTM organizations.

Gena is the author of *Leading Inclusion*, an award-winning guidebook that shows how to counter the typically disappointing outcomes from "diversity, equity, and inclusion" work. Her TEDx Talk, "Yes ... and Careers," encourages an exploratory approach to building a purposeful career.

Gena is a prominent voice on human-centered leadership, helping leaders see that "inclusion tops diversity" and must be powered by respect at the center. Her nuanced observations of workplace dynamics generate many memorable and actionable insights.

Gena's work has been featured widely, including Harvard Business Review, Fortune, Fast Company, Forbes, Business Insider, Market Watch/Barrons, Business Journals, BBC Worklife, Readers Digest, and The Telegraph (UK).

Gena is an angel investor. She is a member of How Women Lead's #GetonBoard Leadership Committee. Gena holds a Ph.D. in Industrial and Organizational (I-O) Psychology. She is a member of the American Psychological Association (APA) Committee for the Advancement of General Applied Psychology (CAGAP), the Society of Industrial and Organizational Psychology (SIOP), and the Society for Human Resources Management (SHRM). She is an International Coach Federation Professional Certified Coach.

Away from work, Gena and her family enjoy all the lifestyle benefits the sunny state of Florida offers.

MARCIE DICKSON is a respected voice on equity and belonging in alternative dispute resolution. She has served in several executive leadership positions at top alternative dispute resolution (ADR) firms, leading a wide range of strategic initiatives and playing a crucial role in developing prominent mediators and arbitrators nationwide.

During the COVID-19 pandemic, Marcie founded Alterity ADR, the country's first and largest national minority-owned ADR company. In its first couple years of operation, Alterity was voted the "Top ADR Firm in Georgia" and one of Pennsylvania's Top Three ADR providers.

Marcie frequently presents on conflict resolution, negotiation, leadership, and implicit bias, and she has been quoted and published in several national publications, including *Bloomberg Law*, *Forbes*, *The American Lawyer*, Law360, and the American Bar Association. Marcie serves on the board of directors of the Institute for Well Being in Law, as a board member of a theatre company in Georgia, as vice-chair of Diversity for the American Bar Association's Tort Trial & Insurance Practice Committee, an editorial advisory council member of *Southern Lawyer* and *Harvard Business Review*, and a steering committee member of several legal and business organizations. She was recently recognized as one of "50 Women to Watch" by *Corporate Counsel Business Journal.*

JAN ANNE DUBIN is an award-winning consultant with nearly 40 years of experience leading, innovating, and serving as a change agent. She is a legal industry thought leader, board member and speaker; client service, business development, and marketing leader and innovator; executive coach; connector; and diversity champion and ally. She serves as CEO and founder of Jan Anne Dubin Consulting, celebrating nearly 15 years of delivering value and results to clients by focusing on client service, business development and strategic communications.

As an executive coach, Jan provides guidance and counsel to organizations and high-potential individuals.

Jan was the first North American business development director for Baker and McKenzie, LLP, and served as director of Client Relations for DLA Piper US, LLP and its legacy firms, where she held various senior leadership roles.

Jan received StreetWise, Inc.'s award for being a "2019 Inspiring Chicagoan" and was recognized by *Chicago Business Journal* as one of its 2018 Women of Influence. She was inducted in 2017 as a Fellow into the College of Law Practice Management (COLPM); and in 2016 into the Legal Marketing Association Midwest Chapter's Hall of Fame.

Jan has been recognized by *Today's Chicago Woman* magazine as one of "100 Women Making a Difference" and received the Anti-Defamation League's Distinguished Community Leadership Award.

In 1994, Jan was recruited by former First Lady Michelle Obama (then executive director of Public Allies Chicago) to join its board of directors. She then became its board chair and serves on the emeritus board. Today, Jan serves on the i.c.stars Chicago board and Streetwise advisory board.

A strategic business partner to the Association of Corporate Counsel and the Thomson Reuters Legal Executive Institute, Jan is a 1994 MBA graduate of the University of Chicago, Booth School of Business; she also holds a B.S. degree from the University of Kansas, William Allen White School of Journalism.

DAPHNE TURPIN FORBES, assistant general counsel and managing attorney, is a trusted legal and business advisor at Microsoft with 20+ years of practice in the U.S. public sector and commercial regulated industries. Her corporate experience spans in-house at companies like Microsoft, Discovery Communications, ACS State and Local Solutions (formerly Lockheed Martin IMS), Hyatt Hotels, and General Motors.

Daphne is lead counsel and managing attorney responsible for supporting Microsoft's Health and Life Sciences and Public Sector businesses (HPSI)—an $11.8B enterprise operating unit composed of three business segments of Microsoft's U.S. Industries (State and Local Government, Education, and Health and Life Sciences)—advising clients on various legal matters, including complex technology and professional services transactions, legal, compliance and regulatory issues, data privacy and security matters, critical infrastructure considerations, government and enterprise cloud, Artificial Intelligence (AI), public sector contracts/procurement law and ethics, public policy considerations, matters raised by U.S. Attorneys General, and health and life sciences regulations. Prior to her role in HPSI, she also supported the company's financial services and federal government business verticals.

Daphne is a diversity, equity, and inclusion (DEI) champion and has served on various nonprofit boards and advisory councils nationally and in the Washington, D.C., metropolitan area. Daphne recently served as chairwoman and county commissioner of the Liquor Board in Prince George's County, MD. She also has served as an adjunct law professor at Howard University School of Law where she co-instructed a class on Technology and Law.

Daphne is a member of the Maryland State Bar and National Bar Associations and is the corporate recipient of the Microsoft MVP Circle of Excellence (Gold Club) Award, the National Bar Association's Clyde E. Bailey Corporate Leadership Award, and is the 2020 recipient of Michigan State University's Distinguished Alumni Award. She is a graduate of Michigan State University, and the American University Washington College of Law. Daphne lives in Prince George's County, MD, with her husband and their two young adult children.

SUSAN E. FRANKEL is a healthcare attorney with over 25 years' experience in law and management. Her legal career has encompassed healthcare transactional and regulatory law and litigation at renowned law firms in New York and New Jersey, as well as in-house counsel for a large New York hospital system and a multi-state medical practice. She also spent nearly a decade as director of operations of a large New York City law firm.

Susan earned her law degree from the University of Pennsylvania Law School, and returned to law school 20 years later to earn her Masters of Law in Health Law. She proudly sat for and passed her second bar exam at the age of 48 alongside students half her age.

Susan is passionate about supporting and empowering women both professionally and personally, particularly those in midlife confronting the inevitable changes in their physical and mental well-being. She is honored to be a speaker and author about her menopause journey, with the hope of educating women and men alike and encouraging those who see themselves in her story to seek out help.

Susan is the mother of two beautiful, strong, young women whose bright futures inspire her mission and mantra of women supporting women. She is the founder of the law firm, Empower Healthcare and Legal Solutions, which proudly embodies this principle.

ANNE STARK GALLAGHER is a writer, actor, and communications professional. She is the executive director of the Luxury Law Alliance and an editorial team member of its parent company, Global City Media, publisher of *The Global Legal Post*. She has spent her career consulting, writing, training, and creating strategies for business and legal organizations and their professionals.

As a SAG-AFTRA actress, she has appeared in film and commercials, narrated countless voice-overs including the audio book, *Her Name Shall Remain Unforgotten*, the story of a holocaust survivor whose mother was murdered at Auschwitz.

Anne's debut book, *Two Weeks to $10 Million: A Memoir of Financial Infidelity, Fraud and Redemption*, tells the story of how her marriage to a charismatic con man devolved into a true crime story rife with forged loans, mob hits, federal indictments, and a criminal trial. For many years, she wrote "Anne on Fire," a blog about an early childhood burn accident victim and her search for the truth of what happened.

A native of Green Bay, WI, she received journalism and law degrees from the University of Wisconsin–Madison. Based in Chicago, Anne enjoys spending time with her two adult children and is an avid tennis player, constantly seeking to perfect her game. Visit www.annegallagher.com for more information.

ALEXIS GLADSTONE is a two-time breast cancer "thriver" and the founder of Intelead, a Chicago-based consulting practice dedicated to aligning people strategies and business results. She designs strategies and programs to help clients develop current and next-generation leaders and drive organizational change that delivers results.

Alexis is passionate about gender equity, empowering women, and helping them succeed. She is a sought-after voice, trainer, and executive coach on women and leadership, sales, and helping clients attract and develop female talent.

Her approach to leadership development incorporates her belief that everyone combines personal and professional strengths on their road to success. One skill she thinks is paramount to anyone's success is building relationships. It's about building our network and communities so that we have the support in place before we need it. Combining who we are as a person with our skills and expertise in our work is a win-win combination. Alexis helps individuals bridge this gap using resources that build confidence and trust.

Alexis has spoken to, trained, and coached thousands of individuals in public and private companies, higher education, and not-for-profit organizations. These clients are in financial and legal services, hospital/medical, and manufacturing industries. Internationally, she has spoken and trained at several organizations in Melbourne, Australia, for business and government leaders in Harbin, China, and corporate leaders in the United Kingdom. She is a frequent podcast guest around the globe, talking about all things' leadership.

LINDSAY GRIFFITHS, the executive director of the International Lawyers Network (ILN), is more than just a seasoned professional. Outside her demanding role, Lindsay leads a diverse and enriching life.

A dedicated runner, she's completed four marathons, a testament to her resilience and determination. At home, Lindsay shares her life with two loyal canine companions, adding warmth to her daily routine. Her role as an aunt is cherished, providing her with joy and precious family moments.

Lindsay's creative side shines through her passion for photography, capturing the world's beauty through her lens. She's also an avid reader, constantly exploring new horizons through books. With an extensive travel history covering over 40 countries, Lindsay's global experiences enrich her work at ILN. As executive director, she skillfully manages the ILN's international programs, fosters a global community, and expands the network's membership base with her strategic acumen and project management skills.

Lindsay's professional achievements, including "Thought Leader of the Year" recognition from the Legal Marketing Association, highlight her commitment to excellence. Her unique perspective, influenced by her diverse interests and experiences, makes her a dynamic force in her professional life and beyond.

JUDY HOBERMAN is president of Selling In A Skirt, a company focused on empowering professional women. She is an award-winning international speaker, best-selling author, trainer, and leading authority on women in leadership and sales. With over three decades in business, she combines wisdom and humor with her behavior-shaping strategies and is often described as "transformational."

Judy is a TEDx speaker, as well as the author of four books, including *Selling in a Skirt* and *Walking on the Glass Floor.* She was named one of 14 "Sales Pros Building Trust" from LinkedIn, Coach of the Year from Powerful Professionals, and was selected as one of the 10 "Inspirational, Accomplished and Engaging Women of Tarrant County" 2023.

Judy's mission is ... to help one woman a day by following an important philosophy—"Women Want To Be Treated Equally ... Not Identically®."

HOMEIRA IZADI is a quadruple board-certified medical doctor with over 25 years' experience in variety of settings from top medical centers where she had the most advanced technology to the war zones where her stethoscope was her only tool. She is board certified from American Academy of Anti-Aging and Regenerative Medicine, American Board of Integrative Medicine (American Board of Physician Specialties), American Board of Pediatrics (American Board of Physician Specialties), American Board of Holistic Integrative Medicine, as well as multiple certifications from Age Management Medical Group, Stanford

University (in Genetics and Genomics), Harvard Medical School: HMX Fundamentals, certificate of completion (autoimmune disorders). She has worked in the hospital setting for over 25 years before joining Cenegenics in San Francisco.

Homeira has her medical practice in San Ramon and Los Altos, CA. She was divorced in 2008 and has twins, one boy and one girl, both in college. She spends her free time learning about new developments in the field of medicine, and traveling is her hobby to explore other cultures and learn from experts from all around the world.

NORI JABBA's career spans 30 years in corporate real estate, community development, and affordable housing. In 2012, she started consulting to have more flexibility and time with her family. After several successful years and when her kids were grown, she decided to look for employed work again. Unexpectedly, she realized she'd lost her seat at the table when no one would hire her, despite relevant experience, a master's degree, credentials, and several awards, including "Businesswoman of the Year" from the Chamber of Commerce.

After multiple disappointments, Nori abandoned her job search and began a quest to better understand why job hunting was so challenging for middle-aged women. What she learned was eye-opening—and too valuable not to share. Through her journey, she gained her seat back at the table, landing the job she was looking for in her field, and launching a new chapter in her life as a writer, professional speaker, and mentor.

In *Keeping Your Seat at the Table*, Nori shares her eight-step journey of growth and transformation. Is ageism real? Yes. Was

there something she needed to do differently? Yes. Did it work?
Yes.

Nori now works for a Bay Area city managing housing programs. She is the mother of three adult daughters and a rescued
Doberman, "Nessa." Her passions are writing, walking her dog
while escaping into a great audiobook or podcast, and empowering women.

APRIL JOY, also known as the Woman on Fire, is an entrepreneur, public speaker, author, and professional coach who helps
women stand in their authentic power and live their purpose.
April spent 10 years in the advertising industry developing pro-
motional marketing programs for blue chip companies like General Mills, Pepsi Co., and Jergens and works today protecting and
empowering business owners and their employees with best of
class legal and identity theft services with Ladies of Justice by
LegalShield.

Through her work with Ladies of Justice, April found her passion in public speaking and began the April Joy Empowerment
Group. She believes in living out loud and if someone can't handle
it, feel free to pass them a set of ear plugs.

April is the author of the book, *Woman On Fire: 12 Ways to
Harness Boldness, Authentic Power and Stand in Your Truth*,
and is a sought-after speaker on stages all across the country.

April is a plant-based enthusiast, a Toastmasters International Public Speaking Champion, loves traveling, all things red
wine, reading autobiographies and most enjoys teaching women
how to share their stories to create freedom and liberation for
themselves and others.

DREW ISSERLIS KRAMER, lawyer turned ad woman turned boy mom turned artist and writer, is a cat with nine lives. With a master's in Transformation, she is writing her own script. Her art and writing focus on food, families, and faith.

She is the founder of Lady & the Floofs, a cross-platform story that encourages Floofs of all ages to try things. The Lady, a quirky and bohemian British caretaker of Floofs, encourages bravery to discover this sometimes scary, wonderful world. With a particular emphasis on food, The Lady addresses mealtime tension between grown-ups and Floofs. In print, in-person, and online, her story time and food play experiments create openness through fun.

Her illustrated songbook, *It's Hard to be a Baby*, is a babies' lament that calls for compassion for Floofs as they embark on the difficult journey of growing up. Sharing her own path from fearful Floof to bold Lady, the book encourages trial through joy and empathy.

Drew began her career in creative digital agencies like Edelman and Vice Media. There, she helped major corporations like Target and Unilever create conversion and community through content. She took risks, moving into roles at the intersection of technology and media to think about how big corporations evolve their businesses from the physical to digital world. Today, she continues to push the boundaries of storytelling from live scene to screen to page.

CAROLINE MARKEL is a trauma-informed coach, three-time international best-selling author, and one of the "20 Most Inspiring Leaders of 2022." Caroline's depth of leadership skills with billion-dollar brands in Fortune 500 companies empowers her team, individuals, families, and communities to achieve substantive improvement in their wellbeing, synchronizing solutions which disrupt complacency to create real change.

Caroline's campaigns and targeted training create robust initiatives with over one billion impressions and opportunities for immediate and actionable solutions; receiving numerous awards, including two Manny Awards.

As a survivor of domestic violence, plus revival from a death experience, Caroline uses storytelling to eliminate disparities for historically excluded communities, being featured on Oprah, Forbes, PBS, NPR, *Ms. Magazine*, *Newsweek*, television, radio, and podcasts.

LESLEY MARLIN is a senior in-house attorney (associate general counsel) with a specialty in labor and employment law. She speaks frequently on various workplace issues, including labor and employment law topics, psychological safety, diversity and inclusion, resilience, and career development. Lesley serves on the Advisory Board for Women, Influence and Power in Law (WIPL). She is also a certified Wayfinder Coach.

Lesley's in-house experience includes work at a nonprofit self-regulatory organization in the financial services industry, a Fortune 100 company in the aerospace and defense industry, and an information technology services company that was a subsidiary of a Fortune 100 aerospace and defense industry company.

Prior to her in-house roles, Lesley worked in private legal practice at an AmLaw 100 firm and served as a law clerk to a U.S. District Judge in the Eastern District of Virginia.

Beyond her professional work, Lesley gives back to her communities. She has served on the board of directors of the Wendt

Center for Loss and Healing for many years and is currently the board president. She also helps women in her network, often connecting them to each other.

Lesley is a "Double Hoo," having received her juris doctor and her Bachelor of Arts (with high distinction) from the University of Virginia. While at the University of Virginia, she received the honor of living on the lawn and also served as the president of the Raven Society.

Lesley lives outside of Washington, D.C., with her husband and three sons (two of which are twins). She loves spending time with her family and friends and cheering on her children in their activities. She is an avid runner, and she also enjoys traveling, cooking, gardening, doing puzzles, and spending time at the spa. Connect with Lesley at https://www.linkedin.com/in/lesley-marlin/ or www.lesleymarlin.com.

SERENA MASTIN's journey is a testament to the indomitable human spirit, serving as a beacon of hope for those grappling with self-limiting beliefs. Her life began in the shadow of witness protection and unfolded in the tumultuous landscape of foster care, where she navigated the treacherous waters of nine different homes. The challenges she faced led her down a path of teenage addiction and homelessness, culminating in the heart-wrenching tragedy of her husband's suicide. Despite these harrowing trials, Serena's story is one of triumphant ascent.

What truly sets Serena apart is her unwavering strength, resilience, and authenticity. Her career spanning over two decades in the corporate world is a testament to her unyielding determination. She weathered setbacks, repeatedly climbing back to executive leadership roles within Fortune 500 companies.

In 2013, Serena boldly carved her own path by founding Pulse Marketing, Inc., a venture that has since flourished into an award-winning marketing and advertising agency. Serena's agency excels in creating content that forges meaningful connections between people and brands, utilizing purposeful graphics, thought-provoking web designs, and heart-touching advertising campaigns.

Beyond her entrepreneurial acumen, Serena has penned her compelling life story in a memoir titled *Exposed: You Can't Heal When You Hide*. In this raw narrative, she delves into her experiences with assault, addiction, homelessness, infidelity, mental health challenges, and, ultimately, profound healing. Her memoir is a powerful testament to the human capacity for resilience and growth.

Serena's story resonates deeply with audiences, offering a thought-provoking reminder that challenges can be confronted with passion and purpose. She has dedicated her life to personally and professionally empowering others, demonstrating that self-limiting beliefs can be shattered and replaced with unwavering self-compassion. Serena's journey is a living testament to the power of the human spirit and inspires all who encounter it.

SHEILA MURPHY is CEO of Focus Forward Consulting and chief learning officer of WOMN, both of which help lawyers, leaders, and legal organizations achieve their career and business goals. After 20 years of litigating, developing, and coaching talent in corporate America and law firms, Sheila helps others reach their full potential.

In 2018, Sheila retired as senior vice president and associate general counsel at MetLife. As a well-respected thought leader,

Sheila was an executive sponsor to the U.S. Women's Business Network, served as a member of the U.S. task force on diversity, and co-chaired the Legal Affairs Academy, providing developmental opportunities to professionals worldwide. Previously, Sheila was at the law firm of Thacher Proffitt and Wood.

Sheila has served on the board of directors of the National Association of Women Lawyers (NAWL), Read Alliance, and PowerPlay. Sheila serves on the advisory board of Transforming Women's Leadership in Law. She co-chairs CARE's Women's Network of New York, which works on eradicating poverty through empowering women and girls.

Sheila received the "Women, Influence, Power in Law, Lifetime Achievement" Award for her commitment to advancing and empowering women. Women's Venture Fund awarded Sheila the Highest Leaf Award for her commitment to helping others. She was named a "Most Influential Irish Woman" by the Irish Voice, a "Leading Women Lawyer in NYC" by Crain's New York, a "Business 100" honoree by Irish America, and one of 250 "Inspiring Women Entrepreneurs."

Sheila received the "Benchmark Litigation In-House" Award at the Americas Women in Business Awards, NAWL's "Virginia S. Mueller Outstanding Member" Award, and a "First Chair" Award for significant professional contributions.

Sheila graduated from the University of Pennsylvania Law School and Binghamton University's School of Management, where she graduated magna cum laude. Sheila earned her associate certified coach and certified professional co-active coach designations from the International Coaching Federation and the Co-Active Leadership Institute, respectively.

Sheila frequently speaks on talent, career and business development, leadership and diversity, equity, and inclusion.

JENN OCKEN is a creative powerhouse with a lens in one hand and a journal in the other. With over two decades of experience as a photographer, she's not just capturing moments, she creates visual stories.

For Jenn, yes, it's about the moments, but also turning chaos into clarity. With her keen problem-solving skills armed with a graphic arts management degree, she ventured into the world of business early on. Her blend of creativity and entrepreneurial spirit soon had her thriving as a professional photographer, even though she never formally studied photography. Talk about unconventional success!

Jenn's story took an inspiring twist when she launched her consulting firm, specializing in creative business practices. Drawing from her own experiences, she began guiding others on their path to success. That's when her love for journaling and strategic planning merged as the ThrivFOCUS Journal.

With the ThrivFOCUS Journal, Jenn is on a mission to help individuals harmonize their goals, actions, and responsibilities. It's not just a journal; it's a transformative companion that empowers you to live a balanced life on your terms.

But Jenn's journey isn't just about business; it's about giving back. In 2020, when the world was grappling with the pandemic, she pioneered The Front Porch Project. Gathering 40+ photographers, they documented 4,000 portraits in just three months, injecting $1.2 million back into their local economy. It was a testament to collective community action.

As the host of the ThrivTALK podcast, Jenn continues to inspire with her interviews and insights and is also a three-time published author.

In Jenn's world, chaos is an opportunity waiting to be seized. Whether she's behind the camera, consulting with creatives, or cultivating projects, Jenn Ocken is proof that with focus and determination, you can turn visions into reality.

SAMEENA SAFDAR is a personal branding and digital media strategist. A former practicing lawyer and federal clerk, Sameena spent years in legal technology sales and marketing before founding Amplify Your Voice LLC in 2021 to help companies and individuals find and share their voices in the world.

Sameena helps clients overcome their imposter syndrome to intentionally and authentically share their personal brands with others. She believes you cannot enjoy professional success without a life incorporating a healthy well-being and living authentically. She coaches lawyers, legal professionals, and others on how to use social media to authentically share their brands to boost visibility, drive business development, and enjoy the well-being of living authentically.

Sameena writes and speaks nationally on personal branding, social media, legal technology, diversity, equity, and inclusion. She also serves on the advisory boards of The Blue and Black Partnership, Justice Technology Association, and Citi Arbitration. She has served as a co-chair of the Women's Bar Association of the District of Columbia since 2019.

Additionally, Sameena raises teens in Washington, D.C., taking advantage of all the museums, festivals, national parks, theatres, and restaurants the city offers, and spends far too much time on LinkedIn, Instagram, and X (f/k/a Twitter).

NITA SANGER is a transformational C-Suite executive with expertise in working with investors (VC and PE) and fast-growing companies, and complex global businesses in professional, financial, legal, and business services to guide them on their growth strategy (organic and inorganic), go-to-market approach, post-acquisition integration, and to transform business processes and operations for sustained revenue growth or a liquidity event. She is currently the CEO of Idea Innovate Consulting.

Nita's experience includes working as a director with a mid-market professional services firm driving business strategy and digital transformation, as the head of global innovation of a legal services provider, a director in a Big Four consulting firm focused on strategy, innovation, and operations transformation, and a partner in a boutique strategy consulting firm.

LAUREN A. TETENBAUM is a therapist, advocate, and writer whose mission is to build community and connection, particularly among and on behalf of women.

A licensed social worker since 2011, Lauren spent a decade in the legal industry supporting individuals facing various life transitions, including new parents and immigrants. A first-generation American herself, Lauren practiced immigration law at top global firms in the United Kingdom and United States before transitioning to roles managing professional development and pro bono programs.

Lauren currently uses her experience, empathy, and emotional intelligence to empower young adults, millennials, parents, and professionals via support groups, coaching, and counseling. She is a proud parent of two children (born in 2016 and 2018) and resides outside her native New York City.

Lauren is actively involved in numerous efforts benefitting at-risk women and families in her area and abroad. She is regularly featured on women's issues media platforms and writes for magazines and other publications, including as a contributing author to the book, *Women in Law: Discovering the True Meaning of Success* on Amazon. Lauren has led workshops and psychoeducational panels for a wide range of businesses, law firms, nonprofits, and professional associations.

Lauren holds a bachelor's degree (magna cum laude) from the University of Pennsylvania, a Master of Social Work from New York University, and a juris doctor from the Cardozo School of Law. She received advanced training in maternal mental health from the Seleni Institute and Postpartum Support International and studied "Motherhood and Work" at Stanford and "Women in Leadership" at Yale.

Lauren is certified in the Fair Play method, a system designed to alleviate the maternal mental load. She trains executives and other mental health professionals in topics including gender equity in the home and women in the workplace. Learn more about Lauren at www.TheCounseLaur.com.

JENNIFER MARINO THIBODAUX is a keynote speaker, writer, podcast host, frequent podcast guest, and attorney. She is the founder of JMT Speaks, LLC and a senior specialist editor at Thomson Reuters Practical Law.

As a professional speaker and writer, Jennifer uses the power of storytelling to share the lessons she has learned throughout her career, from identifying and embracing your authentic self, setting boundaries and saying no, avoiding burnout while staying productive, quieting the imposter voice and amplifying authenticity, and communicating effectively.

Passionate about empowering other women, Jennifer co-chairs the Programming Committee for Women@Thomson Reuters in the New York area, is the co-editor of the *Women Lawyers Journal* for the National Association of Women Lawyers and is on the executive board of the Women's Leadership Committee at Seton Hall University School of Law. She is a proud member of the Freeman Means Business #EmpoweredWomen community, including serving on the event, anthology, and book club committees.

Jennifer is also a trustee of Partners, a nonprofit dedicated to providing pro bono legal services to low-income survivors of domestic and sexual violence. She was previously a partner at the law firm of Gibbons P.C. in Newark, NJ, where she practiced for 11 years.

Jennifer graduated Seton Hall University School of Law, magna cum laude and Order of the Coif, and Bucknell University, cum laude. She has served as an adjunct professor of Appellate Advocacy at Seton Hall Law.

A lifelong New Jersey resident, you can often find Jennifer out for pizza, a hike, or some other adventure with her husband and son.

COURTNEY THOMAS is a strategically wired visionary, complex problem solver, public speaker, and people motivator. Her entrepreneurial approach and leveraging innovation to grow both business and people have been the key ingredients to her successful career in business turnarounds. Courtney has transformed the customer + staff experience, delivered award-winning marketing campaigns, and unlocked new revenue opportunities for four Kansas City, MO, organizations.

Courtney is a native of North Carolina. In 2002, she moved to Kansas City to join the executive leadership team at Wayside Waifs.

Following her successful eight-year tenure as COO at Wayside Waifs, Courtney led the merger of two Kansas nonprofits to form Great Plains SPCA (Society for the Prevention of Cruelty to Animals), the country's first bi-state animal welfare campus. As president and CEO, she grew the budget by 290% and mission impact by 350% during her six-year tenure.

In February of 2017, Courtney took the helm at Central Exchange, a leadership development organization, delivering a revitalization campaign that shifted losses of ($539K) to $75K net income in 22 months. She also led the annual conference with over 1,200 attendees, interviewing national names such as Daniel Pink, Maureen Chiquet, Elizabeth Smart, Carla Harris, and others.

In December 2019, Courtney joined the team of Newhouse, Kansas City's first domestic violence shelter. Amid a global pandemic, she led the cultural, physical, and financial transformation of the agency and has grown the budget from $2.3M to $6.1M.

Courtney is also the founder and CEO of Thrive 360, a growth acceleration practice. She's a proud wife of 18 years, the mom of three children, and serves on the board of directors for the Big Shifts Foundation, InnovateHER KC, First Interstate Bank, and the Global Diversity and Inclusion Council for the YMCA.

Courtney is a Silver Stevie Award winner, and in 2023, she was named to the "Top 50 Women Leaders" in Missouri.

JING WANG is born and raised in Shanghai, China. She was academically trained to be a journalist in the best journalism school in China: Fudan University. Jing started her career with China National Radio as a reporter focusing on economics.

After a short period of the real journalist life, Jing decided to pivot her career toward data-driven decision-making and joined Ipsos Marketing Research Company, focusing on qualitative and quantitative consumer research. The consumer insights experience opened eyes for Jing to the consumer packaged goods (CPG) industry. She worked for L'Oreal and Johnson & Johnson Pharmaceuticals and on many iconic brands including la Roche Posay, Vichy, and Tylenol.

Following her middle school sweetheart to the United States in 2012, Jing completed her MBA degree from the George Washington University and joined Mars, Inc. through the Graduate Leadership Development Program in 2014. Jing has worked for different Mars business units in the past 10 years, including brand manager for Uncle Ben's Rice, finance manager for Mars Chocolate North America, marketing manager for My M&M's, and strategy deployment head for Mars Retail Group.

Jing currently serves as the activity management director for the Mars Snacking Business, overseeing strategic initiatives in the areas of regulatory, sustainability, value leadership, and freedom-to-operate.

Outside of work, Jing loves photography, cooking, and recently gardening. Jing and her husband, Yikang, have a beautiful 7-year-old daughter, Meliora, and reside in West Orange, NJ.

BECKY WHATLEY is a marketing and public relations professional in Southern California. After graduating high school, she joined her father in starting a franchise printing company and spent more than 30 years engrossed in print, Adobe products, and Apple computers. She still owns and manages the company, as well as her boutique PR firm, Whatley Strategies. Today, in addition to print and design, she supports her clients with community outreach, government advocacy, and social media campaigns.

Becky graduated from Cal State University, San Bernardino, with a bachelor's degree in both English and Philosophy, and later a master's degree in Public Administration. She loves both reading and writing and was a contributor to publications for the National Association of Quick Printers and the Business Press. She was previously featured in *Connections: The New Currency* (2011).

Becky's perceptual style is VISION, which leads her to perceive the world as a place of infinite possibilities, full of options and opportunities, that build toward her vision of the future. She maintains an optimistic perspective that a solution will be found, and confidence that if one is not, there are always other alternatives to explore. Becky lives, works, and plays in Riverside, CA.

MICHELLE WIMES is the inaugural chief equity and inclusion officer at Children's Mercy Hospital in Kansas City, MO. She is a strategic leader and former practicing attorney who has developed paradigm-shifting professional development, health equity, and diversity programming in both the legal and healthcare settings.

She is a nationally renowned presenter and author and has received numerous awards for her many professional contributions.

She was recognized by Becker's Healthcare as one of the "Top Chief Diversity Officers in Healthcare to Know" in 2023 and her alma mater, Tulane Law School, also presented her with its inaugural Deans Kramer and Clayton Award for Leadership in Equity, Diversity, and Inclusion in 2023.

Additionally, Missouri Lawyer Media honored her with their inaugural award recognizing 20 state-wide individuals and organizations "for significantly advancing diversity, inclusion and dignity of all people in Missouri's legal profession."

Michelle's life has been a series of defying expectations. She has marched to the beat of her own drum for as long as she can remember, carving her own path when there was no blueprint for girls who looked like her. With each risk taken, she's grown stronger and stronger, and now those risks have changed the trajectory of her life. The secret to her success has been to carefully tend to her mindset, maintaining positivity in the face of setbacks; to own her own power; and to surround herself with an empowering village who lifts her as she seeks to lift others.

Michelle is a mom of three beautiful daughters, a wife, a daughter, a sister, and a friend, but most importantly she is a fearless champion of social justice, a global citizen, a seeker of light and inspiration, and a connector who strives to empower women by living an empowered life of abundance.

A Tribute

by Susan Freeman

DEAR SHEROS,

I write this letter as a tribute to your courage, a celebration of your strength, and a testament to the power of your voices. Each of you has embarked on a journey that many would find daunting, navigating through the complexities of life with a resilience that inspires awe. You have opened the doors to your inner worlds, sharing your stories with a raw honesty that moves the heart and stirs the soul.

To each of you who dared to lay bare your triumphs and trials, know that your bravery does not go unnoticed. Your tales are not just narratives; they are beacons of hope for others walking similar paths, searching for light in the darkness. You have shown that even in the midst of adversity, there is a strength that can be forged, a resilience that can be built, and a voice that refuses to be silenced.

Your stories are a mosaic of the human experience, reflecting the beauty and pain, the joy and sorrow, the defeat and victory that life entails. Through your words, you have painted pictures

of perseverance, of defiance against the odds, and of the indomitable spirit that defines the essence of being a woman.

To you, the valiant women who shared your hero journeys,
know that you have not only contributed to this book; you have
contributed to the fabric of humanity. You have offered solace to
those who felt alone in their struggles, you have provided
strength to those who needed it most, and you have ignited a
flame of empowerment that will burn brightly for generations to
come.

May you always remember the impact of your bravery. Your
stories are not just chapters in a book; they are landmarks of
courage, etched into the hearts of those who read them. You have
inspired change, fostered understanding, and paved the way for a
world where the voices of women are heard, honored, and celebrated.

Thank you for your bravery. Thank you for your vulnerability.
Thank you for your contribution to a legacy of strength and resilience. May you continue to inspire, to thrive, and to shine your
light upon the world.

And to you, the reader, I hope you take from these stories permission to be brave and bold as you take each day one day at a
time.

With deepest admiration and gratitude,
Susan

Our Stories Light Fires; They Break Molds

by Eugina Jordan

IN JANUARY OF 2021, right in the middle of the COVID-19 pandemic, I took a virtual personal storytelling class. At the end of the four-month program, all the students were supposed to do a TED-style virtual performance telling our stories on camera in front of live audiences.

Seemed like a good idea at the time, right?
Little did I know it was about to flip my world upside down.

For the first six weeks, I worked tirelessly with the coach to write "my story," which I proudly called "From Russia to the American C-suite." I am a well-known telecom CMO, I started a new market category, I have 12 patents, I have written over 100 articles in the industry, and I even penned an award-winning leadership book.

Sounds pretty epic, right?

But even after the 10th draft, my "story" felt fake and off, very off. I was at a loss. Then I emailed a draft to a trusted friend of 12 years, and she called me and explained that the very reason it felt fake was that all I was showing was the "triumph" and not "how" I got to it.

So here's what I was keeping under wraps: I grew up dirt-poor in communist Russia. I endured six years of hell in an abusive and controlling marriage when I moved to the United States in 2000. And when I finally broke free, I became a single parent by choice, sleeping on the floor with my 2-year-old by my side after we moved out. All while trying to build a career in marketing.

Yeah, it's heavy stuff.

But you know what else? It's real. And it doesn't take away from what I achieved in my career and life.

And that is MY story. Full, raw, unedited.

******

Why is it that, as women, we don't share our stories enough? We put in the work, we go through the highs and lows, but we often do it all in silence, feeling like we're on our own island.

But here's the thing: when we finally open up and share our stories—whether they're filled with triumph or struggle—that's when the magic happens. That's when we reclaim our power.

And let me tell you, there's nothing more empowering than owning your narrative.

Like a boss.

Our stories are that powerful "how." It's those "how" moments that shape us, that define us. And that's where the magic happens.

So often, society tries to box us women in, telling us to stay quiet, play nice, and be that "good girl." By holding back, we hide our authenticity.

So, let's not hold back. Let's share, inspire, and show each other how vital it is to speak up and own our narratives.

Like me telling my story.

Like Jennifer and Lesley, co-authors and editors of this anthology, did by telling their powerful stories and inspiring many other women to tell theirs.

You see, for the better part of two decades, Jennifer was chasing this dream similar to mine, gunning to become a partner at a law firm. And you know what? She did it. But here's the thing: when she finally got there, something felt off, like me in my storytelling class. There was this gnawing disconnect between what she thought she wanted and what truly made her happy.

That is why she took a step back, did some soul-searching, and you know what she realized? Her passion lies in helping others find their own path to fulfillment through storytelling.

Now, meet Lesley, a powerhouse in the legal realm specializing in labor and employment law.

What sets Lesley apart is her understanding of the power of storytelling. She knows that behind every human, there's a story waiting to be told.

Lesley's passion for storytelling isn't just about captivating an audience—it's about connection. Whether she's speaking internally to her colleagues or externally to a crowd, Lesley's words resonate because they're grounded in real stories, real struggles, and real triumphs.

Jennifer and Lesley have seen firsthand the power of storytelling. That is the "why" behind this book for Jennifer and Lesley.

By sharing their journey, struggles, and all on multiple physical and digital stages, they took their power back; they continue to inspire others to embrace their authenticity and tell their stories.

So, consider this book a love letter from Jennifer and Lesley to all of you wonder women out there, helping y'all navigate the choppy waters of career and life with permission to become free through the power of storytelling.

Like many women did with their stories in this book.

This is what this book is about:

- 32 stories from remarkable women.
- 32 raw, unedited stories.
- 32 authentic voices.

They came together to share with you their "how."

Sure, it's scary putting yourself out there. I know it all so well. That is why I hid my messy story for so long. But our stories are what make us who we are. And when we embrace them fully, without judgment or comparison, that's when we truly shine.

Like I did. Like women in this book did.

And soon, you will, too.

******

Taking back our power isn't just about living our best lives; it's about helping others do the same.

When one of us speaks up, it shows all of us that our Stories, Voices, and Experiences Matter.

When we share our stories—no matter how messy or imperfect—we break down barriers and inspire those around us to do the same.

Our stories light fires; they break molds; they show the world what's possible when we dare to use our voices. That's where empathy comes in. When we hear someone else's story and truly understand where they're coming from, it's like a lightbulb moment. Suddenly, we see each other as fellow humans, not just random strangers passing by.

And that's exactly what this book is all about. It's a treasure trove of authentic and vulnerable stories, each one a chance to learn, to connect, and maybe even find a little piece of ourselves in the process.

So go ahead, dive in, and let these stories inspire you to share your own. After all, your story is worth telling, too, and needs to be heard:

To see you as a role model.

To support women out there with your advice.

To show all of us how, through being vulnerable about your challenges, you can rise above them and succeed.

To inspire the sisterhood.

To let every single woman out there see and believe that they can be anything they want to be, just like YOU.

We need more women's stories to be told. By telling YOUR story, YOU help to close the gender gap, the pay gap, the impostor gap, and all the gaps that we, as women, are facing today.

So let's keep lifting each other up, celebrating our wins, and closing those gaps for you, me, and all of us by sharing and owning our stories.

Because when we, women, share our stories, we stand together, and we can do so much more.

With love and respect,

Eugina Jordan

Award-winning CMO and author, a Russian-born American, a domestic abuse survivor, a mom, and a wife

Acknowledgments

TO BE HONEST, putting this book together was like building a plane while flying it. This anthology would not have been possible without the help, patience, and grace of countless people who supported it every step of the way.

Thank you to each chapter author. This anthology would not be possible without you. We asked you to tell very personal stories—some of you for the first time—and you rose to the challenge. Some of you participated in personal storytelling for the first time; others of you told a new story for the first time. Each of you has been authentic and vulnerable.

Your individual and collective efforts showcase the power of storytelling. We are forever changed by reading your stories. You made us cry, smile, laugh, reflect, and most importantly, feel. We saw ourselves in you and you inspired us with your courage. We are eternally grateful and empowered by your stories.

We would be remiss if we did not thank our chapter authors' friends and family. Our chapter authors gave us their time and talent when they could have been doing other things with their loved ones. We understand the sacrifice their loved ones made so each chapter author could hide away for several hours working on their story, emerging with all the feels after putting pen to paper. Thank you for supporting them so they could support this project. We see you.

Thank you to Tatia Gordon-Troy for guiding us on this journey. This book was a pebble of an idea from several women who had never authored a book before. We had no idea where to start or what to do and you expertly navigated the process and educated us along the way. Notably, your expertise allowed each story to shine and for the collective project to have impact.

Thank you to Laura Rubinstein for her expertise on promoting this anthology. We wanted the chapter authors' voices to be heard so we can effect change—but we needed to make sure the world knows about the book in order to achieve that goal. Our refrain seemed to be, "We don't know what we don't know," but you told us and helped us get where we needed to be.

Lastly, our sincerest thanks to Susan Freeman. Words do not suffice to show our support, admiration, love, and respect for all she does to empower women. She repeatedly says her life's work is to support women, and she walks her talk. Freeman Means Business amplifies women's voices through this anthology, the Wonder Woman in Business podcast, wellness events, and its signature annual #EmpoweredWomen storytelling event.

It would not be an understatement to say that meeting Susan has changed our lives personally and professionally. The #EmpoweredWomen events were transformative for us. We knew we had to capture the event's magic and celebrate the power of storytelling.

Now, we have a book—and a friendship—to show for it.

Own your story!
Jennifer and Lesley

The Art of Storytelling

by Susan Freeman

STORYTELLING IS AN ART form that has been around for centuries. As humans, we have endlessly been drawn to tales and lore. Stories make ideas "more readily manifest as reality in people's minds" because they help the reader visualize the author's circumstance while sharing in the author's trials, tribulations, and triumphs.

Personal storytelling is a powerful communication tool. It helps us bring emotion to our ideas, share our values, make more authentic connections, and give people reasons to believe in us. The power of storytelling lies in its ability to "humanize" us and provide others with the opportunity to share in our journey.

Crafting a personal story is also a way to reconnect to ourselves and possibly uncover, or rediscover, a governing set of principles to guide us or expose outgrown beliefs that no longer serve us.

In this way, our personal story is more than just a communication tool; it serves as an exercise to take stock of where we've been, where we are, and where we're headed. In essence, it helps us begin to live a more examined life—the benefits of which are innumerable.

The stories you will read in this book, *Own Your Story: Empower. Connect. Create Change.*, are profound, moving experiences capable of teaching powerful life lessons. The authors have chosen to share their stories using their own voice to inspire, engage, and connect with you, the reader.

******

Everyone has one ... but what is "voice," really? Voice is our ability to communicate and the manner and reason in which we do so. It is expressed through the filter of our attitudes and personal perspectives shaped by our life experiences, beliefs, values, and what we find most meaningful.

In a piece for *The New York Times* entitled "The Voice of the Storyteller," Constance Hale describes voice as

> *...the ineffable way words work on the page [...] Reflecting a combination of diction, sentence patterns, and tone, voice is the quality that helps a writer connect with a reader....*

With this definition, we can see that voice describes the tone or personality of a story or moment in a story—whether ironic, humorous, carefree, somber, etc., and is created through a strategic choice of words, grammar, and sentence structure.

When you begin to craft your personal story, remember that when the tone or personality of your story reflects your own, and supports rather than distracts from the content, you give strength and consistency to your authentic voice.

******

Practicing introspective awareness is the first step in the ongoing process of crafting our personal stories and discovering our authentic voices. Introspection happens when we look inward and examine our thoughts, feelings, and motives. It helps us understand who we are, not who we think we should be.

Introspection is the basis for self-awareness, appreciating what makes us unique, acknowledging what experiences have moved us, and understanding how we've changed over time.

Understanding our values, motivations, emotions, and mindset is crucial to recognizing the dominant patterns in our lives and relationships. Additionally, when we practice deep awareness, we pick up on subtle clues and insights that might have gone unnoticed otherwise; valuable insights can help us make our stories shine.

******

A good story should be full of color and details that people aren't going to get from searching online for you. But what if you don't think you have an interesting story to tell? Everyone has had at least one experience that others might find fascinating or a personal breakthrough that could inspire others to find strength when they need it most. Don't underestimate the value of your experiences. They might be old news to you, but to others, they're brand new.

Start by thinking back through your history to identify key experiences and pivotal moments that have led you to where you are now. Write these down and backtrack if you need to. What transpired? How did you handle it? What did you learn? What experiences prompted a change of mind, strengthened your values, or inspired a new path or idea? Fill a notebook if you can. These explorations are valuable to the process and will help you get started.

******

What have you learned in your life that might help others? What are the events that prompted these discoveries? Don't just stick to the last decade; go back to childhood and dig deep to find the memories and events that have shaped who you are now.

A touch of vulnerability adds to your relatability. Don't be afraid to open up about your past. Readily share your struggles, mistakes, and other life foibles if they help you tell your story.

Think about how your story might connect to your audience's own experiences. How might your story resonate with them? Most people know what it's like to find themselves at a crossroads, surprised by a change they weren't expecting or struggling to find footing in a complex situation. Look for the common moments that you have lived—and share those.

You can also draw from the lessons you've learned from your parents or grandparents. Throughout human history, storytelling allowed us to pass down lessons from previous generations so we don't repeat their mistakes and can build on their successes. It would be a shame to omit these now.

******

Writing our personal story is an invitation to delve deep into the recesses of our souls, to uncover the narratives that shape our existence. As we navigate the labyrinth of our experiences, we unearth the raw material of our stories, each one a mosaic of triumphs, tribulations, and profound insights waiting to be shared.

Let us not shy away from the canvas of our lives, but instead, with courage and conviction, paint our stories with vivid hues and intricate brushstrokes, knowing that in our narratives lie the power to inspire, to uplift, and to connect with others on a profound level.

So, let us embark on this journey of self-discovery, armed with the wisdom of our past, the clarity of our present, and the hope of our future; for in our stories lies the essence of our humanity, waiting to be shared with the world.

Chapter one

Finding My Tribe

by Cheryl Aufdemberge

I SPENT THE BETTER part of my life searching for my tribe, a community where I felt loved and needed. The road was bumpy. But I persevered; sometimes I wasn't sure how or why. By sharing my story, I hope to inspire and encourage others who may be wandering or have lost their way. Never give up. There is a tribe for all of us.

******

I was born in a small blue-collar town in Kansas to a devoutly religious mother and father. Dad tolerated Mom's beliefs but chose to live his life according to his Cherokee upbringing. I didn't know much about my father's heritage except for the family story that he had been the medicine man for his clan at a young age. I didn't see much evidence of this at home except for times when I was sick, and he would try to cure me with medicinal herbs instead of the traditional over-the-counter medicine.

Mom hid our Cherokee heritage from me and my siblings for years. "It's not right to make money off your heritage," she said, referring to the monthly stipends and other benefits we could receive because we were Native Americans. I knew my father's mother didn't like her and often wondered if Mom said this out of spite toward my grandmother.

In my strict, Bible-based home, you turned the other cheek and kept your opinions to yourself. The word "no" was not allowed. Mom was a very loving and caring woman to others but that didn't extend to me. It seemed that I could never please her, so I started to learn how to be the perfect child, the good girl who never got in trouble. But deep in my soul, I knew that wasn't who I wanted to be.

Instead, I always felt the need to be unique so that I would stand out from others and be noticed. "You cannot have friends who aren't in the church," Mom emphasized, though it seemed this rule didn't apply to my siblings. Why was I being singled out?

As I approached my teenage years, the desire to escape my boring life and travel to Europe motivated me to look for any opportunity I could find to move out. But I never received my parents' support, and the lack of parental love and support had left me lacking the courage to do anything on my own.

When it came time for me to go to college, my mother informed me, "You will go to a Bible college," and sent me to a small Iowa town where I hated the weather and was not allowed to pursue my dream of being a lawyer. This college mirrored my mother's church where hard work, prayer, devotion, and a strict dress code were part of the daily routine.

Once again, I tried to be the good girl. After less than two years of this masquerade, I dropped out of college and set out on my own to be a rebel in a new city where I thought life would be easy and my dreams would come true. Little did I know that it would take years to find my own peace, discover true love, and have a career that combined my skills and passions.

******

My first job was as a receptionist for a local employment agency. The owner always seemed to find an excuse to rub up against the single young females in the office with an "oops, pardon me." Mom always said, "If a man abuses you, it's because of the way you dress." I thought this was my fault. But it happened again, and I started to doubt her words. I had done nothing to entice him by wearing my power suit. So, I decided to call his wife. It never happened again.

I left the agency soon afterward and worked a series of jobs where I tried to get ahead but always struggled to make ends meet. I was playing the role of the good girl again, pleasing bosses, trying to get along with difficult co-workers all while trying to reach the glass ceiling. But I was missing that coveted promotion again and again because I didn't have a college degree.

My parents were not college educated and always told me, "Work until you die." I didn't want that to be my legacy so I persevered, working hard to obtain as many promotions and certifications as I could at every job I held. I was always looking for that company where I would fit in, with co-workers and bosses who were like me and would accept me for who I was. But I didn't find them until years later when I started working at a law firm.

To ease my stress from the daily struggles and to have some fun along the way, I became a disco queen. Dancing the night away was a great way to meet men and get exercise at the same time after a long day at work. That's where I met my first husband who was handsome, divorced, and had custody of a 10-year-old daughter. I had no desire to be a mother and never really wanted children of my own. Yet, I pursued this relationship with the thoughts of marriage and family, which came true two years later.

Everything was fine for six months; and then the honeymoon was over. He was verbally abusive, controlling, and an alcoholic. Once again, I found myself in a relationship where I had to win approval from someone who should have loved me unconditionally. Less than three years later, the relationship was over. During a 12-hour alcoholic rage, my husband threatened to kill me. I was terrified. I left my home feeling as if my heart had been ripped from my chest.

I was on my own, still struggling and embarrassed that I had failed yet again. It wasn't until midway through the divorce that I discovered his affair with a co-worker, which produced the child he had always told me he never wanted. Years later, I heard he'd married her, divorced, married again, and had a stroke.

******

Being divorced was a watershed event because it led me to do the inner work I needed. I told Mom about the divorce and she replied, "It's your fault." She died many years later and never forgave me.

Her cruel words finally forced me to go to therapy for the first time. The therapist reminded me of Stevie Nicks, the same flowing gowns and attitude toward life. She held sessions in her garden and was kind but direct. "Enough," she said. "You have to realize how beautiful you are. It's not you, it's him. Let him go and move on to your dreams."

Those words resonated deep within me. In therapy, I learned to value myself as well as my dreams and desires. I began to love myself for who I was and not for who I was trying to be to please others. It also dissolved my need for perfection. As a child, I felt that I would not be accepted until I was perfect. Therapy helped me realize that humans are not perfect. I was always trying to be something that I could never be.

This was an "aha" experience that led me years later to meet a widower with two young children. He invited me to a party where everyone wore white. We had a great time and got along so well. The party lasted until early morning.

I lived out of town at the time and was too tired to drive home, so he graciously let me stay at his house. He slept on the coach so that I could sleep in his bed. That kind gesture made me feel special and I decided to get to know him better.

Over time, our relationship grew into love. We learned that we were very much alike with common backgrounds, beliefs, interests, desires, and dreams. We moved in together and were married four months after we met. Kind and compassionate, David believes in the value of hard work just like me. The "new" me finally met a person I could love and rely on who loved me back. My life was changing and evolving in wonderful ways.

Devoted to my new stepchildren, I soon learned they had "holes in their hearts" from losing their mother at an early age. From my first marriage, I learned that I couldn't replace their mom so I did the best I could to be the mother figure they needed. It wasn't easy and at times I wondered if I could do the job.

Today, they are both successful adults with their own families. I just celebrated my 30th wedding anniversary and couldn't be happier with the man I chose to spend my life with.

I knew I needed to apply the positive lessons from my marriage to my career. As a dyslexic child, I worked hard but I didn't learn easily. As an adult, I discovered that not only did I love learning but had developed the ability to apply myself in every work situation.

Learning and advancing myself became my passion. Through hard work and diligence, I earned two associate degrees. I am now working toward my goal of achieving a college degree.

******

One day, I saw a job posting for a law firm position in the marketing department; I applied and was hired. I felt like I was realizing a long-lost dream to be in the legal field. After I had worked there for a while, an opportunity arose for me to manage the department alone for two weeks. I threw myself into the challenge of leadership by enrolling immediately in courses to further develop my skills.

Finally, I had found my tribe of like-minded people who had an interest in the law. I thrived in this environment and became the go-to person for all things digital. I learned how to be a trainer and a leader. Many times, I had to conduct a last-minute meeting or training session. As my skills increased, I was given more responsibility to lead website projects, database rollouts, and blogging/social media training for the attorneys. I loved my job. I stayed and advanced at the firm for a decade.

As so often happens in law firms, one day our entire department was laid off.

Remarkably, I saw this not as a setback but as an opportunity to advance myself. I took more courses to learn how to run a business and successfully handle every role in a company. Since I was a child, I had dreamed about having my own business. I wanted to be my own boss and do things my way. I knew that I had the ability to be successful. I finally had the confidence to live that dream.

With a decade of experience in legal marketing, I confidently opened my own business. For me, being a legal marketer is the next best thing to being a lawyer.

******

Helping others seems to be ingrained in my DNA. As a business owner, I am making a difference in the world. I have been fortunate to be a part of business groups where my experience, willingness to help, and mentoring skills have provided value to many people. Having my own business brings together all the experiences I had at previous companies and lets me offer meaningful services and support to a wide range of clients. I am blessed to work with amazing clients, some of whom have become part of my personal tribe.

During my many dark years, I would not have believed how my life would evolve. But the legal marketing field is where I found my tribe. I am now part of an international association of professionals who are caring, compassionate, and wickedly smart. I have found colleagues that support and lift each other up. I have been fortunate to volunteer with the Legal Marketing Association for many years, serving on several local and regional committees, and I look forward to serving them wherever they need me.

******

There is a Cherokee proverb that says, "The soul would have no rainbow if the eyes had no tears." My tears have helped me find my purpose in life, which is to help others with their problems and show love to them with that help. Having a tribe can be both life changing and comforting. It is my rainbow.

If my life serves as any indication, you can let go of your past and look forward to new beginnings.

"The secret of our success is that we never, never give up"
–Famous Cherokee saying

Chapter two

A Unicorn in an Ordinary World

by Rebecca Baumgartner

THERE IS NO COMMUNITY like a community of women. I didn't always believe this as fervently as I do now. My experience with other women, for the most part, always had an undercurrent of competition. When I began my professional career, I was the youngest multi-unit manager at a large casino in the Midwest. Not only the youngest, but one of only a few women. I was surrounded by older white men. The few women who worked in my department were older and not all that interested in friendship.

The executive responsible for the department seemed to be an inspiring leader; he constantly shared leadership theory, books, thoughts, and suggestions. And I soaked it all up. But as I began to rise through the ranks, there seemed to be a bigger and bigger disconnect for me. I was given all the information on what a good leader looks like, but I wasn't given the tools and skills to be that leader. I felt like I was simply treading water, and nobody was helping me swim. I desperately needed and wanted somebody to help me make the connections.

I decided to seek out another woman leader because maybe that was it. Maybe I wasn't grasping this because I hadn't figured out how to crack the male code. There was a newer woman executive in another department who was seen as a superstar, and I knew my own bosses highly respected her. I saw her as almost my North Star, right? A woman leader who male executives respected. (And maybe I had some visions of mani/pedis and champagne brunches with my fabulous new mentor dancing through my head.)

I saw her walking through one of my areas one day and when she spoke, I went for it. I don't even remember what I said. But it was generally "I would love to get your advice or bounce some ideas off of you." She kept smiling at me and gave me some vague responses about continuing to grow.

I was a bit taken aback. This is what everyone was so enamored by? Surely, I must have just caught her at a bad time. I did kind of ambush her as she was walking past. Maybe she was running late to a meeting or had a lot going on at that moment. I decided I would give it a few days and then email her, schedule some time to sit down and talk. I never got the chance.

The very next day, my direct supervisor approached me and asked, "Did you ask Julie to help you do your job yesterday?"

"Uh, that's not exactly what I asked. I just wanted her advice on something. Why?" I inquired.

"Well, she came up to me this morning and told me that if you can't do your job, she's not going to do it for you."

What?! Liquid hot lava was pouring over my body. My face, I'm sure, went beet red and I almost cried. Not only did another woman brush me off when I asked for help, she actively trashed me to my boss! Julie never acknowledged me again.

This was a pivotal moment in my life. Before, I was a confident and dedicated leader who wanted to continue to grow and advance. I focused on developing my team and making them stronger and more impactful. Coming into work every day, I felt challenged but not overwhelmed because I was happy with who I was and how I showed up every day. I wanted to collaborate with others and focused on building strong relationships with colleagues, co-workers, and my team. This is not to say that everything was perfect. Reflecting, many years later, there were signs I was too young and naïve to see.

There was an award given to recognize a huge overhaul of our department that took well over a year to complete. Every leader, from the supervisors to the executives, worked tirelessly to make it successful. There were long days and long nights, short and even non-existent weekends for that entire year. We were all so proud of the work we did.

However, when the award was given at a huge dinner and reception, only the department executives (all men, of course) were named and recognized. The executives didn't even mention anyone in the department during their speech, only praising the company and the company's president. I kind of shrugged it off, explaining to myself that of course they would be named, they're the leaders. They thanked us in their own way. This is a department award, and I am still proud of our accomplishment.

During our annual Employee Opinion Survey, instead of focusing on our individual and department scores, we were almost pitted against other leaders. Comments like, "This person got a better engagement score than you and they have a more difficult department," were thrown around. Well, I thought, what a great way to highlight the strength of another leader and recognize his hard work. I just need to do better and get a better score than him next year.

******

My entire life was wrapped up in work. I had no social life, no friends, or acquaintances outside of work because I was always working. Since most of my colleagues were men, I had no female support system. This was sort of intentional. My situation with Julie showed me that I couldn't trust women in the workplace, right? But I had no real outside friend group to talk to, who I could vent my frustrations to in a safe, loving environment. This wasn't something that registered at the time but, again, looking back, this had a huge negative impact on me.

These and other moments began to chip away at my optimism well before my encounter with Julie; I just didn't realize it. These small papercuts, almost invisible over time, slowly began to sting and this interaction finally opened my eyes to the pain.

But instead of trying to heal, I worked hard to numb myself. I decided the reason I was feeling this way, that I wasn't quite feeling connected to the work, was because I wasn't playing the game right. Instead of keeping my focus on helping and developing others, I needed to toughen up my own skin. I needed to act more like Julie. That was how a woman got ahead in this company.

I began to take on a different persona to project what I thought others needed and wanted me to be. I was the superhero who had to work the hardest, the perfectionist who worked to eliminate the slightest error, the soloist who had to do everything by herself. I was focused on me, my needs, and how others perceived me and my usefulness. My team and our performance were just a byproduct.

Instead of making me feel better, I felt wrong. I glanced around at my colleagues, each engrossed in their tasks, seemingly confident and assured. Meanwhile, a voice inside my head whispered that I was just pretending and that sooner or later, everyone would discover I was a fraud. The accolades and achievements I received felt like a carefully constructed façade, ready to crumble at any moment.

Meeting deadlines and surpassing expectations didn't provide the satisfaction they once did. Instead, they fueled the belief that I was merely stumbling through, fooling everyone around me. I began to scrutinize every aspect of my work, searching for signs of inadequacy. Any mistake, no matter how minor, became evidence that I didn't deserve to be here. I questioned every decision, replaying conversations in my mind, searching for hints that others had caught on to my perceived incompetence.

The irony was that the more I doubted myself, the harder I worked to prove my worth. Yet, no amount of success or positive feedback seemed capable of dispelling the imposter syndrome. It clung to me like a shadow, whispering that I was out of place and unworthy of the opportunities before me. I began to work 18-hour days, six days a week. If I just put in more time and worked harder and longer than anyone else, nobody could doubt me, right?

This toxic situation began to take a huge toll on my well-being, a fact I hid from everyone including my husband. The constant stress meant I was always on edge, making sure that in any given situation I was on top. Every interaction with my colleagues and bosses felt almost like a fight that I had to win instead of an opportunity to strengthen a relationship. I needed to come out on top in every scenario and when I didn't, I beat myself up mercilessly.

One day, I was especially tired. My stomach felt off and I couldn't keep any food or water down. I thought it was just a bug so I kept on working, fighting through the discomfort because I couldn't let anyone see me less than perfect. I wasn't going to be the emotional woman who couldn't handle herself. Suddenly, my stomach started cramping. It wasn't subtle, it was extremely painful, and I felt liquid in between my legs. I thought maybe I was finally starting my period. I had been working so much lately, my stress levels had caused my cycle to become irregular.

I went to the bathroom, and I almost screamed. There was blood everywhere. My cramps were almost debilitating. I was too afraid to face what I knew was happening. I stayed in the bathroom for almost an hour praying that this would pass and freaking out that I wasn't working, that someone would notice I was not around and think I was slacking.

When I felt strong enough, I snuck to our wardrobe department and borrowed a pair of black uniform pants that some of the departments utilize. Then, I went back to work. I couldn't say anything to anyone. None of the male colleagues I worked with would understand. They would treat me like I was broken. I stuffed the shock of what just happened and my anxiety about it into a box, shut the lid, and stuffed it into a dark corner of my mind. I worked for another seven hours, taking frequent bathroom breaks to clean up.

I went to the emergency room after leaving work. The doctor confirmed my suspicion. I had just experienced a miscarriage. I didn't even tell my husband where I was, he just thought I was working an extra-long shift. I felt like a failure, I couldn't bear to disappoint him like that. Shockingly, this wasn't the straw that snapped me out of this spiral. That came a few years later during the Great Recession of 2008.

******

I was finally pregnant again, after a lot of worrying and crying that my body and mind were too damaged to create life. At the same time, my company, like many others, began massive layoffs. However, the layoffs were random. You never knew when one day someone wouldn't be there. Everybody was walking on eggshells and my anxiety was through the roof.

One day, I had my regular touch-base with my boss, and I still remember what I was wearing—a gray cowl neck sweater, black slacks, and black slip-ons. My hair was in a bun. I sat down and realized the head of Human Resources was there. I thought, "This is it. I'm done. They've found me out." They told me that they were eliminating a leadership role between the two properties. I felt water rushing in my ears and I could barely hear what they said next. I had to ask them to repeat themselves.

My response was, "But, I'm pregnant. This can't happen." I was almost eight months at the time. Turns out, they weren't exactly laying me off. They were asking me if I wanted to oversee both units. I felt like I couldn't breathe.

Later that night, speaking with my husband, I told him I was done. I couldn't do it anymore. He still didn't know the extent to which I had been struggling for years, but he already had a pretty good idea. We spoke previously about my need to change something once our son was born. I spent that night tossing and turning, thinking back about my experiences. Was I really going to continue this way? Why was I feeling this need to stay and prove myself? Did I really want to be the type of mother who was never home?

I had already made the decision to cut back my work hours, but this new role would mean even longer hours than I was currently working. I was at a crossroads, and I had nobody outside of my husband to help me figure out in which direction to go. I felt so incredibly scared and alone.

The next morning, my husband and I spoke again, and we decided that I needed to turn down the offer. I needed to take the severance package they would offer and take care of myself for a change. It was hard, I felt like I was a quitter, a failure, a weakling—everything I was determined not to be in front of my colleagues. I was scared I had made the wrong decision and that I just messed up my entire life.

Then a funny thing happened. The next morning after my last night at work, I felt light. The squeezing in my chest and the buzzing in my head were almost gone. I hadn't ever noticed that before. I didn't know what to do with myself, home alone all day with my newborn. But in those six glorious months that I wasn't working, I learned more about myself than I had in all my previous years on earth. I realized I loved helping people grow and develop. I felt fulfilled by helping others realize their potential.

I hated dealing with customers, I was not fulfilled by operational tasks. I was hiding in a role that was not using my potential because I was afraid of failure and rejection, so instead, I sought approval from others who didn't even appreciate me. While coming to the realization that others didn't love and accept me for who I was, the fact that they made me not love and accept myself hurt even more.

******

When I returned to work, it was in Human Resources and diversity, equity, and inclusion. This work and my new employers were exactly what I needed. I felt encouraged, finally, to be myself. I didn't feel like I was constantly hustling for my worth; my work and contributions stood on their own merit, and I wasn't being compared to anyone else. This experience allowed me to finally open up and create authentic connections with other women. At first, I was skeptical. I never had strong, professional women in my orbit that supported me. My experience had always been that women were catty, competitive, and that we were all fighting for the same space.

Well, I had just been hanging around the wrong women.

I surrounded myself with strong, amazing women who truly want to lift each other up. They are my "sister circle." They listened. They guided. They called me out. They let me see how strong I am. When I came up against another difficult issue at work, they helped me. The old me would have suffered through it and worked harder. They listened to me cry and helped me understand that I needed to move on; and they helped me search for new roles. When I was asked to give references to my new employer, they were first on my list. My boss said that he had never received such thoughtful and thorough references in his career.

This is what a community of women should be. The hands that lift you up when you fall. The hands that clap for you when you succeed. No competition. No gaslighting. Just pure "I got you" vibes all around.

My sister circle continues to grow and strengthen as I meet women who want nothing but the best for me and other women. I couldn't have gotten here without doing the internal work I did when I was laid off and the support of amazing women. I learned about myself and how to live and act from a place of authenticity—a healthy alignment between my values and behaviors. I discovered that authenticity isn't a trait, it is an active balance of intentionally reviewing my values and priorities and choosing my behaviors that match as circumstances change.

And so I leave you with this passage that I copied into my journal a while back; it has been my mantra ever since:

> *You are a unicorn in an ordinary world. This simple truth requires an acceptance that you will not please everyone. Be okay with this. Do not fear your own greatness. Surround yourself with people who appreciate your magic. Stand tall, shoulders back, and confidently speak your truth. Avoid trying to win the approval of others. And for the love of all things, don't ever allow yourself to play small to satisfy the needs of someone who cannot stand in your light.*

Chapter three

Unbreakable

by Natalie A. Borneo

TO MOST OF MY co-workers, friends, and associates, I've always been the confident successful woman of color sitting in the room. I'm sure they would be surprised to learn that 15 years ago, I experienced the most devastating humiliation of my life. Literally, overnight, I went from being one of the most senior young women of color in a regional leadership role to being unemployed.

I lost my identity.

What changed was my reporting line. I found myself reporting to a manager who said that my position should be held by someone with a law degree. He ended up penning a performance evaluation that attacked my "written and oral communication skills" and used the evaluation to justify my termination.

And just like that, I was out of a job!

The experience was even more devastating because the alliances I thought I had developed over my 30-year career failed miserably. It was a hard lesson to learn, but I saw the mistakes I had made in not holding my network accountable for promises made and not being bold enough to make "asks" that would have elevated my brand and protected me. There was a lot of humiliation on my end, but I had enough sense to find a strong attorney to speak for me and she held that global organization responsible for enabling the abuse of power that destroyed my career.

Sadly, this situation happens to professional women all the time. We are constantly under attack. I knew this and had supported others experiencing similar assaults. Yet I want to take you on my journey to share where I started and what I had to come to terms with to be able to evolve, find myself, use my voice, and put pieces of a different dream together.

******

My family comes from Jamaica—not Jamaica, New York, but Jamaica, West Indies. I am a naturalized citizen of the United States and enjoy being able to experience the rich cultural diversity of two countries. My sister and I moved to the United States very early in our childhood and traveled back and forth during different phases of our lives. I often use the phrase, "My mother fathered me," because she did. In fact, my mother walked both my sister and I down the aisle when we got married.

My mother lost the love of her life unexpectedly at the age of 36. My father, who was the same age, died the year I was born. I was born in June, and he transitioned in August, after months of being treated for an ulcer that actually was stomach cancer. He left behind a wife and two young girls under the age of 4. My father wrote my mother a heart-stopping letter encouraging her to move on with her life. She was young, beautiful, and deserved to find happiness. Instead, my mother decided to remain single and poured herself into making a life for her children. She made the decision to migrate to the United States with her girls in tow, to forge a career in nursing. We were Ena's girls, or Ena and her girls, or Lady Nurse Mrs. Lawson's daughters.

Our mother taught us to strive for excellence, exceed expectations, and be seen and heard at the right times and in the right places by the right people. As young women, we were very active in our local church and found security and comfort during challenging times in our ministers and our community of faith. I believe that my faith has taken me to places and through spaces that I never expected to be in. It has led me to be deliberate about being purpose-driven and feeds my moral compass.

Growing up in an all-female household had its benefits, but there were also moments of regret and sadness. I always wondered what it would have been like to have my father with us. There were many events and family gatherings that made his absence more pronounced for a young girl growing up.

We had an extensive family and were blessed to have uncles as male role models, including a special uncle whom we called "Daddy Les." He was kind, jovial, compassionate, and graciously accepted the assignment of being the "social father" for road trips and adventures, and the beneficiary of our Father's Day gifts and cards. But in the late midnight hours when I was alone and the voices of loneliness and grief tugged at my heart, I would ask God why he took my father away so soon.

******

While I can't specify the age, I began dealing with unresolved trauma by changing the endings of stories. I wouldn't say that I fantasized, but it was important to me that everyone had a happy ending, and I would do everything in my power to change the outcomes of others. It may sound idealistic, but I understood the pain of not "being". It was not trivial or silly. It was survival.

I grew up in a single-parent household while my friends had both parents. I was an immigrant with a strange accent that people didn't acknowledge or respond to. I was often invisible in a crowded room and was never missed after I left. Finally, I was the friend and colleague who never made the special invitation list but got to hear all about the great time everyone had. There were many painful moments and disappointments that I had to work through secretly, and the only thing that was clear was I needed to prevent others from experiencing the same things.

Over the years, I intentionally put myself in spaces where I could help others confront pitfalls that can disorient, displace, and derail them. As a woman of color, being in strange seasons was not unusual and being the only one in the room was a common occurrence. I learned to strategically change outcomes by observing, challenging the model, befriending, and using my very polished voice to inspire and spark change. I followed the golden rule that I learned from my mother—to strive for excellence, exceed expectations, and be seen and heard at the right times and in the right places by the right people.

So how did the maneuverer become out maneuvered?

Leadership guru John C. Maxwell wrote that "most people want to change the world to improve their lives, but the world they need to change first is the one inside themselves," something I've only realized in recent years. I was fueled by disappointments in my life and launched head-first into hero mode and missed the reality that while my actions helped others, they worked against me. I seemed to follow a pattern of self-sabotage, putting the needs of others ahead of my own. It was exhausting.

******

I had an abysmal experience in my first year of college, followed by several negative personal relationships. I found myself on academic probation after being among the brightest and best. A professor told me I would never pass his class, and he was right. He didn't care for my accent, and I had trouble writing journalism jargon. I had met the enemy, and he destroyed me. I ended up transferring to another university.

I dated someone in college, and everyone knew his girlfriend except me—that is until she introduced herself to me on campus. Then my most serious relationship resulted in my phone being tapped so that he could monitor my calls and my movements. My friends joked that I had a "scum magnet" and attracted the worst of the worst.

But while my personal life may not have been going so well, my career began to take off. I was hired by one of the top three insurance brokerage organizations in 1986, promoted to vice president in 1998 and senior vice president in 2000. I was awarded the Black Achievers in Industry Award in 2000 and received a Professional Excellence Award in 2001. I was elevated to managing director in 2004.

I had cultivated a reputation of strategic collaboration, with a keen specialty of repairing tenuous client relationships. At one point, I managed a team of 22 professionals. I trained colleagues and senior leaders for the National Casualty Practice and the

North American Compliance Practice. I supported, mentored, and encouraged others to lead with their strengths.

It was all going so well ... until it wasn't. My promising life fell apart when I got a new manager who wasn't impressed or satisfied with anything I did.

Then came the review. It didn't go well.

When I realized that this was going to be career-ending, I kicked into high drive with outreach to leaders in other areas of the organization to find options, but learned that as an at-risk employee, I could not transfer to another department. How was it that only months before this, I had been nominated by the same organization for an award for excellence?

I emailed copies of the weaponized performance review, previous performance reviews, and a correspondence trail that was a smoking gun to the U.S. Human Resources manager who told me that he was in the middle of a global transformation initiative and was fully booked with meetings. I went to the employee relations team to discuss my situation, yet all roads led me to retaining an employment attorney, something I never thought would ever be in my future. I had to make a choice, so I decided to adjust my perspective. I was under attack and there were no reinforcements coming to save me.

After years of neglecting my personal growth and self-promotion, I was defined by an arbitrary rating that could not be defended. Instead of challenging the manager, the company leaders agreed to write a settlement check and move on. I was stunned and numb. I didn't recognize who I had allowed myself to become, and I wasn't in control of any aspect of my professional career. I was unemployed for the first time in my life. I had been the major breadwinner in my household and my daughter was starting her senior year in high school. College was on the horizon, and I was in financial chaos.

I remember wondering how I would recover from this and doubted that I would ever be able to show up in the same industry network again. It took almost a year to find "meaningful" employment. I often wondered if my name was on a blacklist somewhere because promising outreach, assurances, and referrals went nowhere.

I felt betrayed, confused, and alone. I remember standing up in church one Sunday to give a testimonial on stepping out on faith after falling from grace. I shifted any reliance on human intervention and focused on a higher power—the only one who could make a difference.

******

When I talk to women and groups about self-clarity, I emphasize knowing your attributes and giving yourself permission to leverage them whenever you need to. The person who achieves self-clarity is not influenced by situations; instead, they have influence over situations. Getting clarity helped me control my personal and professional influence. I had to rebuild my sense of self by asking myself four questions:

1. What do I bring to the table?
2. What outcome do I need to achieve?
3. What boundaries do I need to feel safe?
4. Does the work bring me personal joy and is it worthy of my energy and focus?

I believe that our careers and personal lives are not linear, but circular in nature. Your knowledge and experience are only good enough to get you started, then you must continually build and expand your foundation and network to remain relevant and competitive. I ask myself these questions before every performance discussion and job opportunity.

You also need to be clear about your identity and personal brand. It comes down to what people say and think about you when you are not in the room. Intentionally shaping your narrative and planting those seeds are crucial to your identity and journey. If you suspect that there is a disconnect between your brand and the water cooler conversation, pump the brakes, and make the correction.

I am still a work in progress, so it is important for me to use my voice to advocate for myself. I don't allow anyone to speak for me without my express permission. I have always been multidimensional and that's what makes me unique. My passions and activism are important to my brand and can be leveraged to support individuals and organizations that I may work with and for. I work IN my environment; I am not A PRODUCT OF my work environment. I work to ensure that everyone understands and is comfortable with who I am.

Failure is hard and it is easy to blame others for negative experiences. My fall from grace was a very hard lesson to learn; but I recognized the importance of being able to recover and lean into what I could have done differently. Although uncomfortable, I've changed my strategy to include fail-forward actions, such as maintaining a positive attitude, taking new risks, being open to solutions that challenge the norm, and learning something from every mistake.

No one expects failure, but it happens because we're not perfect. Sometimes it's unexpected, and other times there are warning signs. As I reflected on my situation, there were signs that I could have acted on to change my outcome, but I was comfortable and naïve in thinking that my tenure, seniority, and impressive network would protect me. I was so wrong!

I never had to play chess in my professional career because the positions I held were based on referrals and recommendations. Bells and alarms should have gone off the moment my new boss regurgitated my statement about "adding value." He seemed amused, but I ignored it because I was a managing director, and he was a senior vice president.

I have learned that you should always be looking ahead for the next challenge or opportunity, whether you propose an innovative change to your existing role or explore growth opportunities elsewhere. Everything has an expiration date including your job. The first day in any new job should also be the first day to begin to explore.

A job should never be a destination; it should be an opportunity that you outgrow and a path to your next great step.

I am reinventing myself and making decisions based on the colors of my parachute. The journey I am choosing to go on will require constant tuning and refining. I am putting pieces of a new dream together, and if you are reading this story, it's possible that our paths may cross in the future.

This sister is "fearfully and wonderfully made" and the dreams I have are bold and scary but necessary. I am moving forward by putting my happy ending in motion, and I am inspired to unleash everything I have to take my next great step.

Even if I fail, I'll always strive for excellence, exceed expectations, and be seen and heard at the right times and in the right places by the right people.

Chapter four

What I Was Made for

by Michelle M. Bufano

IF YOU WERE TO ask my mother, she would insist that my destiny was to become a lawyer. She always believed, as did I, that being a lawyer was "what I was made for." My mother would also point to my last day of second grade as the day when my path was first set in stone. If I go back and do the calculation, that would have been mid-June 1979.

The last day of school at John Hill Elementary always doubled as "Move Up Day." "Move Up Day" was when you found out who your new teacher would be for the following school year and would spend an hour or two with him or her.

Miss Merner asked us to answer a few questions about ourselves and put our answers on an index card. One of those questions was, "What do you want to be when you grow up?" My answer was a "lawer" (sic). I am not sure why I even chose that profession, whether the choice was random or because my mother had planted the seed; it must have been an important moment because I still have that index card somewhere in a box in my basement.

As a 7-year-old, I did not appreciate that this moment in Miss Merner's sunny and yellow-painted classroom was the beginning of anything other than summer break. I also had no idea that the path to becoming a lawyer that was set in motion that day would not end once I started practicing law and that life rarely proceeded in a straight line. Instead, practicing law would ultimately be the start of a series of journeys, eventually leading me to my best self and the many things I was made for.

As time went on, I learned the correct spelling of "lawyer," and it became my mother's fervent wish that I become one. As I have gotten older and reflected on my mother's motivations, I think her desire was not so much that I become a lawyer per se, but that I have a career that allowed me to support myself without the need to depend on anyone else financially. I think that for her, who had grown up without money, money equated to power and freedom. I think the luxury of independence is what every mother wishes for her daughter. I know that is what I want for my own daughters.

Consistent with my mother's dream for me and, in fairness, my dream for myself at the time, I ultimately went to law school. I had moments of uncertainty about whether the law was the correct path for me when I was a senior in college. I ended up deferring law school for a year. I spent that year working most days as the world's worst legal assistant (no joke) from 9:00 am to 5:00 pm and as a Star Market grocery store cashier from 6:00 pm to midnight.

After about six months of that routine, a diet of ramen noodles, student loan payments, and an often-negative bank account balance, law school seemed to solve my problems. I would live with my parents, where I would not have to pay rent, would have food to eat, and could defer my undergraduate student loans.

Although it was something I always wanted to do and how I planned and dreamed of my future, I think I may have ultimately become a lawyer because it was the easy path. I had already applied and gotten in. As I reflect, my ultimate choice to become a lawyer was influenced by the convenience of it at that time.

I graduated from law school in the spring of 1997, passed the bar exam, and worked as a judicial law clerk that first year. I spent the following 25 years working at law firms. I toiled away as an associate and later as a partner.

When I left the full-time practice of law in the spring of 2023, some may say that I was at the pinnacle of my career and that it was silly to leave. I was in my seventh year as an equity partner at an Am Law 200 firm based in New York City. And in theory (but not reality), I was positioned to become the head of my practice group. Ironically, even though outwardly I had reached the "holy grail" for a lawyer, the three years leading up to my departure were the most unfulfilling of my life.

******

It began in early 2020, just before the start of the COVID-19 pandemic. I was 48 years old when I asked myself, "Is this all there is to life?" I believed I was having what I thought was "THE" existential crisis at the time. Some might refer to it instead as a "midlife crisis" or a "midlife awakening."

I was too naïve then to understand that midlife did not come with a single identity crisis, having a distinct beginning and ending. Instead, this was the start of a period that would go on for the foreseeable future. I also did not know that figuring out my life's purpose would be an endeavor that would change over time and last for the remainder of my life. All I really knew was that I did not like how unsettled I felt.

Brené Brown refers to this as "a midlife unravel": ongoing low-key anxiety and depression that is just enough to make you uncomfortable but not uncomfortable enough for anyone else to notice your suffering or prevent you from convincingly pretending life is perfect. And for me, that ongoing feeling was also punctuated with short periods of more acute depression and anxiety.

I suspect my "unraveling" was kicked off by having too much time during the pandemic for self-reflection, which resulted in uncertainty about my place in the world, my values, and my life's purpose. The cherry on top was a heightened awareness of my mortality. I woke up one day and realized I had now been a lawyer longer than the time left before my firm's mandatory retirement.

Oh, and my 50th birthday did not help either. Good times. It was when I really began to appreciate that I did not have endless time to live my life. It was when I first concretely realized that someday life would end.

I have since learned that what I experienced (and am still experiencing) is typical for midlife adults. It seems that all of us, at some point, question the meaning of life. I believe, though, that my unease was exacerbated by feeling the full impact of being a middle-aged woman in a profession dominated by white men. I felt marginalized and disenfranchised.

For the first time in my life, I was acutely aware of the enduring presence of a patriarchal workplace culture that dominated law firms and corporate life. This culture included outdated norms, biases, and a lack of diversity in leadership positions, which led to my sense of exclusion.

The most challenging aspect for me professionally was that I do not believe my peers excluded me purposely. I experienced what I now term as "negligent bias." I was finding it more and more challenging to have the opportunity to connect with and/or access influential male decision-makers. Not because anyone consciously decided to exclude me. Instead, it was more that no one ever thought to INCLUDE me. As a result, I missed out on valuable opportunities for mentorship, sponsorship, and professional growth. I felt invisible and completely detached from the inner circles of my firm and the legal industry.

In the last weeks before leaving my firm, it felt as though the "negligent bias" and related microaggressions worsened. An instance that stands out is when I was part of a panel of "mock judges" for a moot court argument in a case that raised several constitutional due process issues. I had been the supervising partner on the case for years, working with a female associate who masterfully and brilliantly presented the issue in a way that caught the attention of the New Jersey Supreme Court.

Before the start of the practice argument, where the associate would be mooted by the mock panel of judges, a young, white male partner in the room started to praise an older white man, also in the room, on the strength of the briefs submitted to the Court. This older white male had zero previous involvement in the case and in writing the briefs. Yet, he said thank you.

I had already announced my departure from the firm, so I did not really have a "dog in this fight." Except that I did.

I stood up and set the record straight. I did not do it for recognition for myself. I did it for all the women who would come after me. I hoped to save other women from constantly having to prove their competence in the face of subtle discrimination and from struggling to earn the respect and recognition they rightfully deserve.

I am not sure my actions changed or will change anything going forward. All I could hope was that there would someday be another female partner in the room who will not feel quite as alone, while standing up for herself and other women, as I did in that moment.

Thus, I ended my full-time legal career disillusioned with the patriarchy and feeling isolated and powerless. At the ripe old age of 51 years and 256 days old, on a partly sunny morning on the last Friday in April, I walked away from my 21st floor, east-facing office and the alleged prestige and actual money that came with equity partnership.

The following Monday, two days later, I started my own business, six days before my 52nd birthday—and it was the first time in a very long time that I felt I was about to do something that really mattered. The business would focus on providing risk management advice to female entrepreneurs to level the playing field for women starting businesses. My mission is to create a world where every woman thrives and NEVER feels marginalized by a lack of access or resources. I would make sure they got what they needed to succeed.

I was excited and felt like I was finally fulfilling my destiny—even if it was not the destiny my younger self had imagined or the linear path my mother had hoped for me.

******

I was beyond prepared for this new phase of life. Typically, I do not just have a Plan B for most things, but also plans C, D, and E. I hope for the best but expect the worst, a philosophy that has served me (and my clients!) well. Starting this new business, one that took me off my previously linear career journey, was no different. I WAS PREPARED. I WAS READY.

For this reason, the morning of that last Friday in April came as a surprise. I entered the office early that morning to drop off my keys, building pass, and laptop. And to send the "farewell" email I had already drafted.

I was so laser-focused on moving forward that it was almost like I had tunnel vision about the future. I had packed, and the boxes were ready to ship. I had completed all exit forms and written my departure memos. I had formed an LLC for my new business, obtained the EIN, and opened the business bank account, along with dozens of other pre-launch tasks. Out with the old, in with the new! I was SO ready to start my new endeavor. At least, I thought I was.

The unexpected happened as I sat at my desk for the last time and looked out at Bryant Park. I started to cry. The crying quickly turned into outright sobbing. All the while, three letters kept going through my head: WTF! Why was I grieving a life I was choosing to step away from?

In all my planning and preparation, I failed to appreciate something: I was leaving the full-time practice of law. I was so excited about the future that I forgot that I had spent more than half my life either as a law student or lawyer. Being a lawyer was a vital part of my identity for so long. I had dreamed about it since I was 7 years old. While I was still going to practice law part-time in addition to consulting, I was leaving behind the only way of life I had ever known as an adult. I was deviating from the path I had planned 40-plus years before. The significance of this pivot never even crossed my conscious mind in the lead-up to it. It took me turning into a sobbing mess for me to see it.

In tort law, there is a concept called "proximate" cause. It means that "but for" a specific action, a particular result would not have happened. But for being a lawyer, I would never have conceived of, created, and launched my new business. But for feeling marginalized as a woman, I would never have made it my mission to make sure other women never felt marginalized as I had. I would not have wanted it to be any other way. And as I thought more about it, it occurred to me that almost every path we take in life is the result of proximate causation, in addition to actual causation. Every choice we make in this life is predicated on a prior experience.

Change is hard. But I have learned that leaving parts of your life behind that no longer serve you does not mean forgetting everything you have been through or throwing away your whole identity and ties to the past. It simply means transforming yourself, integrating your past, present, and desire for the future into something different and better as you start down your new path.

While I may not have been prepared for the loss I would feel, I was ready for the future. I just needed to grieve the loss of my old self as part of letting go of "what is" in favor of "what can be." And "what I can be" would never have evolved but for my past. I am happy that being a lawyer has shaped my identity. I would not have been able to pivot into risk management consulting otherwise.

******

With this acknowledgment that I could feel a sense of loss even when I made the choice to take a new path, I, yet again, thought I had put my middle-aged angst behind me. I was wrong. I continued to fumble and figure out my way in this new world. Life was far messier than I had ever realized.

Even with all the angst and the mess, I have not regretted my choice to leave the full-time practice of law and become an entrepreneur. I love that I was doing something that matters to me so much. My happiest moments have been when I avoided or solved a problem for one of my clients and knew it made a meaningful difference in her life.

That does not mean the fear has gone away. I continue to be scared shitless by the uncertainty of my new life where nothing necessarily goes according to plan. It has taken me some time, but I have finally accepted that life is messy and that roads take unexpected turns. The perfect life path does not exist. But that is okay because feeling fulfilled beats perfection any day!

In the end, my mother was correct that being a lawyer was my destiny. But we both had to learn that life's path is not a straight line and that we all have multiple destinies to fulfill. Human existence is multifaceted and dynamic. While we may set goals and make plans, our journeys are influenced by a complex interplay of factors, experiences, and choices, each stacked upon the other. And although life may be messy at times, it is that nonlinear yet meaningful path that leads us to the most self-discovery and growth. It is what leads us to be our best selves. It is what gives us the courage and power to do the many, many things we were made for.

Chapter five

On Hospice: Life After Death

by Sara Burke

I SHOULD HAVE DIED FIRST.

We had an agreement. He promised me, and I believed him. Our friends did, too. You see, I was dependent on my husband, Jack. We both liked it that way. Jack took care of me. Coffee in a thermos every morning with a note of love. He filled my car with gas, put air in my tires, grocery shopped, and cooked. He was a great cook. Jack was my "driver." He dropped me off at meetings and picked me up.

We really did have a good thing going. We had a grand romance. We traveled the world. Danced in the streets of Brazil. Sat in Parisian cafés. Dined on pasta in Italy. Rented a houseboat in Amsterdam. We traveled to Croatia, Estonia, and Russia, to New York for theatre and dance. We held hands through it all. Arm in arm, we sauntered the streets of the world. We had such a love for each other.

And then in June 2021, Jack fell and broke his hip. He was 77. He has COPD. He had been on supplemental oxygen for a few years at that point. He would not survive surgery. His lungs were too damaged. He almost died right then in the hospital.

We called our families; everyone came to say goodbye. Jack was ready to die; but incredibly, he rallied. He came home, went into hospice, and was expected to pass away within a few weeks.

Jack, on hospice.

How did this happen, to him, to me, to us?

A few weeks turned into nine months. Long enough for a birth. Nine months of days, of seconds, of minutes and hours. We tried to stay in the moment because it was all we had.

******

This is our life now. He is not in pain. He is mentally alert, emotionally available. He is still my great love.

I try to see this as our new adventure. Me learning to lean on myself, and him leaning on me. It breaks my heart. Our roles are reversed; they're in the wrong order. This is not how we roll.

He always took care of me, but now he can't. So, I rise up. I will do so for him—every day, no matter how hard. This, I promise.

Our friends are in shock. No one thinks I can do this—take care of Jack, at home, every day, all the time. But I summon all my strength hidden deep within me, and I rise up.

But I am tired, so tired, exhausted, and spent. I want our life back. The life we had before. He thinks I am doing great, even if

I am not. He is encouraging, supportive, brave, and courageous. But when I wake up, it starts all over again. I want to make this work. I am happy to be his person ... until I drop to my knees, in despair.

Always, I wake up to the same thought, "Is he still alive? Oh, please be alive." I wake up to the same grind: rush to empty the urine bottles, wear a mask to avoid the smell, pray nothing spilled overnight. I am the hamster on the wheel.

******

Every morning, I heat the water for the tea. I put four small do-nuts on a plate. Add a *pain au raison*, a napkin, and some fruit.

Next, I wash the dishes, clean the tray table, and hand him his pills one by one.

I fluff his pillow. I straighten his blankets. I hug him, I kiss him. I love him so much.

I place a photo on his table of us when we got married in City Hall 35 years ago. I put fresh flowers in a small vase next to his bed. I buy a cute runner to decorate his table, something festive, hopeful. I pick out a t-shirt with a message on it: "Vote." Or "Black Lives Matter."

Now it is mid-day. Time for yogurt with fruit in a bowl. I bring it on a tray. I take back the donut plate and return with a protein drink. I remove the tea.

I empty another urine bottle. I hand him more pills.

For dinner, I heat a spaghetti Lean Cuisine. I add a roll with butter. I give him a generous glass of Jack Daniels on the rocks. Maybe I will add a brownie or a cookie. It is the best I can do right now.

It is 2:30 am and I am cleaning up poop. I am changing his sheets. I am reassuring him. I tell him it's a privilege to take care of him. It truly is.

I don't tell him my pain is crushing. My herniated discs are on fire. I have done this two times tonight. The poop: runny, huge, and smelly. I scrub the toilet. My hands are raw. I use candles and incense to get rid of the smell. Nothing helps. I double mask. I carry on and pray for grace. I need grace. I really do.

Every moment of every day, he cannot help me. He can no longer cook, no more emptying the dishwasher, turning lights on and off, no more taking me to the doctor. Instead, I call an Uber and travel far for a procedure. I am alone. I want to pretend Jack is with me but that is magical thinking.

The life I had is now irretrievably gone.

******

I want Jack to still be able to drive me, to share the work, to walk, to cook, to travel. I really do not like this altered life. In my dreams, I try to escape. It never works; and when I wake up, it is time to empty the urine bottles. Again. I check on him. Tonight, he is disoriented, not sure of where he is.

I reassure him that he is safe and at home. He is comforted. But he asks where he was today, and of course he was in bed. I think his carbon dioxide is rising, which means he cannot expel the poison from his body properly, so he mostly sleeps.

I have flashbacks from when he got ill in Russia three years ago and almost died. I fought for his life and to get him safe passage back home. I would do it all over again.

I find courage to continue fighting for him; but then it leaves me. I feel invincible; then I am not. I hate the word "caretaker"— I banned it from my vocabulary.

But now I say: "I am the taker of care for him."

I love him and he loves me. He wants my pain to go away, and I want him to walk again. Sometimes, I dream he is walking or cooking again in the kitchen. Or I think I see a light on in his bathroom—only it was me, I forgot to turn it off.

Jack is still with me, but only in one place. I navigate the world alone. I fill my own gas tank; I know all the aisles in the grocery stores. I don't even need a list.

But one day, I start sobbing in the aisle because I cannot find one single thing. The manager comes to me and says, "Where is Jack? He does the shopping." I say, "He won't be coming back again." The small kindnesses loom so large. The manager takes my list, tells me to sit down, and finishes my grocery shopping for me. This was our neighborhood store and Jack was revered. I get offers of help, recipes, and good wishes. Still, if only ...

******

It's Thanksgiving already, and my brother and his husband are here from Wisconsin. Jack always says: "They bring the sunshine." They come every year. Jack always made the turkey. "Best ever turkey," everyone said. This year, someone else will make the turkey. It will not be as good; I can promise you that.

Jack has been working so hard with a physical therapist. He is determined to be able to sit in a wheelchair at the table with us for Thanksgiving. He was insistent: "I am going to dine with everyone just like last year. I know I can."

When the dinner is ready, the candles lit, flowers placed on the table, and the wine is poured, Jack, with the help of Steve and Wayne, tries to get from the bed to the wheelchair. He just cannot do it. His face is red from the exertion, and he is struggling for air. He becomes anxious, he cannot breathe. We assure Jack that he did not fail. He gave it all he had. He could not have tried any harder.

We make a tray for him and turn the hospital bed toward the dining room table so he could be with us. But I would be lying if I didn't admit that my heart breaks a little—this is just so hard.

Jack will never be able to sit at the table again.

I buy TV tray tables much to my own horror. I swore that if I ever used a TV tray, I'd know my life was over. In some ways, it is. Those tables are a symbol. A harbinger.

******

The hamster wheel continues as the days go on. I make break-fast—the same thing every day. I empty the urine bottles, and I give Jack his pills. He sleeps more. Sometimes, he does not want lunch or cannot eat lunch, so I give him protein shakes or a milk shake. He is losing so much weight. He bruises so easily. I cut his nails, shampoo his hair, and massage his feet.

Jack was always so handsome, so good looking. He would dress to the nines. I know he hates being this way. In just a T-shirt and a diaper. It is unthinkable.

I go into my bedroom closet, throw myself on the floor and weep, tears streaming down my face. I want to get off the hamster wheel. I really don't think I can do this anymore. I just don't think I can do one more day.

I see the door, and I wonder if I should leave. Could I? Just walk out the door and leave. I am horrified by this feeling, but it is real.

I am in such pain. I agonize for us both. This is so hard. I pull it together and I remember that Jack is still here—with me.

I ask him how he copes with the hospice nurses changing him, strangers, and he says he just goes somewhere else in his brain. The nurses and aides are lifesavers, especially for me; but they can only come three times a week. I pick up the slack. I rise up; I really do.

Jack never complains, not ever. His main concern is for me: am I ok? How is my pain? He says how sorry he is that he fell. It seems I can never reassure him enough that I am here for him in any way he needs me. That it is my honor to care for him.

He is still Jack. And we are still us. I feel grateful.

******

And just like that, Christmas is here. Our niece, Zoey, is on her way to St. Louis from New York. We are both so happy. I plan a meal. She helps. We put out the TV tray tables, pull them around Jack's bed, and enjoy being together.

January comes, he is eating less, sleeping more, and experiencing hallucinations. I sleep on the couch near Jack now. Most nights, I stay with him. He is restless. He moans. Sometimes he thinks he can walk, and I just get to him in time before he falls.

I am with him most of the time. I go out less. I stay home more.

February is upon us. I call Jack's doctor. I report on his condition. The doctor comes by, we share some whiskey, and he talks with us about dying. About the death process.

Jack wants to know if he will suffer. What it will feel like when he cannot breathe. Jack was afraid to die for the longest time. He never wanted to talk about it; but since hospice, he is completely at peace. He is ready. But I am not sure I am. We are never ready, those of us left behind.

We discuss endlessly what I would do alone. He helps me plan for his absence. He suggests I go to the ocean after he dies, go to Paris, Wisconsin, or New York. Take his ashes with me. Live my life fully. Carry on. Be fearless.

It's February 28. I call Anne, my goddaughter, and Zoey, and I tell them they should come if they want to see him one more time. I can tell that we are entering the final phase of his long and beautiful life—of our beautiful life together. They both come in time.

Jack is getting ready. Getting ready to take that journey where, for the first time in our lives, I cannot follow.

His body begins to shut down. Little by little. And then, he just peacefully drifts off. It is like he wafted away on a cloud, on the wings of love. I unplug his oxygen. The air is still. It is so final. I am really alone now.

It is March 2, 2022.

******

Now what?

For the first time in my life, I have no back up, no safety, no cheerleader. I am out here on a tight rope without a net. Who will

I be now that I am no longer reflected in Jack's eyes? Now that the one person who thought I was "perfect" is gone. Just who will I be? Can I have a second act? Without him? As one person, solo, by myself?

I go to the ocean. Alone. Then, I travel to Paris. Alone. I dine in a Paris café we both loved. I have Jack's ashes in my pocket. It is like we are having one last dinner together.

Then I take him to the *Seine*. I did not know I could do this. I marvel at myself. "Look at you," I think. "You are going to be okay. Yes, you are bereft, you are sad. But you might just be able to do this."

I still believe I should have died first, though.

Chapter six

Permission to Live Out Loud

by Tiffany Castagno

OUR STORIES HAVE THE power to shift the way we react, think, feel, and respond. Our stories can impact others but only if we first believe in ourselves, in the way we see and think about ourselves, and in the stories we tell ourselves.

There's a quote by Charles Bukowski that asks, "Can you re- member who you were, before the world told you who you should be?" This quote sat so resonant with me when I heard it, as I thought about the life I had and the life I wanted. It's very fitting of the story I'm sharing now about my own "Becoming" along my Journey. This Journey is not just my Journey; it's one for all of us, built to share and inspire confidence in others. The Journey to confidence was difficult until I challenged the narratives I was telling myself.

I've been in spaces where I wasn't wanted, seen, valued, heard, or appreciated. It shook my confidence. I had to establish my own values and I learned to fiercely advocate for them, and for myself, which ultimately led to advocacy for others.

I had smart, confident parents who could hold their own in any situation. They each (and collectively) taught me to be honest, to not back down, to stand up for myself, that I could be and do whatever I want, to educate myself, and to have a good job. Some of these came easier to implement in life than others. I was a good student, did what I was told (mostly), have worked since I was 15½, and have progressively built my career.

As I'd come to learn, building that career didn't come as easily as getting good grades in school. Trying to kick off my Human Resources (HR) career was bumpy at best. "You don't have enough experience." I frequently heard that, but no one was willing to give me the opportunity to get that experience and showcase even my transferable skills. Joining a board and getting my master's degree and HR certification ultimately became launching points to build some momentum.

******

I grew up in a generation where children were there to be seen not heard, what adults said is what went, and you didn't dare talk back or assert an opinion. When that's the framework you grow up in, you hide in the shadows, afraid to come out and live out loud; afraid to advocate for yourself, afraid to "Become". As a result of living within this framework, I became self-doubting, a perfectionist, afraid to make a mistake and disappoint.

But the irony of striving toward perfectionism is that it only illuminates our imperfections and makes us feel worse about ourselves. All of this caused me to overcompensate and subsequently to be on the other side of heartbreak and naïveté.

For example, I'm on my second marriage. I stayed in my first one at least three years too long, and that marriage and its aftermath sent me into my first depression. My whole identity was wrapped up in this man, in this relationship, in the vows I'd taken; but where were the vows to myself?

I was operating under societal "norms" of love being "enough". We loved each other; until we didn't. My ex had left me to try to sell a home by myself. I later found he also didn't pay certain bills he claimed he was paying. Lesson learned there to always know what's happening with your own household's finances.

After moving out of a home we only lived in for six months before divorcing, I moved in with a roomie whom I'd made fast friends with in an online chat room. Hello, AOL. It was a mistake to room with this woman I'd not known for long. She ended up leaving me high and dry with a huge rent bill without a second thought. I nearly lost the apartment because I was still trying to recover financially from the divorce. While living together, she also broke most of the rules we agreed on as friends and roomies to respect each other and our home. It wasn't the first time promises to me had been broken, and it certainly wasn't going to be the last.

I nearly lost my job, too, after the roomie situation, because my depression was in full swing and was impacting my attendance at work. Thankfully, I had an empathetic boss who was supportive, honest with me, and didn't let this bad patch of life I was experiencing overshadow my typical high performance and the dependable person she always knew me to be.

And through her grace, I encountered the Employee Assistance Program (EAP). This was pre-HR career for me, so I didn't know what it was until she told me and handed me a brochure. It came in handy as I was trying to reckon why I was feeling so bad about the divorce. I came to learn through therapy that even asking for a divorce you want is still a loss and there is still a grieving process.

******

A core piece of the life I knew was shifting and I wasn't prepared to deal with that. I thought it would be easier, liberating. Eventually, it was. But that took some time. It was only through my depression that I realized how truly lonely I was and that some of the people I called friends weren't there for me. Where were the people who claimed to be friends when my marriage crumbled and I needed them the most?

I felt abandoned by those who were supposed to care. The friends who always wanted to party and hang out were suddenly absent when asked to prove their loyalty.

I found myself in a few "romantic" (and I use that term loosely) relationships that I thought would fill the void; they didn't. I'm not even quite sure a couple of them qualified as relationships because they weren't even emotionally available. I know that now. I didn't then.

My overly trusting nature and desire to be seen, heard, valued, loved, and appreciated by others had landed me in yet another awful situation. One of those relationships left me held at gunpoint, a hostage in a room for five hours and suffering with some major associated trauma in the aftermath.

Yet another undesirable ending from quickly making acquaintance with bad folks in an AOL online chat room. These were folks I spent months hanging out with, whom I trusted significantly at the time, and one whom I began dating. The "love interest" at the time was nowhere to be found for consolation after such a traumatic incident.

It should also be noted that said "love interest" was family to those connected to my traumatic incident. I also found out soon after that he had a family and another love interest that the rest of the family knew about and failed to disclose to me.

In court, I was victim-shamed and lied on. As if that wasn't bad enough, some of the people in my life who were supposed to be in my corner shamed me for "getting myself into" such a situation. When that trust was broken in such a twisted way, it shattered everything I knew about myself—my judgment, my relationships, my hopes, and my dreams. How could it not?

In another failed relationship, I sensed something was amiss, but I wanted so desperately to be loved and accepted. He said all the right things in the beginning, before sharing that he'd been unfaithful, dumping me over a plate of pasta in a restaurant, then appearing shocked by my very emotional reaction in this very public place.

So much for my plans to enjoy a nice, romantic dinner together, welcoming him back home from being away, and to later share with him the poem I'd written to express my overall feelings for him, where I saw our relationship heading, and how much I'd missed him while he was away.

Instead, he planned a break-up dinner at a nice restaurant. Gross. Wish I'd seen that one coming.

I often thought if I was just "this" or if I was just "that", it would solve all my problems. But they were never mine to solve. I made other people's flaws and insecurities my own. I took them on as my problems. Then I vowed to never let someone hold that much power over me that it would affect my self-worth. Once I learned to set boundaries, people didn't always react so well when they couldn't take advantage of me and my feelings. I learned very quickly that people will turn you into the villain of their story when you set healthy boundaries for yourself.

I also learned through this series of failed relationships to love myself. I had to pull myself out of the depths of deep despair and reinvent myself—literally. Who was Tiffany without these people? Who was she before and who and what no longer served her? What did I need to let go of or bring in to become this new version of myself? Who could I Become?

******

I've had my fair share of corporate encounters and traumas. Make no mistake: Workplaces can cause trauma. And the toxic ones certainly do! Enter my second depression brought on by bad bosses who were condescending, who didn't give me a voice or hear my voice, lied on me, gaslit me, didn't stand up for me; bosses most focused on workplace "politics"; and bosses who asked me to do unethical things.

I've certainly experienced my fill of places and spaces where I felt like I didn't belong—organizations that were about profit over people, who meant well but didn't offer a realistic job preview because they had no clue what they even wanted or needed, who didn't see, value, or appreciate my talents and potential, to misogyny and racism, microaggressions, stolen credit for work I did that was deemed "a bad idea" or "not going to work or fly."

Apparently, that fire brimming inside of me full of truth, light, power, influence, and impact was "too much" for some people, spaces, and places. I stopped letting that hold me back.

******

The old me would've found excuses not to tell my story or would've believed it wasn't "good enough" or "important enough." The past me was too afraid to come out of the shadows. So many times in my life, it felt like no one loved me and that I couldn't get anything right. I wondered why these things had to happen to me and what I'd done to deserve to be mistreated.

I hadn't yet built up my confidence. When I finally did, I elevated myself above others' expectations, and even my own. I pleasantly surprised myself and I showed up for myself in ways I never had or felt I could before.

My advice to my younger self would've been not to stay in a marriage for fear of what people would think because that kept me miserable. Present and future me know that's not the way. I would've told younger me to stand up and advocate for herself and to discard those expectations of others.

Present me is 48 years old, living her best life at work and at home, has a successful business, and is more surrounded in love (and the right love) than ever. It's empowering. I've taken back my power and I'm fully living into it in everything I do. Power is a funny thing. It, of course, serves those who have it most. But when you reclaim your power (because we all have more than we often give ourselves credit for), you come into your own. You Become.

I wrote this for all the past-life Me people out there so they can learn from my story of Becoming and challenge the narratives they may be telling themselves. We can become anyone and anything we want. Just let THAT version of you be the version you create, not a version someone else creates for you.

I want you to give yourself permission today to live outside the shadows. I want you to live out loud. I'm granting you permission to Become!

Here is my advice to you to own your shine as you move from outside of the shadows and into your Becoming:

1. Create, acknowledge, and OWN your value and your Values.

2. Be unstoppable and don't let anyone tell you you're not a force—you ARE!

3. Instead of questioning yourself when self-doubt arises, question the self-doubt that has arisen. Read that again and hold onto it.

4. Believe that you can before you believe that you can't.

5. Set your intentions for where you're going. Don't get stuck in where you've been.

6. Take pause, rest, and reflect when needed. It will be one of the greatest gifts you give yourself.

7. Share your shine with others on your Journey of Becoming. Don't hold that light back from the world.

Chapter seven

A 'Yes ... And' Career Model

by Gena Cox

I WAS DELIGHTED WHEN Sammy, a woman executive I had known and admired for years, invited me to apply for an open position on her leadership team. A couple of months later, I was working with my small team on a strategy and grabbing some quick wins.

So, I was virtually speechless when, about a year later, the head of Human Resources told me, "One of your team members has reported that you are treating him poorly and slacking on the job."

Wow! After all those long days (and nights), instead of appreciation or recognition, I got a pie in the face. The complainer was right about one thing: I was dissatisfied with his performance. It is also true that I had to push him to deliver the promised work regularly; however, I was never abusive in any way.

This humiliating complaint was a wake-up call. It signaled that I would be unsuccessful no matter how much I tried to correct or fix this lie. I had never been part of the inner circle (of which my team member, the complainer, was a part). I was an outsider. I knew I needed to find another job and I would be more cautious and thoughtful about this next move.

Now that the reality of my situation was apparent, I pretended all was well, but I was traumatized and speechless. Though I was still capable of physical speech, my brain and emotions were so raw that I simply could not speak.

For months, I sat through work meetings in a daze, wondering how to center myself, regain my confidence, and move forward confidently toward the future. And then, I found the solution in an unexpected place. I took an improvisation class.

******

"Each of you must share a story with the class tonight. Don't even bother trying to hide," the man proclaimed, as I sat in my first improv class that fall. "Who was this man who wanted to control my life," I thought, "I'll slip out quietly, and no one will notice I am missing!"

That self-indulgent and cowardly idea was also irrational because, in a room of 25 improv newbies where I was the only Black woman, my classmates would quickly notice I was missing. Plus, I had paid all this money, cleared my calendar of other commitments, and craved the healing energy I hoped improv would provide.

So, instead of hiding, I heard myself say aloud, "I'll go first!" And so it was, for each class in the four-month program, I pushed myself to go first, speak out, share, and be vulnerable.

I dared to experiment. I dared to improvise.

On the last night of the course, during the public showcase, I performed improv in a red sequined blouse (which I still own) in front of my embarrassed teenage daughter!

I regained my voice through improv.

******

As a graduate school intern, my manager paid for me to attend a leadership development seminar called "Introduction to Supervision," held in the enormous local convention center. I felt special because she had chosen to spend some of the department's discretionary funds on me. As she handed me the ticket, she said, "I think you have the potential to be a great manager. This seminar could be your first step."

I learned a lot of helpful stuff that day, but the one teaching point I never forgot was, "Dress for the job you want, not the job you have." I took that to the extreme in the following years when I started my corporate career. I didn't just dress for the job I wanted; I behaved for the job I wanted. I worked hard, followed each organization's norms, and kept my head down.

But when several years later, a manager told me I didn't get the promotion because "it was my male colleague's turn," I realized I couldn't rely on someone else to illuminate my direction.

Not my boss. Not my parents.

I needed to take charge of my own story. I had to design a career that seemed purpose-built for me. But where would I begin?

******

"Purpose" is one of those concepts, like "love," that we all appreciate but have difficulty explaining. In each class, the improv instructor chanted his "Yes ... And" appeal to the next person who should add to the story. The essence of improv is to take what your partner said and add something. In the beginning, I would yell out 'oh gosh, that was so stupid!" after each of my utterances.

Improv felt like torture because I had become so accustomed to my corporate "fitting in" ways that I felt uncomfortable uttering my thoughts! That's ridiculous, isn't it? I was rejecting my own thoughts. I was denying my truth.

But as the weeks progressed, I internalized the instructor's support. I stopped trying to come up with logical responses to improv prompts. I learned to let go and "trust the process." I learned to believe that something good would come as long as I had a brain and emotions. I had those in spades.

And each night, as the pathos and tears poured out, I got closer to me. The laughter came, too! And then a larger truth emerged: improv helped me suspend the present so I could imagine a potentially incongruous but brighter future.

Brighter because I defined it. Brighter because I defined something that no one else could. Could that have something to do with my "purpose" on this planet?

I saw myself more clearly after improv, and two questions began to pick at me like harpies: "What change do you want to see in the world, Gena, and what will you do to be part of that change?" Improv had taught me that I need not fear the answers. And now, it was up to me to show I was ready to meet the challenge.

The answer to the first question came easy. I want a world where we all see that human variation is normal. And with that inclusive understanding of normal, I hope we can each take small and significant actions to connect. But I was struggling with the answer to the second question.

Then, in March 2020, police officers murdered Breonna Taylor. As the crime scene photographs emerged over time, I became obsessed with the facts of the case. I did not know Ms. Taylor, but I had a daughter her age. I wondered if she was at risk of having a similar experience. And, for the first time in my life, I could feel a mix of terror and depression beginning to rise.

When George Floyd was killed two months later, I had what my mother might have called "a nervous breakdown." The powerlessness I felt helped me answer that second question: "Gena, what will you do to be part of the change you want to see in the world?"

I broke this down as a formula to help me make it more concrete. I knew my purpose had to do with building a more inclusive world. Now, I had to figure out what concrete steps I could take. I took out a piece of paper, drew three columns, and began an exercise that became my North Star.

The heading in the first column read, "The change I want." The second column read, "What I know or can do," and the third was "What I will do." This careful exploration is how I knew I needed to pivot to entrepreneurship, write an award-winning book on inclusion, and land a TEDx speaking gig, among other dream projects.

I defined all these projects in my improv-inspired purpose plan. And then I accomplished them.

******

As a psychologist and executive coach, I have worked for decades to help leaders optimize their influence and impact. But it took starting my firm, speaking on stage, and writing a book to crystalize my purpose: helping leaders build workplaces where all employees can thrive. Discovering my purpose was a winding 20-year journey, not a lightning bolt moment.

The more my work aligns with my purpose, the brighter my inner light shines. Suddenly, the clients I attract share my values, my work brings me joy, and I no longer feel burdened.

I smile more.

I am finally making the difference for which I was put on the planet!

You can unlock your purpose by answering those questions, too. Explore what issues matter most to you. Ask yourself, what is the unique "And" you add to the "Yes." If you had unlimited time and money, what would you do? When do you most feel alive and energized?

You unlock your highest potential when your work aligns with your unique talents and sense of purpose. It's not easy to do this, but you can do it with the power of "Yes ... And" thinking. Remember that the process requires you to be spontaneous. The process requires you to stop self-editing. The process requires you to trust yourself!

Say what you need to say. Do what you need to do. You can always edit later!

******

Purposeful career and life changes are a big deal and, in my experience, usually come with unanticipated challenges. But having a clear purpose can help you handle those, too. Having a purpose didn't prevent me from feeling overwhelmed at times, but it helped me persist. To write my purpose-driven book, I had to break it down into manageable bits. I started by writing 250 words each day.

I was terrified the first time I gave a keynote speech to an audience of executives. So, I controlled what I could: I wrote a powerful speech. I rehearsed and rehearsed. I arrived at the venue a day early and surveyed the meeting room like a world-class espionage agent. Then I went back to my room and watched a romcom. Feeling the power of "Yes ... And," I breathed out, lived in the moment, and hit it out of the park!

There were times when I felt alone, even with a clear purpose. That led me to create a "personal board of directors" composed of friends who believed in me but were not afraid to give me a kick in the butt. Sometimes, the encouragement came in the form of a hug. They would hold me accountable, too! Above all, they cheered me on!

Having a purpose didn't eliminate financial challenges, but it helped me persist in finding solutions. I learned to value my services in line with the market. Still, in the early days of entrepreneurship, I sometimes reduced my fee or gave away services to get access to decision-makers who could finance my higher-priced services. Sometimes, I bartered services for other valuable outcomes such as publicity or testimonials. I did what it took to keep moving on my purpose journey.

Purpose did not eliminate my fear, but I used my "Yes .... And" belief that I would find a way through.

Purpose did not prevent me from getting tired, but it allowed me to practice self-care and put my seatbelt on first. I learned how to block my time so I would have the space to think, not just "do." I learned how not to say "Yes" in ways that would maintain relationships and still leave time for me to recharge.

When I felt lost in the face of a seeming national disregard for my chosen purpose, I would seek a booster dose of purpose by redoing my purpose exercise. And I would find a new way forward.

It took courage and tenacity to own my career. But now that my work and life are aligned with my purpose, I can't imagine living any other way. I hope you, too, can get out there and manifest the impact only you can make!

Chapter eight

Breaks Don't Define You, They Refine You

by Marcie Dickson

WHEN I WAS 17 years old, my mother and I lived in a motel. It was one of those unexpected situations that no child, or anyone, should ever endure. At the time, no one outside of my family knew what was happening. I carried on with my studies, friendships, and sports activities. And I told no one. During this same time, I helped lead my high school basketball team to a second state championship. I developed into an All-American, Blue-Chip recruit.

All this while homeless.

I've never spoken about this period of adolescence until recently, nearly 20 years later. During that period of deep

71

uncertainty and scarcity, I was determined to move forward and not become a statistic—to not let a series of unfortunate events shape the trajectory of my life or mindset. And for a while, this worked. I thought for sure I'd developed the muscle to suppress shame, trauma, and fear and transfer these feelings into grit and self-protection. Or, at 17, perhaps I simply understood Maya Angelou's words:

> *You may encounter many defeats, but you must not be defeated. In fact, it may be necessary to encounter the defeats so you know who you are, what you can rise from, how you can still come out of it.*

But, of course, vestiges of these early core memories emerged at different points throughout my adolescence and beyond. Sometimes they came as gentle reminders in the still of night or as a flood of fear and anxiety that soaked my ancient bandages and allowed me to see and feel the dozens of wounds that were still there.

******

I came of age in a spiritual home. Every Sunday, my mother would usher my brothers and me to Sunday school, followed by a two-hour service at our quintessential, vibrant African Methodist Episcopal church. On weekdays, sounds of Mahalia Jackson and other traditional gospel music filled our home. Of all the songs we listened to, the one song that stayed with me was a live rendition of "The Potter's House" by Tramaine Hawkins.

As I got older, when I needed an inspirational tune or a comforting message, I turned to this song and the idea that even in our brokenness, we can still heal fractures and restore our lives in beautiful, unexpected ways. But it took two decades and lots of stumbles, betrayals, and hardship for me to truly understand the song's meaning.

The duality of triumphs and tribulations did not end with my transition into adulthood. During the COVID-19 pandemic, I launched a groundbreaking dispute resolution company with a bold vision to improve the industry. The venture scaled rapidly and generated traction. The mission was clear, the drive relentless, and the beginnings promising.

But once again, the façade of success was marred by bullying and misalignment at the hands of my male business partners. In a space where I should have stood as an equal, I was often reminded of "place." I was micromanaged, disrespected, and reminded to be grateful.

It took several advisors warning me of what was happening, and the likely outcome, before I decided to end my suffering. My decision to wind down the company came as a surprise to the venture's many supporters and champions. The aftermath nearly broke me. And despite my best attempts to keep moving, it felt as if the experience had carved the most painful scar of my existence—straight down the middle, from my temple to my heart, and over all the existing faults and wounds.

My awakening as an entrepreneur had seemed like a grand moment at which all past and future experiences merged into a calling and true purpose. I was ready for the moment. I'd "paid my dues" with long hours and nights helping others. I'd read dozens of books on startups and building long-lasting businesses and devoted countless hours to collecting customer discovery. Everything was in place to succeed. But I had no clue that a fundamental shift still needed to happen. Because how could I expect to build something entirely new from brokenness?

******

There is something powerful, even magical, that happens when you're operating in your purest form. Vulnerability transmutes to courage, and you come to understand that you're just scratching the surface and know nothing at all.

It was during this period of winding down my company and searching for the meaning of it all that I rediscovered Kintsugi, the ancient Japanese art form known as golden joinery. Kintsugi is a mending practice that repairs broken pottery with lacquer mixed with powdered gold, silver, or other precious metals.

Instead of concealing the cracks and fractures, Kintsugi embraces them and transforms the broken object into a unique and arguably more beautiful piece of art. Like "The Potter's House," I was instantly drawn to the idea of viewing brokenness as a way to see more clearly. The cracks let the light in.

As a silly healing practice, I started collecting old bowls and mugs; and in fits of rage and sadness, I'd go to the garage and break them. I never quite got around to mending these pieces with lacquered gold; but for the first time in my life, I started to do the work of looking at my own perceived brokenness. I say "perceived" because there was a pivotal moment during this period when I stripped down everything. I wanted to see myself as I truly knew myself: as a woman of color with wounds so deep you could almost see the light shining from the other side.

The other side is where I'd always wanted to be, but I'd never quite grasped that getting there would often require a lonely and sometimes troublesome path of interminable darkness and uncertainty.

The scars and old wounds were not impediments to living a holistic and healthy life; they were reminders, fraught not with pain but with possibility. My journey over the years is a testament to the tenacity of the feminine spirit. We can bear enormous burdens as we play the roles expected of us by society. Yet, I've learned, much like the philosophy of Kintsugi, that concealment is not the same as healing. Acknowledgment of seeming brokenness is the first step toward genuine strength.

The process of Kintsugi serves as a powerful symbol of healing and transformation. Kintsugi teaches us that what is broken can be made whole again and even more valuable. Similarly, in life, our ability to regenerate and come back from adversity and turn our past struggles into sources of strength and wisdom can lead to a more wholesome and authentic way of being. Trials can add depth and character to our lives, and we have the power to remake ourselves into something new.

Friends and loved ones are often shocked by how freely I share past traumas and experiences with them. One day while having lunch with a female business executive who works for one of the most influential companies in the world, I shared an experience that happened during college. It was the first time I'd ever disclosed that life event to someone other than my therapist. Her heartfelt response prompted her to reciprocate by telling me what she'd been going through. We spoke through intermittent moments of laughter and tears for over two hours.

As our meeting drew to a close, we embraced in a warm hug, expressing our shared gratitude for the safe space we had created to share our authentic truth. We parted with a pact to one day muster the courage to share our stories more widely, aspiring to connect with and support other women who may be enduring their struggles in quiet resilience or masking their pain without solace.

In addition to breaking pottery and embracing opportunities to speak my truth, I also discovered new works of art that nourished and restored my soul beyond measure. One such piece is a soulful book by Sarah Lewis, *The Rise: Creativity, the Gift of Failure and the Search for Mastery*. Every word is a masterpiece:

> If we fail to cultivate grit, it is also because we often grant little importance to the practice of making and the process that it can teach us throughout our lives. Inventions come from those who can view a familiar set of variables from a radical perspective and see new possibilities.
>
> Creative practice is one of the most effective teachers of the spry movement of this perspective shift. It offers agency, required for supple, nimble endurance that helps us to sense when the bridge is about to collapse. It lets us shift our frame, like a painter who stared at a set of canvas stretcher bars for years and one day saw its potential to be an original communication device. And then persisted for decades to realize its full application for the world.

Through her work, Lewis shares the beauty and importance of embracing the "near win," and her belief that the pursuit of mastery is an "ever-onward almost." I've started gifting this book to founder friends and anyone ready to explore the value of ideas and concepts like power of surrender for building resilience, the role of play in fostering innovation, the motivational force of almost reaching a goal, the near win and the significance of perseverance and creative practice on the journey toward mastery.

Lewis argues that many of our greatest achievements are not direct accomplishments but result from learning from and transforming past failures.

Each experience, no matter how harrowing, contributed to the person I am today—a mother, an entrepreneur, a warrior in her own right. And it is through these experiences that I learned the power of impermanence—that nothing, whether joyous or painful, is ever fixed.

******

In the lessons of my past, I have found instructions for my children's future. I teach them about the transience of life, the importance of embracing failure, and the courage it takes to stretch beyond their comfort zones. We talk about the value of solitude, the strength found in moments of quiet self-reflection; yet we also acknowledge that connection with others is a pillar of a well-rounded life.

My leadership style, both in business and in my personal life, is a testament to my journey. I have learned to run toward fear rather than away from it, a seemingly counterintuitive sprint that has been the catalyst for growth and change. And this has manifested in tangible ways—from running marathons to starting new ventures and advising other founders.

Starting new ventures, for me, is not just about business acumen; it is about chiseling away at the unknown and sculpting it into something magnificent. It's about taking the rubble of past pains and seeing within it the potential for creation.

With every new challenge, I strive to embody the principles of Kintsugi, repairing what was broken with something precious.

And I trust that the scars left behind do not signify ruin but rather a complex form of restoration.

As Ernest Hemingway said, "The world breaks everyone, and afterward, some are strong at the broken places." These words resonate with a truth that I have lived. I have been broken many times, in many ways. But it is in my fractures that I have found my greatest strength, in my wounds that I have discovered healing.

The world indeed breaks everyone in different measures; and how we rise from those breaks, how we fill them with hope (or gold), is what defines our character.

I keep moving, not despite the traumas and setbacks but because of them. I stand with my cracks filled with gold, a living Kintsugi, embodying a resilience that whispers that there is beauty and strength in our brokenness, that the scars we bear can become the marks of our truth and power.

To anyone who may see their reflection in the fragments of my life shared here, know this: Your breaks do not define you; they refine you. May you find solace in shared stories of resilience and remember that in every scar, there is a story; in every crack a place for gold to rest, making you stronger, making you whole— not despite your brokenness, but because of it.

Chapter nine

Grateful: A Life Well Served

by Jan Anne Dubin

IN A WORLD OFTEN captivated by grand gestures and towering achievements, my journey is subtly contrasted, marked by the steady rhythms of kindness, gratitude, resilience, and compassion. These quiet yet powerful forces have shaped my life's trajectory, forming the core of my beliefs and actions.

This story isn't about monumental achievements; it's about the small yet impactful acts that form the essence of who I am and the values I hold dear. This is a tale of finding strength in softness, seeing the extraordinary in the ordinary, and understanding that real change often begins with a single act of kindness.

******

My story begins with the foundation laid by my family. I was born into a home where love, strength, and moral integrity were the cornerstones. My parents, Joan and Dave, were remarkable not just in their accomplishments but in their character. My mother, a Wellesley and Northwestern alumna, managed our finances gracefully and joyfully. My father, an esteemed architect and a Fellow of the American Institute of Architects, was a formidable presence in our lives and his profession. He and his partners founded the first racially integrated architectural firm in Chicago in the early 1960s, setting a powerful example of inclusion and diversity in a time of social upheaval.

The ethos of my family went beyond mere words. It was a living, breathing part of our daily lives. I remember the many evenings spent around the dinner table where discussions weren't just about our days but often turned to the importance of empathy, understanding, and giving back to the community. These lessons were not just taught but were embodied in the actions of my parents.

My father's favorite quote from Sir Winston Churchill, "We make a living by what we get; we make a life by what we give," was a mantra that resonated deeply within me, igniting a lifelong commitment to service and philanthropy.

******

My initiation into the world of giving and community service began quite early. A school-sponsored food drive in the second grade was my first encounter with the stark realities of inequality and need. I still vividly remember the confusion and sadness, wondering why some people needed help with something as essential as food. That experience planted a seed in my mind, sparking a desire to understand and alleviate the disparities in the world around me.

As I grew older, this desire only strengthened, influencing my choices and career path. In 1989, while working at the law firm of Rudnick & Wolfe, I observed the changing landscape of corporate gift-giving and initiated a shift from traditional corporate gifts to charitable contributions. This strategic philanthropic shift not only distinguished our firm but also set a trend that was soon emulated by many nationwide. The success of this initiative was a testament to the power of tiny changes leading to significant impacts.

My journey of giving and community involvement took an exciting turn with my participation in Public Allies Chicago. An interesting twist of fate led me to this organization. In the mid-1980s, I had the pleasure of working with a Michelle Robinson during her first year in law school when she was a summer associate, later known as (First Lady Michelle Obama,) at the law firm of Chadwell & Kayser Ltd. Little did I know this connection would come full circle years later when I was recruited to join the board of Public Allies Chicago by Michelle who served as the executive director and its then development director Julian Posada.

Serving on the Public Allies Chicago board for nearly three decades, including several stints as the board chair, was a gratifying experience. It allowed me to contribute to shaping young leaders' lives and be part of an organization that has had a profound impact on the community.

In 2009, following a couple of professional setbacks, I embarked on a new venture by founding Jan Anne Dubin Consulting (JADC). This turn of events, while challenging, allowed me to reevaluate my path and focus on what truly mattered to me.

At JADC, I combined my expertise in legal consulting and executive coaching to assist individuals and organizations in realizing their potential. This venture allowed me to continue my commitment to diversity, equity, and inclusion and provided a platform to encourage and empower others in their personal and professional growth.

One of the most poignant chapters in my journey of giving unfolded in 2020 when I joined the i.c. stars Chicago advisory board. This role enabled me to contribute to bridging the opportunity gap for underserved communities by connecting young adults with the high-growth tech sector. Co-creating the "StarGazing" program series and bringing influential speakers on board was an enriching experience, further fueling my passion for creating equitable opportunities.

However, during the challenging times of the pandemic, I found a unique way to make a difference through the Milk Made project. The project was born out of a simple yet profound realization of the need for milk in our community. Partnering with local farmers and organizations, we provided thousands of gallons of milk to those in need, especially children and families affected by school closures. The success of this initiative was a powerful reminder that, sometimes, the most basic acts of kindness can have the most significant impact.

******

Throughout my life, I have learned the importance of small acts of kindness and the ripple effect they can create. Serving on various boards, including Streetwise, and collaborating with organizations like the Association of Corporate Counsel and Thomson Reuters Legal Executive Institute has reinforced my belief in the power of community and collective action. These experiences have taught me that anyone motivated to help others can make a tangible impact, no matter how small the act may seem.

My journey has also been one of personal challenges and pivotal moments. Growing up in Highland Park, Illinois, I grappled with shyness. I faced bullying, experiences that left deep scars but also instilled in me a fierce resolve to stand up for the vulnerable and fight against injustice.

These challenges, coupled with the loss of my parents and the toll of balancing a demanding career, led me to a critical point in 2021 when I embarked on a transformational health journey. Losing more than 125 pounds over 18 months was not just a physical transformation but a journey of self-discovery and of learning the importance of well-being and putting myself first.

******

My life's journey has been shaped by believing in the power of kindness, empathy, resilience, and compassion. These values have guided me through various roles and experiences, from my early days of philanthropy to my current consulting and board service endeavors. They have taught me to strive for authenticity, embrace risks, learn from failures, and, above all, be kind.

As I continue on this path, I hope my story inspires others to recognize their superpowers and use them to create positive change in the world. In the end, it's the small acts of kindness and compassion that truly make a life meaningful.

Chapter ten

Grace, Grit, Grind, and Gratitude

by Daphne Turpin Forbes

STORIES HAVE THE POWER to build communities. They can bring people together around shared experiences or common goals, fostering a sense of belonging and solidarity. In the context of leadership and diversity, sharing my journey as a Black woman can have profound impacts. It can challenge stereotypes, highlight the need for inclusivity, and pave the way for others who will follow in my footsteps.

With this in mind, the tapestry of my life is interwoven with threads of challenges and triumphs, each strand representing a pivotal moment that shaped who I am.

******

I had several troubling racial experiences when I moved to Saginaw, Michigan, at the age of 7, but I found solace in sports and education. Together, they became my refuge and where I first discovered my love for leadership.

I joined student organizations, and excelled in sports, which helped me make friends and create a space where diversity was valued. My high school years were marked with establishing several "firsts" for a young Black woman in our predominantly white school.

For instance, I was the first Black woman to be nominated for our school's homecoming court. Several white moms, whose daughters didn't receive a nomination, loudly criticized and argued with school officials that my nomination did not belong to the exclusion of their privileged daughters. They suggested that I was not good enough to be in this space. And while I did not become the homecoming queen, the reaction from these white parents to my nomination was incredibly impactful. I decided then that I wanted to devote my life to creating change and to making a difference.

It was something about "their" lack of confidence in me that caused my confidence to increase in ways that have influenced my identity today. That experience confirmed my passion for promoting diversity, equity, and inclusion. The experience was empowering; but at the same time, it showed me the bitter truth of how others would exploit my race to put me at a disadvantage.

Reflecting, this was the first time that I understood some people would use unfair stereotypes about the Black community to try to limit my personal ambitions. From then on, I was determined to become a "successful" person to inspire other women of color and to use my platform to advance diversity efforts all throughout my life's journey.

College was a continuation of this journey. Attending a predominantly white institution, I was enveloped in an environment that did not nurture my identity. It was here that I truly began to understand that the power of my voice was necessary and required. I supported campaigns for student rights, organized community service initiatives, and was a well-known figure in the student community. These experiences were formative, teaching me the importance of advocacy, teamwork, leadership, and strategic thinking.

******

Upon entering the corporate world, I was quickly confronted with the harsh realities of bias and inequity. I saw firsthand how Black women were often the most qualified yet the least recognized. This reignited the flame of advocacy within me. I became involved in diversity and inclusion initiatives, often advocating for change as the only Black woman in the room. These moments were daunting but also empowering. I realized that my voice could bring about change, however incremental it might be.

Black women in corporate America often face a sense of invisibility, which is a byproduct of systemic biases and cultural misperceptions. This invisibility manifests in several ways. One of the most striking ways in which Black women can feel invisible is through our lack of representation, particularly in leadership and decision-making roles.

When there are few or no Black women in positions of power, our unique perspectives and voices are often missing from important conversations. This absence can lead to organizational blind spots where the specific challenges and contributions of Black women are not recognized or valued.

Black women frequently encounter stereotyping and unconscious biases that can lead to fewer promotions, developmental opportunities, or challenging and visible projects. There are pervasive stereotypes that can affect the way Black women are perceived, such as the "angry Black woman" trope, which can unfairly characterize us as difficult or confrontational when we assert ourselves. These stereotypes can prevent us from being seen as potential leaders or from having our ideas taken seriously.

The concept of intersectionality is also crucial to understanding the invisibility of Black women in corporate settings. As both women and people of color, Black women face a dual burden of gender and racial discrimination. The combined effects of sexism and racism can compound our experiences of marginalization, making it harder for us to gain visibility and recognition.

Without a critical mass of peers or role models within the organization, Black women may find it difficult to build the networks necessary for professional growth. I have personally experienced this. In my career, I did not enjoy the luxury of making a mistake. That's a privilege afforded to white people. This isolation limited my visibility and access to informal channels of influence and support that are often crucial for career advancement.

Daily encounters with microaggressions—subtle expressions of racism or sexism—can make Black women feel undervalued and invisible. These experiences can range from having our judgment questioned in their area of expertise to being mistaken for someone at a lower professional level.

When Black women do achieve success, our accomplishments may be attributed to external factors or dismissed as a result of affirmative action policies or "D&I" initiatives rather than recognized as the result of our competence and hard work. This can diminish the visibility of their achievements and undermine their contributions.

This feeling of invisibility is not only a reflection of the many barriers we face but also a signal to organizations that much work remains to be done to create truly inclusive and equitable workplaces. Addressing these issues requires systemic change, including targeted efforts to increase representation, combat biases, and create environments where diverse perspectives are genuinely valued and leveraged for organizational success.

******

I also faced personal struggles that tested my resolve. Balancing a demanding career with a personal life was a constant challenge. There were times when self-doubt crept in, whispering that I was not good enough or didn't belong. But each time, I silenced these doubts with my achievements and the support of my family and mentors. Their belief in me was a powerful motivator, reminding me of my worth and potential.

The pinnacle of my journey came when I was appointed as a leader to our Blacks in Legal steering committee at my company. It was a moment of triumph, validating my years of hard work and dedication. I played a key role in helping to implement initiatives that fostered a more inclusive workplace for this underrepresented community, from mentorship programs specific to this cohort to bringing awareness to company leaders on effective ways and policies that promoted equity and inclusion. This role was more than an appointment; it was part of my mission to make a difference.

But the journey did not end there. I realized that my impact could extend beyond the walls of my workplace. I began speaking at conferences, sharing my story and insights on leadership and diversity. I started a mentorship program for young Black women, guiding them through the intricacies of professional life. My aim was to be the mentor I wished I'd had during my early career.

Throughout this journey, I faced numerous challenges. There were moments of frustration when it seemed like progress was impossible. But each obstacle only fueled my determination. The lessons of grace, grit, grind, and gratitude were not just philosophical concepts but practical tools that helped launch me over every hurdle.

******

My journey through the legal landscape of corporate America is both extensive and dynamic. With over two decades of legal practice, I have established myself as a trusted advisor at the intersection of law and business. My role as assistant general counsel and managing attorney at Microsoft is a testament to the breadth of my expertise, especially within the U.S. public sector and commercial regulated industries.

Navigating the corporate terrain, I have had the opportunity to contribute to various industry giants, from Microsoft and Discovery Communications to General Motors. At Microsoft, I spearhead legal strategies and manage a vast array of legal matters for the U.S. health & life sciences and public sector businesses, which is a substantial enterprise. My counsel is pivotal in complex technological transactions, compliance, and other legal matters concerning data privacy, security, AI, and public policy.

Prior to that, I played a significant role in supporting the company's financial services and federal government business segments, showcasing my versatile command over corporate legal affairs.

Beyond my corporate commitments, diversity, equity, and inclusion are not just buzzwords but principles I actively champion. Serving on various nonprofit boards and advisory councils, I strive to make a difference, advocating for equitable representation and inclusive practices within the legal field and beyond.

In my local community of Prince George's County, Maryland, my leadership extends to public service as the chairwoman and county commissioner of the liquor board. And my dedication to education is evident in my role as an adjunct law professor at Howard University School of Law, where I co-instruct a class on Technology and Law. This allows me to impart practical wisdom and insights to the next generation of diverse legal professionals.

Recognition from my peers, such as the Microsoft MVP Circle of Excellence Award, the Clyde E. Bailey Corporate Leadership Award, and being honored as a distinguished alumna by Michigan State University, serves as affirmation of my professional contributions and community impact.

As a member of the Maryland State Bar and National Bar Associations, my commitment to the legal profession is unwavering. But beyond the accolades and positions, what truly matters to me is the legacy I leave behind—both as a legal expert and as a beacon for change in diversity and inclusion.

Living in Prince George's County with my husband and our two young adult children, who both attend historically Black universities, I am reminded daily of the importance of nurturing future leaders who value justice, innovation, and community engagement. My story is one of relentless pursuit of excellence, driven by a passion for justice and a dedication to serving both the corporate world and my community with integrity and purpose.

I share these details on my accomplishments as a Black woman in corporate America, so you will see me, hear me, know me. This is my story, a journey of grace, grit, grind, and gratitude. A journey of a proud Black woman as a beacon of hope and inspiration for others embarking on similar paths. I hope sharing my story will help you clarify your values, beliefs, and the essence of what makes you who you are.

My story is a path fraught with challenges but also filled with immense rewards. To be a leader is to be an agent of change, to have the courage to stand up for what is right, and to inspire others to do the same.

My story is one of many narratives, unique yet interconnected in the shared experience of striving for a better, more inclusive world. The journey is ongoing, and the path ahead is filled with endless possibilities.

To those who walk this path with me, I say this: Embrace your identity, lead with your values, and never underestimate the power of your voice. Your journey is your own, but remember, you are not alone. Together, we can create a world where diversity is celebrated, and everyone is empowered to reach their full potential.

On behalf of marginalized voices, sharing my narrative is an act of empowerment, as it asserts my presence and perspective in spaces where others may have been underrepresented or overlooked. My personal story contributes to human history, preserving the richness of diverse lives and ensuring that different narratives are included in the collective memory of society.

Chapter eleven

Breaking the Stigma

by Susan E. Frankel

I SAT ON THE edge of my bed alone, trembling and paralyzed. I couldn't think, I couldn't move. All I felt was dread and panic. I had to break the news to my teenage daughter that the delicate surgery she was scheduled for that day, which had been months in the planning, had been canceled because our insurance company denied coverage as "medically unnecessary." A stressful situation, to be sure, but my reaction was not at all a proportional response.

I've always been the problem solver, the fixer. I'm an attorney, a former litigator, and should have taken the gloves off to prepare for battle. But I couldn't. I was frozen. I couldn't summon the strength to move or to deal at all with this problem, or anything else for that matter. I thought I was losing my mind. I had been slowly spiraling for months; but on this day, I hit rock bottom.

And I was scared.

I know now that I was not losing my mind. But too many women in their forties and fifties are quietly suffering, as I did. I don't use the term lightly or to be melodramatic. The crippling anxiety and depression, it's real suffering. And to make matters worse, these women think that there's no help, that they're all alone. They're wrong, as I was. I just wish someone had told me sooner.

These significant mental health changes are, in fact, common symptoms of menopause. Yup, I said it. Bring on the chuckles and the jeers. The butt of jokes for years and stigmatizing for those who dare to complain out loud. The harsh realities of menopause for many women have for too long been neglected from our social and medical discourse. This, even though virtually every woman—regardless of race, wealth, or geography—will experience, to some degree, the life altering symptoms of menopause and its precursor, perimenopause.

******

I'm 53 years old. I'm a professional and a mother of two girls, now 18 and 21. In my late 40s, I started noticing changes in myself. Unexplained digestive issues. Unusual persistent fatigue. Poor quality sleep. Memory problems. Reduced concentration. But my periods were still regular, so I didn't initially connect the dots. I was trying to balance the work stress of demanding clients and working late nights and weekends with parenting two teenage girls (which should require no explanation). So I dismissed my symptoms as stress-related and did nothing about it.

Eventually, I mentioned my symptoms to my gynecologist. A woman my age, she said I was in perimenopause, but that full menopause—defined as 12 consecutive months without a period—was likely still a couple of years away. She said if the symptoms became disruptive to my life, we could talk about some treatments, including hormone replacement therapy, or HRT.

I shut that right down. Hormones = high risk of cancer, heart disease and stroke, right? At least that's what the news had been telling us for the last 20 years or so.

Time went on and my symptoms progressed. By the time I was 50, my period cycles began to change. While I used to be able to set a clock to my periods, 28 days on the dot, they started coming closer together around every three weeks, and then further apart to five or six weeks. On occasion, I missed a cycle completely. Hot flashes had now crept in, particularly at night, brain fog seemed constant, constipation was now a chronic problem, and a good night's sleep was not to be had.

And let's not forget the uninvited pooch appearing below my belly button, obliterating, seemingly overnight, years of efforts for a flat stomach despite no change in my diet. At my doctors' suggestions, I tried probiotics, melatonin, and attempted "vigorous" exercise to relieve my symptoms (good luck with that when you're exhausted all the time).

But as bad as these symptoms were, I was not prepared for what came next. I noticed that I was less able to cope with stressors in my life, even the minor ones. Irritability and mood swings are notorious hallmarks of menopause, but this was way beyond that. I felt I was in a constant state of panic. My heart was always racing. I felt a pit of dread in my stomach. I feared the worst outcomes of every problem. The daily anxiety became debilitating. I didn't want to get out of bed. But I didn't seek help. I thought it was all due to situational stress—a perfect storm of my Type A personality self-struggling against the isolation of COVID, on-going work stresses, my daughter's own health issues, family turbulence, and the fiascos of a new home construction.

I confided to a friend about the severe anxiety, and apparent depression, I had been experiencing. To my surprise, she told me she had a similar bout with anxiety and depression the prior year and had gone on HRT, with great results. I had no idea. She told me about colleagues of hers who were also on HRT along with anti-anxiety/anti-depressant medications and were getting their lives back.

I kept thinking to myself, how did I not know about any of this? I consider myself an educated person but had no idea the true toll that menopause and perimenopause could take, especially on mental health. It had been a taboo subject, even among the closest of friends.

I made another appointment with my gynecologist. The moment she walked into the treatment room, I started bawling. I couldn't get a single word out, but she knew. Once I regained my composure, we talked about my options. Turns out, she subspecialized in menopause. A unicorn for sure, but I was so grateful. Like me, she believed in medication as a last resort. But I was worried and afraid. We decided to first start me on an anti-anxiety medication. Not necessarily forever, but for right then, I needed the help. The plan was to address my mental health first, and we would discuss the physical symptoms later.

******

I joined Facebook support groups for women with similar mental and physical symptoms from menopause and perimenopause, and quickly realized I was far from alone. I also read studies and was stunned to find that almost 50% of women suffer from anxiety and depression leading up to and during menopause, and women with low baseline anxiety before menopause are at significantly higher risk of anxiety in the transition to menopause. But most women do nothing about it. For too long, I, like so many, put on my fake smile and pretended to the world that I was okay.

After about six weeks on the anti-anxiety medication, I started feeling more like my old self again. Clarity returned. We tinkered with dosages and eventually found my sweet spot. My only regret was not starting it sooner.

But the physical symptoms of perimenopause remained, and were still a severe disruption to my life, both personally and professionally. My doctor and I discussed the pros and cons of HRT, and I did my own extensive research as well. What I learned shocked me.

In the 1990s, nearly 15 million women were given a prescription for HRT, with exceptionally positive results. HRT is a form of estrogen, which is naturally depleted during the menopause transition. In the late 1990's, however, a large-scale study began on the safety and effectiveness of HRT. In 2002, the bomb was dropped. Headlines soared that the study had been paused due to a determination that HRT causes an increased risk in breast cancer, blood clots, heart attack, and stroke. Practically overnight, women abandoned their treatments and doctors stopped prescribing HRT.

For the next 20 years, women went back to suffering in silence with perimenopause and menopause. They were advised by their doctors to just deal with it; it's a rite of passage, nothing can be done. Menopause was barely being taught in medical school, and women in general were not being educated on what to expect from this inevitable phase of life.

It has only recently come to public light, however, that critical nuances of the HRT study were not publicized. The actual increased risks of cancer, heart disease, stroke, and blood clots from HRT were, in fact, nominal. For example, while alarming headlines read that the risk of breast cancer increased by 26 percent, the actual likelihood only increased from 2.33% to 2.94%. Not to be ignored, but certainly not an increase warranting the wholesale abandonment of HRT.

But women were not even given the chance to balance for themselves the risks of HRT versus a reduced quality of life by doing nothing. The studies also showed that the increased risks were found in women over age 60 and those who had taken HRT for more than five years. But for most women in their 40s and 50s, without family histories of those conditions, HRT could be a safe and effective option.

I discussed with my doctor the pros and cons, given my personal health history, and decided to start on HRT. The hot flashes dissipated. My energy and sleep improved. The weight gain is still a stubborn reminder, but I try to remember my doctor's words: "Be kind to yourself."

******

In January 2023, another obstacle was thrown my way. A large benign but painful ovarian cyst required the surgical removal of my ovary. My other ovary had been removed nearly 20 years earlier. With no ovaries and now an empty tank of natural estrogen, full blown menopause kicked in within 48 hours. I was already on

HRT, so there was some cushion for the fall, but all my physical symptoms significantly worsened. We again played with dosages of HRT, which took some time, but thankfully most of the symptoms abated.

Then, yet another curve ball came my way. Post-menopausal women on HRT who still have their uteruses are strongly advised not to take estrogen therapy without also taking progesterone to prevent endometrial cancer. While spotting and occasional bleeding is normal and expected with progesterone, some women have difficulty adapting to progesterone and will experience regular bleeding. I was one of those unlucky ones, and I experienced daily bleeding and full menstrual-type cramps due to the progesterone. Ironically, the glorious, and only, benefit of menopause is no more periods; but that was taken away from me with menopause treatment.

Completely frustrated, I once again did my research and spoke with my doctor. I discovered there is an effective alternative hormone replacement therapy for post-menopausal women with a uterus (meaning that they have not had a hysterectomy) and which does not require progesterone. It is an estrogen-based therapy combined with another drug that protects the uterine lining from thickening and becoming cancerous. Sold under the brand name, Duavee®, and manufactured by Pfizer, it has been on the market for about 10 years and has been shown to be safe and quite effective.

But my excitement was short-lived. Duavee® had been pulled from the market during the pandemic due to packaging issues, and production had still not resumed. So what does a desperate menopausal woman do? Naturally, I called Pfizer every week for updates on when it would relaunch.

Duavee® came back on the market in June 2023 (and I enjoy thinking that my incessant phone calls had something to do with it), but only in a low estrogen dose. I tried the treatment for several months but, unfortunately, the low estrogen was not enough to curb my symptoms.

I needed to manage my severe menopausal symptoms without the side effects of progesterone. As radical as it sounds, one option was to have my uterus removed, eliminating the risk altogether of endometrial cancer and allowing me to safely manage my menopause symptoms. This, of course, opens another can of worms in the space of women's health: elective hysterectomy is not typically covered by health insurance for purposes of menopause because it is "medically unnecessary." I wonder who in the insurance industry is making that determination—not likely a woman in menopause. But I digress.

After discussions with my doctor, who in turn discussed my situation with Pfizer representatives, we decided that I would remain on Duavee® and supplement it with a low-dose estrogen patch. While elective hysterectomy may still be an option for the future, I am happy to report that my physical symptoms—the night sweats, sleep issues, digestive problems, etc.—are currently well-managed. I will, of course, be diligent about routine gynecological exams and mammograms to monitor for side effects or changes.

One last significant struggle that I've experienced during my menopause transition is brain fog, a combination of forgetfulness and inability to concentrate. Candid conversations with friends, colleagues, and online menopause support groups revealed how common a complaint this is leading up to and during menopause.

Unfortunately, brain fog is a menopausal symptom that does not typically improve with HRT alone.

I did some research and discovered fascinating recent studies out of the University of Pennsylvania Medical School, which found that the effect of estrogen loss on focus and memory is the same as those who suffer from ADHD. Studies were therefore conducted to treat menopausal women who suffer from this "loss of executive functioning" with Vyvanse®, a highly effective ADHD medication. Not surprisingly, the results were strongly positive. I discussed the studies with my doctor to see if Vyvanse® might be right for me, and we decided I would give it a try.

******

I need to pause here for a moment. I really struggled with my decision to reveal in this writing that I started taking Vyvanse®, along with the other medications I've discussed. I feared being ridiculed or dismissed or labeled a "pill popper." But I realized that if I did not honestly share my complete experience, I would be succumbing to the same stigmatization that women have experienced for years when discussing help for severe menopause symptoms.

I am NOT writing this chapter to suggest that women should start taking medications for menopause. They are not right for everyone. And I also do not intend to stay on any of these treatments long term. But I can't stress enough: find a doctor who will listen to you, not dismiss you, about the changes to your mental and physical health, and who will discuss the options that are right for you.

I urge you to find a Certified Menopause Practitioner on the website of the North American Menopause Society at www.menopause.org.

And please, talk to your friends, talk to your family, join online support groups, do your research, whatever you need to convince yourself that you are not losing your mind, and that you are not alone.

Chapter twelve

Unexpectedly Redirected: Loss to Possibility

by Anne Stark Gallagher

"THANK YOU FOR JOINING US," my boss said as I entered the Zoom® meeting room to discuss year-end compensation for my communications team. As the law firm's director of global communications, my days were a stream of endless, back-to-back meetings.

Almost immediately, he added, "The co-managing partners have decided to go in a different direction with your position, and Rick will explain your termination benefits."

My heart started pounding in my chest and my eyes glazed over as I stared into the computer screen. Rick, the company's chief Human Resources officer, was talking but I couldn't hear a word. I simply nodded as he attempted to walk me through the details of my severance package. The law firm had changed its leadership team in the past year and the managing partner I'd worked with for nearly seven years had stepped down.

I thought, "This must be how mosquitos feel when they find themselves flying straight into a truck's windshield with no way to avoid the collision."

"Just keep nodding," I told myself.

"Do you have any questions?" Rick asked.

"Not at this time," I replied.

I mean, what could I ask, as I watched my future slipping away? My mouth was so dry I could barely eke out those four words.

"Is there anything you'd like to say?" piped in the chief administrative officer. She was new to the firm, having joined in the months before the leadership change took effect. I'd worked with her to draft her website biography, and she seemed pleasant enough. But she had never taken an interest in me.

My brain struggled to think.

"Please tell the co-managing partners thank you for the opportunity to work with them," I said.

"Thank you for your service," she responded robotically.

With that, the call ended. I watched as my computer system automatically shut down and shut me out of my job. Fifteen minutes ago, I was part of the law firm's family. Now, that door was firmly shut.

I sat motionless at my work-from-home desk. The quiet seemed oddly loud. I looked at my mobile phone. It was 3:13 pm. I sighed. In less than 15 minutes, my world had changed.

What was I going to do? I had taken this job seven years ago, just one month after my divorce was final. For the 20 years before that, I had my own business as a marketing consultant and media/presentation trainer. I did voice over and acting on the side. My life was full. But an empty marriage and divorce threw me off. With two teenagers to support, I panicked and took a full-time job, telling myself it was best for them. I'd have a steady paycheck, health benefits, a 401(k), bonus, and profit sharing.

But the decision to take a full-time job was more complicated than that. Just thinking about that complication made my stomach turn into a knot.

My husband defrauded me during our marriage, forging my name on about $200,000 of loans and then borrowing $500,000 from a mobster who put a hit on me and the kids as collateral.

He was diagnosed with mouth cancer then stomach cancer; and he blamed the loss of his business on that. The truth was that he was a con man who had bilked dozens of people out of money in a failed effort to hit some big payoff. Instead, his scheme collapsed like the house of cards it was, leaving him broke, sick, and with more angry creditors than anyone should have in a lifetime.

******

I'd never heard of the concept of financial infidelity—the act of keeping money secrets in intimate relationships—until I experienced it. Like any infidelity, financial infidelity is an abuse of trust, and that loss of trust causes a lot of tension in a relationship, sometimes ending it as it did in my case.

As many as one in three couples deal with financial infidelity in the United States alone, according to a January 2022 survey by *U.S. News and World Report*. Other surveys suggest the practice is getting more common with each passing year.

At first, there was shock and shame. I didn't tell anyone what was happening. I couldn't. I was so ashamed. How could my own husband cheat me?

With that first forged loan, he was sincerely remorseful when I confronted him. As always, he was both charming and disarming and said all the right things. I believed him when he said he would make things right and pay me back the $75,000 he had taken as a second mortgage against my lake home property.

But what I didn't understand was that this duplicity was just the first. Lawsuits for his debts were filed against me because I was his wife. The bank called, threatening foreclosure on another loan I didn't know I had after he defaulted on the payment. Unsavory characters showed up at our house and office at all hours of the day and night, demanding money and repayments. Neighbors began telling me about borrowed monies he never repaid on "can't miss" deals with him that went bad.

It's a complicated and unsettling story detailed in my debut book, *Two Weeks Away from $10 Million: A Memoir of Financial Infidelity, Fraud and Redemption.*

Included in the story was my decision to accept the full-time job that had just evaporated like a puff of smoke.

******

Part of my severance package included access to a career coach, and I began meeting weekly with Cliff. "Explore all your options; take your time," he counseled.

But I didn't want to explore my options. I wanted a high-powered, stressful, director-level job like the one I had. After all, I had my knees cut from under me before I was ready to make my own choice to move in another direction.

Despite my stubbornness, I tried hard to follow Cliff's advice. As the days passed, advice started pouring in from family, former colleagues, friends, and other contacts:

- "Think about what you would do if money didn't matter."
- "You've already worked for corporate America, work for a nonprofit and do some good."
- "Well, if this isn't a call to retire, I don't know what is."
- "Don't leave the industry that's been so good to you all these years, stick with it."
- "Have you looked at Starbucks yet? You could work part-time and still get health insurance."
- "It's time to play more tennis. With your days free, you could get really good."

It was a confusing jumble of a time. I hoped for the best and cast a wide, if messy, net.

Cliff encouraged me to network, which I began to do reluctantly and sporadically. I didn't want to talk about being laid-off but that would have to be part and parcel of the work. But as I began talking about it, I was pleasantly surprised that no one cared much; and with the pandemic raging, layoffs were sadly the norm.

"Why that's great news," my friend, Mary, in London chirped when I called her. "You can freelance for the company again." I had been a freelancer for her media company years ago and regularly stayed in touch with her. To my delight, my work with her began that day.

When I gave Cliff the update during our weekly call, he was encouraging. "You are fortunate to be positioned to get consulting work; that's one of the reasons they go back into companies. You've done that before, and doing it again is a good option that gives you both work and flexibility."

I still had job applications pending at large law firms, so I considered this new gig more as a starting point, or as a temporary holding spot, than a final result.

******

"Annie, Jim didn't show up to our lunch today. I'm worried. He's not answering my calls either," my niece, Angie, said when I picked up the phone. There was a twinge of panic in her voice, and I felt it, too. My brother, Jim, would not miss a lunch date with his stepdaughter. When Jim married Angie's mother, she was 4 years old, and he became her father figure. Now in her early 20s and working in Chicago, Angie always met with Jim when she was back home.

When Jim did not respond to my calls or texts, we dialed 9-1-1. Paramedics found him unresponsive in his home and took him to the emergency room. Diagnosed with Type 1 diabetes when he was 21 years old, Jim had fallen into a coma.

I called my sister, Kathleen, who lived nearby, and she rushed to the hospital. Within hours, Kathleen, my brother, Mike, my sister, Susan, and I devised a plan of visits and care as we waited to see if he would survive. We were in crisis mode.

Within the week, we learned more challenging news: Jim had awakened from the coma but with a traumatic brain injury. He would require extensive care, and there were no guarantees that the injury would improve.

As time wore on, more bad news followed: Jim was in the late stages of diabetes and was not likely to recover.

It was a devastating development.

In the early weeks after the incident, my siblings and I addressed his care as well as any immediate concerns, such as notifying his employer and getting him on short-term disability. But we also had to focus on longer-term issues like managing his home and finances, longer-term care, and, sadly, legal and estate planning.

Of the four siblings, I not only had the closest relationship with Jim but I was the only one of us "between jobs." For example, when Jim went through his divorce from Angie's mother a dozen years before, I helped him with a new will and trust, and I knew he wanted me to manage his affairs should anything happen to him.

None of us could have imagined this would take place; Jim was only 54 years old. And while each sibling devoted large amounts of time for visits, assignments, and group planning, we agreed that I would serve as the family point person.

With these added responsibilities and my freelance work, I was busy. I knew that if I were still in my high-powered law firm position, I wouldn't have had this time to spend with my brother. In fact, the reality was that if I still had that job, I would have quit for Jim.

******

A detour is a special route for traffic to follow when a regular route is under construction. In life, sometimes what looks like a setback is really a divine detour—an opportunity or invitation for growth and transformation. Depending on your beliefs, that divinity might be generated by God, spirit, serendipity, or something else.

That year there was a double detour—first, losing my job, then the painful realization that I was losing my brother. My soul ached with sadness. Life did not feel like an opportunity of any sort; it was tough.

Spiritual teacher Eckhart Tolle gives this advice:

> *Whatever the present moment contains, accept it as if you had chosen it. Always work with it and not against it. Make it your friend and ally, not your enemy. This will miraculously transform your life.*

When I thought of this wise advice, my face scrunched into a scowl. I wanted that vibe, but my resistance was stronger. I was angry about my situation. These weren't my choices; these things had been cruelly thrust upon me.

By August, we relocated Jim to an assisted living facility where he entered hospice care. With every visit, there was a glimmer of the "old" Jim—witty and sly, a bit of a jokester. Despite memory issues, he often had an uncanny ability to pick up a conversation from before the incident.

"How's the job search going?" he asked one day. I tried to remain stoic but was amazed he remembered our many discussions about my career angst.

"You know, I have résumés out. I'm plodding along, trying to figure it out."

"You'll figure it out. You always do," he said confidently.

"Yeah, I guess." I didn't feel much enthusiasm.

"Well, there's always the alternative," he said, pointing to himself and laughing.

I smiled at his insight and humor. There was no other place I'd rather be.

We buried Jim in November just weeks after the one-year anniversary of my layoff, which no longer seemed so important.

The following months were filled with "business of death" issues—paying final bills, selling his house, and settling his estate. I stopped applying for jobs in law firms and companies, and I focused on my freelance assignments.

******

Still working with my career coach, Cliff, we talked about my progress. Though he worked for a company, Cliff negotiated a three-day work week and often talked about how he had time to do the things he enjoyed in life.

Right after the layoff, I thought his balanced life was a little silly. But loss and death put life in perspective for me. I thought less about life's unfairness and more about possible next steps. A shift was occurring. It was time to release my resistance and "accept things as if I had chosen them."

One goal languished at the bottom of my list. "I'm thinking about writing the story of my marriage and divorce," I told him. "It's been on my mind for a long time, as you know."

"That's sort of the magic of this process. Things we thought were important change, and that's usually a good thing," he said.

At our next weekly call, I told Cliff I'd hired a book coach. "To write this, I need someone to hold me accountable and hold me to deadlines. That's one of the things you and I have talked about. It's how I work best, having someone to answer to."

Throughout my career, I'd written for and about other people. I'd used that excuse to hide the fear of writing my own stories.

******

During the next year, there were more stops than starts, but I completed the draft of my book. It gave me hope that the pieces of my life were falling back into place, and I could accomplish more of my goals.

There remained an enormous amount of work to get it published and build my platform as an author. It's a story I needed to tell. But as my story played out, I was tormented by the idea that I was suffering alone.

Years later, when I heard the term financial infidelity, I realized that was not true. Some 39 percent of American adults with partners (married or living with a partner), are financially unfaithful—a secret credit card, a hidden bank account, or maybe even a significant amount of undisclosed debt. Whether large or small, money secrets are betrayals.

What happened to me can happen to anyone. I do not delude myself that bad things are actually good. But my story of financial betrayal resolved in a way I could not have predicted. It helped me make sense of senseless events. Finding meaning changed the way I think about and live my life.

It is not the path I planned. Maybe it's better than I envisioned. What I do know is that I would not be here if not for the grace of two divine detours. By writing my story, I hope to inspire others to find meaning in their difficult life circumstances.

Chapter thirteen

The Power of the Girlfriend Brigade

by Alexis Gladstone

LIFE DOESN'T ALWAYS HAPPEN as planned. Things occur in our lives, circumstances change, and we change with them. Many times, our internal changes happen when facing challenges we never imagined.

Growing up, I was always friends with the boys. In high school, I didn't date after my sophomore year because, up until then, I had only dated seniors. The boys in my age group were my buddies. We hung out in classes; I gave them dating advice and cheered them on with their relationships. College was much of the same, though I dated regularly. Even though I lived in a sorority for several years, my closest friends were the men from my classes and the college's fraternities.

When I moved to Chicago and started my first job, while there were women with whom I became friends, I still spent a lot of time with men, both straight and gay. I liked the male energy and what

I saw as no drama. Happy hours, concerts, and baseball games were usually with my male friends. In one apartment where I lived, there was a group of four attorneys I became friends with. We watched Sunday football, cooked dinner, and just hung out together. I never considered dating any of them and vice versa.

Things started to change as this group of friends fell into long-term relationships. Their new partners weren't keen on having a random woman in the group. Eventually, like many friendships do, we drifted apart.

But after my mother died unexpectedly, I moved from New Jersey back to Chicago where I had a support network and strong friendships. I don't remember exactly when I started appreciating my female friends and being around female energy more than men, but I know it was solidified when I returned to Chicago after being absent for five years. Moving back was like coming home; the friends I re-engaged with became even more important. Many of them are, as I call them, my local sisters.

Despite having this solid community of women from various circles, I still didn't rely on them for the hard stuff. I did that alone. I was one of only a few single women in my circle and prided myself on being independent and self-sufficient. I knew that even though I was important to my friends, there would still be times when I had no choice but to figure things out on my own.

******

In 2015, I was diagnosed with breast cancer. I was now part of a club no one ever chooses to be in. By that time, I had cultivated a vast group of women in my life, and once I was over the shock, I started sharing my diagnosis with those in my most inner circle.

Many wanted to help, starting with making sure I wouldn't be alone for doctor appointments, so I "shared the wealth." I chose who I thought could best support me based on the appointment type.

I chose one friend to take me to my initial oncology and plastic surgeon appointments because she is detailed, would ask good questions I may have forgotten, and take detailed notes. Another took me to the plastic surgeon appointment before my surgery because I knew she would be a calming presence. I asked a third friend to take me to my first oncology appointment because she worked in labs and was good with "science" terms.

Then, there were those I assigned to the caregiving jobs. I chose to have a double mastectomy even though the cancer was only in one breast. I didn't want to go through this again. My sister came in to stay with me while I was in the hospital and for a few days after. She kept me company and made sure my needs were met. Once she left, I chose another friend to spend the next few days with me because she is a nurturer.

The experience showed me what a community of strong women can and will do for each other when the chips are down.

I continued to cultivate friendships and be purposeful about staying connected to them. I found different groups of like-minded women to connect with. Women entrepreneurs, check. Women into spirituality, check. Women who love supporting other women in business, double-check. These various groups have sustained me over the years.

******

Fast forward to 2021, when I found a lump. I decided to have it checked out and had a biopsy in early 2022. The first time, my cancer was found during my annual mammogram. (Side note: Ladies, please get your mammogram!) But this time was different. While most of the friends I talked with about the lump were positive and "sure" it would be nothing, deep down, I knew differently.

When I saw my surgeon's name on the caller ID at 8:00 am on a Monday, almost seven years to the day of my first diagnosis, I knew what it was. It was the second time she would say, "I can't believe I'm telling you this," and "I was sure it wasn't cancer." I responded, "Are you fucking kidding me?" and "That's what you said last time."

The first call was to a friend I had hung up the phone with 15 minutes earlier. I hadn't known her during my first go-round, but we had become close in subsequent years. I could barely get the words out, "It's cancer." She had been in the "it's going to be fine" camp, and I think she was as shocked as I was.

She immediately went into task mode, trying to help me focus on taking things one day and one step at a time. I could do that the first time around but couldn't find the wherewithal to do it this time. I couldn't talk to anyone else that day. I needed to process everything. I sent a few text messages telling two other friends and my two sisters the news and telling them I would call when I felt I could talk about it.

The following week was a whirlwind of tests. They threw it all at me because there had been less than a 2 percent chance of this happening (remember the double mastectomy?)—bone scan, CT scan, MRI on the breasts, and an MRI on the pancreas because the CT scan found something concerning.

I had a friend accompany me to my MRI appointment because it was the first one I had ever had and I was nervous; the others I went to alone. There was no reason for anyone to spend a day hanging out in a hospital as I waited between each test.

The day of the tests wasn't without its absurdity. After the CT scan and before the bone scan, I got a call from my surgeon asking if I still had my uterus. When I asked why, she said they couldn't see it on the CT scan. I told her I was sure it was still there unless someone came in the middle of the night and removed it. Regardless, she threw in a pelvic ultrasound for good measure. The week of stress from having five tests in three days wasn't over.

One of my sisters called that Friday night to tell me our father had a suspected stroke. At 89 years old and with health issues you might expect at that age, I had chosen not to tell him about the cancer recurrence, so I at least felt assured that his stroke wasn't caused by the stress of what I was going through. The good news is that it turned out to be minor, and he recovered over time. But his health, of course, added to my stress and anxiety.

Four weeks later, I was scheduled for a lumpectomy, and the stress of waiting continued. As the day of surgery got closer, I kept reminding myself that soon I would be on the other side. I embraced the love of my community, or the "Girlfriend Brigade", as I affectionately called them.

There was a friend who called me every morning to check on me. When she knew I wasn't eating much, she would drop by with French fries, which she knew was my guilty pleasure. There were many offers to stay with me post-surgery from those who lived nearby and others who lived across the country. There were cards, flowers, books, treats, and tokens of strength. All of it was appreciated and received with open arms.

After the surgery, the physical recovery was much easier than the emotional one. I had to wait five weeks for another test result to hear if I needed chemotherapy. Fortunately, I didn't. But while waiting for those results, I had the misfortune of needing emergency surgery for a hematoma 10 days after the lumpectomy. It pushed out my recovery time by a few more weeks. There were then 20 rounds of radiation and new medications. Through it all, the Girlfriend Brigade was there.

******

I've learned a lot as I've traveled this journey, at times on my own and other times with the love and support of the Girlfriend Brigade. This community of women has lifted me and kept me going, and I've taken away some important lessons.

Lean on Your Community: As a single woman, not by choice, I've always taken pride in being able to take care of things myself. I've had to be self-sufficient even when I didn't want to be. I got used to not always having someone around when I needed them, and it was not easy to ask for help. But I learned how to ask. When a significant health crisis arises, you need to lean into your community—and mine showed up in spades. You can't do it alone, especially when you're having surgery that limits your mobility. You also need emotional support.

So, I leaned in. Besides the friends I chose for the various appointments, there were the friends I decided to talk with, depending on how I felt. Sometimes, I needed a nurturer; sometimes, I needed someone I could vent to without judgment; and sometimes, I just needed to cry. I'm lucky to have a community that includes a variety of women who encompass all these traits, and I took advantage of it all.

Laugh With Your Community: I'm also lucky to have friends with a great sense of humor. Friends I can laugh with about things big and small and who can help me see the funny things. The friend with me on the day of my surgery drives an orange car. When the patient transport aide wheeled me to the entrance to meet her, her eyes lit up when she saw the car. She left me on the sidewalk as she ran over, fawning over the car and exclaiming how orange cars are her favorite. There I was, left sitting on the sidewalk, laughing through my drug-induced fog, waiting to be wheeled closer to the car so I could get in. We still talk and laugh about it today.

Another funny moment was when a friend brought me a homemade soup she knew I loved. While carrying it to the kitchen, the bag burst and literally spilled the beans. While she was cursing the bag, I was laughing. I mean, what else could you do?

Love Your Community as They Are: I learned to appreciate what each woman gave, even if it wasn't what I needed. More complicated for me was learning that some people want to do things for you that you want or need, while others want to do what they think you want or need or what makes them feel better and useful. There is a considerable difference, and it took me time to work through it. With 20/20 hindsight, I can see that they were all there in their own way, and it was all done out of an abundance of love.

Life is full of surprises. Some are sweet, and others will knock the wind out of you. Having a community of strong, fierce female friends will sustain you through the good and the bad.

Chapter fourteen

The Survivor's Journey

by Lindsay Griffiths

"NICE VEST!" HE YELLED.

Confused, I took out one ear bud, not sure what he'd said. It was dark, after dusk, as I was returning from my walk with my big, protective rescue shepherd.

His friend had slowed the car to a stop, and he'd rolled down the passenger side window to yell at me in the blue light of evening. I ignored him. Kept walking. Luckily, they drove on.

My heart pounded as I put my ear bud back in. It came to me what he'd said.

"Nice vest." I murmured aloud. I patted my dog on the head.

"Good boy," I told him. A peaceful walk ruined.

It seemed like an innocent interaction—just a compliment on my brightly lit NoxGear® vest, a weapon against the darkness. But every woman knows the statistics: one in four women will be sexually assaulted in her lifetime. And when you ARE one of those statistics, even a small interaction can trigger your PTSD.

Hi, I'm Lindsay and I'm a rape survivor.

In 1998, I began my first year of college, and the administrators did something that now seems revolutionary, but was less about student care and more about litigation avoidance. They brought in a speaker to talk about date rape. As bright-eyed and excited first-year students experiencing our orientation week, we filed into an auditorium. The speaker was Katie Koestner, only a recent college graduate herself—class of 1994.

Katie Koestner may not be a familiar name to many, but she's known as the first reported date rape survivor. To be clear, we all know that she is not the first date rape survivor, she is just the first woman to publicly report her date rape and gain notoriety for it. I'm sure many of us can imagine what happened to the women before her who attempted to do so—and, indeed, Katie herself.

Her story takes place on a college campus. She had been dating another student for about a week and after a dinner out at a lovely French restaurant, she brought him back to her dorm room. When he wanted to have sex with her and she refused, he raped her.

Katie knew that this was rape. Even though they had been dating. Even though she had been to dinner with him that evening. Even though she brought him back to her dorm room. Although it wasn't a word we were using in 1994 or even 1998, she hadn't consented to have sex with him. He raped her. She reported him.

Her college, William and Mary, didn't want her to file a police report and encouraged her to go through the judicial process at the school; unfortunately, this was fairly common at that time and something I saw happen at my own school with another student. Remember, this was before the "Me Too" movement and we, the students, didn't know any better.

The schools were the authorities, and we didn't know how to advocate for ourselves in any great capacity yet—not like kids do today; we didn't have social media or even the internet, really. Schools loved to be able to boast low rape statistics for both incoming prospective students and alumni. So, reporting a rape to the police was regularly discouraged.

In Katie's case, she went through her school's judicial process and the outcome of the hearing decided that her alleged rapist would be allowed to remain on campus. Her friends didn't support her. Her own parents didn't support her. Imagine what that must have been like.

She shared all of this with us during this speech. She spoke about consent, her activism, how a rapist can be a date or even a friend.

We left feeling like experts.

Not only would we be able to spot a rapist, but we would be able to avoid those same situations if they came up in our lives. After all, wasn't that the goal of this assembly?

But life isn't like that.

I remember being at a party a couple of years later when a girl came out of a room and seemed really off. Something was wrong. It was a cast party for a musical I was in, and the cast members were tight. She was very young, younger than I was. I grabbed another woman and we found her and asked her what had happened. She eventually told us—she had been raped. By another cast member.

I spoke to the director who was a good friend. Of course, he wanted to get a group of guys together to beat him up, but that wasn't the right course. We wanted to do what was right by her.

We followed Katie's path and spoke to the school.

"Are you sure you want to report it? It's his word against hers."

For his part, he was devastated. He didn't realize that she didn't want to have sex with him. This was before people started talking about consent and not taking advantage of drunk women. But he still raped her. And he didn't accept what she said.

She decided to press forward. We supported her.

She turned into a shell of herself.

The hearing happened.

It was the same result as Katie's.

The campus allowed him to stay.

How do you run into your rapist over and over and over, and survive?

******

It was a winter night, my junior year of college, and all my close friends were away for the evening. I spent much of my teenage years and all my twenties desperately wanting to be cool, with my self-esteem somewhere on the floor, so I was thrilled to be hanging out with a fun group of seniors who were friends of my best friend's boyfriend.

We partied in their room for a while, listening to music, doing shots of Wild Turkey® because we lived in the middle of nowhere and that's all they had available. I'm sure I was wearing a sweater and jeans because it was the early 2000s and a winter night in central New York. Some women can recall exactly what they were wearing when they were raped, but I am not one of those women.

After a while, we agreed to walk over to the campus pub to keep drinking and see who else was partying. Things got a bit fuzzy from there. I had a few beers, which were never my drink of choice, and at some point, someone said I got a "look" as if I was going to vomit. Adorable. Attractive.

One of my friends, who I thought was cute, decided to help me get home safely. We lived on a small campus—it is said that there are enough acres of land on campus for all the students. And unlike many schools where students move off campus after the first year, at my school, you had to enter a special lottery during your senior year to be allowed to live off campus, which most people didn't do. I lived on campus all four years of school.

This was my junior year, but somehow, we had ended up living in sophomore housing, which meant that I was a bit farther from the main part of school than most people—slightly "down the hill" as we called it. It was dark and cold, but safe for the most part; the only people wandering around the school would be other students.

That night my "knight in shining armor" walked me back to my dorm room. I didn't share it with anyone, and as I mentioned before, my friends were all away for the evening; even my closest neighbors weren't around. Things become a bit hazy from this point, all I can remember are flashes. I know that I was slipping in and out of consciousness, which is, of course, the legal definition of rape. And I also remembering saying "No."

But despite both of those things, it took me 10 years to reconcile what happened to me. It's not that I was in denial. It's just that it didn't occur to me that I had been raped.

I sat through Katie Koestner's assembly and felt confident that I would recognize a tough situation if I were in one.

I had counseled a friend through a date rape situation.

I had even waited to drink until I knew I could trust the friends I had made in college to have my back.

Yet, the next day, I felt confused. Upset.

I talked to my friends about it. I had previously liked this guy and thought he was cute. Collectively, they seemed to think this was a bad drunken night. Maybe he wanted to date me?

I saw him in the dining hall the next day at dinner. He was friendly and acted like things were good between us. He asked me to a party that night, and my friends and I all decided to go. I felt conflicted. But I still went. He was cute after all, and my friends really wanted to go. My best friend's boyfriend was going, and we pretty much did whatever she said when it came to socializing, so that was that.

The guy and I ended up dating for three months, and it ended when he cheated on me with another woman and was upset that I wouldn't allow him to date us both. It took me a long time to get over him, and I didn't have great support around me. My friends felt like I was overreacting and that I should just be fine when he continued to be a part of our mutual friend group.

Later, when one of those friends got married, he turned up for her wedding weekend engaged to the woman that he had cheated on me with, and no one gave me any warning. Instead, one of our friends threw me in a pool fully clothed because he thought it would be funny.

It was still another five years before I reckoned with the knowledge that what had happened to me that night was rape.

In those early days, I was numb. I believed that so much time had passed that I didn't have a right to feel triggered or harmed over it. I didn't want anything to do with my rapist, and I had separated myself from him a long time ago. I also slowly and quietly separated myself from that friend group.

I shared my story with a few people close to me and began to claim it as part of who I am. But it wasn't until the "Me Too" movement first started by activist and writer Tarana Burke and later shared by actor Alyssa Milano, that I started to see so many other survivors' stories. I began to recognize myself in some of those stories.

******

For a long time, I felt like I didn't qualify as a rape survivor. There have been times when I've shared my story with people and they have said,

"Well, you did date him afterward."

"Yeah, it didn't really count."

Those comments felt like gut punches at first. They reinforced every terrible thing I had said to myself about being raped, about what I deserved for being drunk that night, for dating a guy who had raped me.

Two things changed all that.

First, I had a conversation with someone I cared deeply about, and I confessed what had happened. He thought for a moment, looked at me, and said, "Your self-esteem must have been very low for you to keep dating him after that happened."

It made me realize that I could separate the rape and the relationship in my mind and come to terms with both of them. It also made me realize that I'd grown a lot since then, and what I would accept from my relationships in all levels of my life is completely different now.

The other thing was entering into the survivor community and surrounding myself with the right support system, which allowed me to understand that survivorship doesn't have qualifications. I was raped because my rapist raped me. That is a full sentence—no explanation needed.

******

Today, I am surrounded by an amazing group of friends, who offer me incredible support. Truthfully, I wasn't in a place to BE a good friend when I was in my twenties, and probably most of us aren't. But in my forties, I have found these incredible women who offer true community and understanding. We show up for each other in every way—from flying in for celebrations to holding each other in the worst moments you can imagine.

Someone always has the right words of wisdom to share, and when we don't, we can just be with each other. I am so grateful for that, and it is something that I wish for everyone and especially every survivor.

Finding the right therapist has been a game-changer. Therapy as part of healing is essential. Being a survivor is part of who I am, but it is not ALL of me. Yet on the days when it becomes a louder voice in my head, it's something that I talk to my therapist about and she reminds me to be present: I'm here now, where I am safe and protected. I have tools that I can use. I have an incredible support system that I can ask for help. Speaking to her allows me to breathe a little easier and untangle the knots in my brain.

Being a survivor of sexual assault and rape feels lonely. Often for the act itself, but also often for the aftermath—the way people treat you, the lack of support from people you thought would be there for you. That silence can be deafening.

So, when someone says, "I see you and I believe you," it is so incredibly critical. It is lifesaving. I have been so grateful this last year just for people to have said, "I see you."

It has been over 20 years since I was raped, and I still have PTSD. It's worse now than when I was 21. I don't know if that's because there are so many publicly shared stories of the horrors that rapists and abusers commit. I feel compelled to read them and witness the strength and bravery of my fellow survivors. I see them, too. I get to speak with some of them in my DMs and other communities that we've created and what has happened to them is often so staggering. They are so strong and brave in ways they shouldn't have to be.

On the hardest nights, my big shepherd will stand by my bed, sigh, and then jump in and snuggle up against my legs to sleep. He has PTSD, too—I have no idea what his history is, but we navigate our shared traumas together and try to find some peace. With a sleep story and my big dog, I can finally relax enough to rest.

My dog has also given me back the night because I can take him for a run or walk in the dark and feel safe. When I am lost, I always turn to movement to find myself again. That's how I became a distance runner. My coach always says that most people don't find running, especially distance running, because they love to run; they find it because they're processing trauma. For me, this has proven to be true.

Footfall after footfall, mile after mile, I claim my body back. I learned to trust it again, to discover what it can do, and what I am capable of. It's a lifelong journey and I'm not finished yet. Many days, it feels like I'm just getting started.

******

Sexual violence is common. Over half of women and almost 1 in 3 men have experienced sexual violence involving physical contact during their lifetimes. One in 4 women and about 1 in 26 men have experienced completed or attempted rape. About 1 in 9 men were made to penetrate someone during his lifetime. Additionally, 1 in 3 women and about 1 in 9 men experienced sexual harassment in a public place.

Sexual violence starts early. More than 4 in 5 female rape survivors reported that they were first raped before age 25 and almost half were first raped as a minor (before age 18). Nearly 8 in 10 male rape survivors reported that they were made to penetrate someone before age 25 and about 4 in 10 were first made to penetrate as a minor.

Sexual violence disproportionately affects some groups. Women and racial and ethnic minority groups experience a higher burden of sexual violence. For example, more than 2 in 5 non-Hispanic American Indian or Alaska Native and non-Hispanic multiracial women were raped in their lifetime.

Sexual violence is costly. Recent estimates put the lifetime cost of rape at $122,461 per survivor, including medical costs, lost productivity, criminal justice activities, and other costs.[1]

Every 68 seconds, another American is sexually assaulted.[2]

1 out of every 6 American women has been the victim of an attempted or completed rape in her lifetime (14.8 percent complete, 2.8 percent attempted).[3]

About 3 percent of American men—or 1 in 33—have experienced an attempted or completed rape in their lifetime.[4]

From 2009 to 2013, Child Protective Services agencies substantiated, or found strong evidence to indicate, 63,000 children a year were victims of sexual abuse.[5]

A majority of child victims are ages 12 to 17. Of victims under the age of 18: 34 percent of victims of sexual assault and rape are under age 12, and 66 percent of victims of sexual assault and rape are ages 12 to 17.[6]

If you or someone you know is a victim of sexual assault, call the 24/7 National Sexual Assault Hotline at 1.800.656.HOPE. It is free and confidential. RAINN.org also has a live chat function. RAINN is the nation's largest anti-sexual violence organization.

---

[1] CDC Facts on Sexual Violence – Last Updated on June 22, 2022.

[2] Department of Justice, Office of Justice Programs, Bureau of Justice Statistics, National Crime Victimization Survey, 2019 (2020). Note: RAINN applies a 5-year rolling average to adjust for changes in the year-to-year NCVS survey data.

[3] National Institute of Justice & Centers for Disease Control & Prevention, Prevalence, Incidence and Consequences of Violence Against Women Survey (1998).

[4] National Institute of Justice & Centers for Disease Control & Prevention, Prevalence, Incidence and Consequences of Violence Against Women Survey (1998).

[5] United States Department of Health and Human Services, Administration for Children and Families, Administration on Children, Youth and Families, Children's Bureau. Child Maltreatment Survey, 2012 (2013).

[6] Department of Justice, Office of Justice Programs, Bureau of Justice Statistics, Sex Offenses and Offenders (1997).

Chapter fifteen

Self-Doubt as a Catalyst for Change

by Judy Hoberman

IT'S TOO TIGHT. It's too loose. It's uncomfortable. People look at me funny. I'll never fit in. Sounds like a conversation we might have with ourselves about clothing in our closet. No matter what I tried on, there were days when nothing seemed to fit.

While I never really had a problem with my clothing fitting, it was more about me ... fitting IN, that is. You see I was cute, not beautiful; I was smart, not Madame Curie smart. I wasn't tall, I wasn't curvy, I wasn't a cheerleader, I wasn't popular. The "what I wasn't" list was definitely longer than the "what I was" list. No matter what I did, I always returned to the same conclusion: I'm just not enough.

Things started to really feel too tight **on** me ... and **for** me. One morning, shortly before I was going to graduate from high school, I was greeted at the breakfast table by a white envelope adorned with ribbons and bows. I excitedly opened it while being careful not to ruin the wrapping.

The message inside read, "Congratulations! You have been entered into Miss Queens Beauty Contest." The note was from my father. To say I was shocked was an understatement. You see, as I said before, I never thought of myself as particularly beautiful. More importantly, I had no interest in competing in a beauty pageant.

In fact, not long before that, I shared my dream to go to medical school, and that was met with my father's response of simply rolling his eyes. What was even more curious was how it was possible to be entered and accepted into a beauty contest without even knowing about it. I wondered, "Should I say something to my father? Should I protest?"

But since I always strived to be "the perfect" girl and didn't want to offend him, I thought, "Maybe I shouldn't say anything and just go along with the program."

Pretty soon, he understood this was not something I wanted to do. He sat me down and said, "You need to do this contest and you need to win, because all you are is pretty, and that's all you will ever be. You won't amount to anything more anyway."

The invisible clothing was now choking me; and although I really wanted to please my father, I also realized that I could NOT go through with the whole beauty pageant thing. So even though it was completely out of character for me to go against my parents' wishes, I withdrew myself from the contest. I was surprised at how good this small act of rebellion felt. Yet my father was undeterred. He enrolled me in another beauty pageant, then another one. The more he enrolled me in these beauty contests, the faster I un-enrolled myself.

My feelings of inadequacy didn't change when I graduated high school.

******

This story was one I had never shared with anyone until I decided to in a TEDx talk. I know, crazy. Many decades later, many careers later, and many personal development programs later, I found myself with an application to deliver a TEDx talk. This was never on my radar; and, for some reason, I started to have the feeling that nothing seems to fit ... again. I thought I had rewound the tapes to that old story, yet those old feelings quickly resurfaced.

My TEDx talk was an opportunity to share my secret and remind others, and especially myself, that enough was clearly enough. But I couldn't seem to get through it without bursting into tears. Those old feelings stung like a swarm of bees. My coach suggested that I reword the story so that it wouldn't be about me but rather someone I knew. I wasn't sure if even that would work, but I did it. And even though my voice started shaking and cracking, I kept going until the very end when I revealed that the story was about me.

That's when the tears poured out. That's when I saw everyone crying with me, not for me.

And when I heard the cheers from the audience, I realized it wasn't rewinding the tapes that I needed to do. I had to release them.

******

Things started to get interesting as I began to "own" my story. It was my story and only I could tell it the way it should be told, which I did, many times, without tears. I called it "The Beautiful One," and I talked about why someone would want to listen to me and what value I could bring. I would share ways to overcome the litany of limiting beliefs that led to my feelings of inadequacy and how to break through those limitations. All the while, I still "owned" THAT story.

My coach asked me why that was the story I chose to tell. I shared the entire background and drama behind it, thinking I had answered it sufficiently and successfully. Then he asked me the same question. I filled in a few other missing pieces, like being an introvert. I thought I was done until he asked me again and added, "But that isn't your story now." I looked at him as if he had two heads and said, "I don't know what you mean."

He then told me that he never saw me that way. He described me as someone who could walk into a room and people would take notice—not because I come across overly confident or cocky but because of the energy I bring. He said that people seem genuinely excited to see me and look forward to engaging in conversation with me. He saw me as someone who was not bogged down by the limiting beliefs that I describe in my story.

Maybe it was time to shift the narrative from self-doubt to self-discovery or even start to transform my self-doubt into empowerment.

There was a lot to think about, but I was determined. Self-doubt is a universal struggle that often holds us back from realizing our full potential. We frequently ask, "Who would want to listen to me?" These limiting beliefs can be crippling, preventing us from pursuing our passions and sharing our unique voices with the world.

Sometimes it's our past holding us back—in my case my father's words, perhaps? Your past is your past, and you might be ready to release it but something or someone is making it too difficult. Whether you want to hold onto it is your choice.

Right or wrong, good or bad, many of us take the lessons we've learned from our past and apply them to our future. But your past doesn't define you ... it prepares you. Just because your past didn't go the way you wanted it to doesn't mean your future can't be better than you've ever imagined. Your greatest talent is so much more powerful than your biggest fear.

What would it be like to reclaim your life? Imagine feeling that power ...

******

In one of my many conversations with myself and others, I realized that my limiting beliefs were merely stories I had told myself over the years. My father's story for me was his story, not mine, and I could choose to rewrite my narrative. I realized that my self-doubt had held me back for far too long. I suddenly understood that when people said I was playing "small," it was because of those stories that kept resurfacing. The muddiness was now clearing up for me.

Many of us have experienced moments in life when self-doubt overshadowed our dreams and ambitions. We've questioned our abilities and wondered if we were "enough." However, it's essential to understand that self-doubt is a common part of the human experience. What truly matters is how we navigate and transform it.

I have always told my clients that words matter; and perhaps this was a case of "do as I say not as I do." In any event, I went back to my original story and changed the title from "The Beautiful One" to "In Demand." My words to the audience became more about being exactly who they need. I believed they would love what I stand for. I shared that I have the privilege of doing what I love every single day!

I realized that this journey wasn't just about what I did but who I had become. Changing my mindset made me realize that my words have the power to inspire and connect with others. I am enough, and the world is waiting to hear my story!

My journey has taught me some valuable lessons.

******

Lesson 1: Embrace Your Uniqueness

I learned that where/how I was brought up was not a limitation but a source of authenticity. My stories are enriched by my experiences, and I have a unique perspective to offer the world. Rather than comparing myself to others, I decided to celebrate my individuality. This uniqueness is such a valuable asset that sets us apart in this very crowded world. I would come to realize that this uniqueness would be the "S" in my company's name, Selling In A S.K.I.R.T., as Standing Out!

Lesson 2: Believe in Yourself

The power of belief has transformed my life. I understood that self-doubt was a natural part of the creative process. Instead of letting it hold me back any longer, I use it as fuel to improve and grow. Believing in myself became my daily practice. I have affirmations that I practice and even on my whiteboard it states: "I am in demand. People are waiting in line to work with me." I see it as soon as I walk into my office, and it shifts my mindset.

Belief in oneself is a fundamental pillar of self-empowerment. As we navigate life's challenges and pursue our passions, self-doubt often creeps in. The key is not to eliminate self-doubt entirely but to learn to coexist with it. It can serve as a catalyst for growth and self-improvement.

When my children were younger, we had an affirmation jar. Each morning, they would each pick one out of the jar and read it aloud. That set the tone for the day. Believing in yourself is a continuous practice, one that requires nurturing and reinforcement. Over time, it can lead to significant personal growth and empowerment. Let's remember that you're never too young or too old to believe in yourself.

Lesson 3: Share Your Voice

The question we still ask is why does anyone want to hear what we have to say? Our words make others take notice. They should be authentic and valuable and make others think. Our words should share our passion and our purpose and should make us think as well. Our word is our bond and our voice shares that with the world. Pretty powerful, isn't it?

But it's more than just the spoken word. It's watching a person and seeing and feeling their excitement. It's what they share with others. It's what makes them stand out in a crowd. It's realizing what is important to us and really owning it. It's about being authentic and intentional. Knowing who we are gives us the time and the reason to do what we love, for the reasons we love, with the people we love.

My journey taught me that my voice mattered. I stopped striving for perfection while hiding my opinion. I have a message to share, and there were people who needed to hear it. By sharing my stories, I connected with others on a deeper level and created a sense of belonging. Remember, it's not about finding your voice. It's about giving yourself permission to use it.

As my community grew and my business success continued, I used my platform to inspire others. My greatest joy is to mentor young women starting out in their careers. I share my experiences of being the only or one of the only women in my chosen career, with executive women who need support and guidance to advance and excel. I learned that the privilege of doing what you love also comes with the responsibility of giving back and preparing the next generation of leaders.

******

So, what's your story? What narrative are you ready to change? When something doesn't feel right, think about why it doesn't. When you felt that, did something change? There is someone in your life probably feeling the same way or has felt the same way or possibly will be feeling the same way. Reach out to a friend, a colleague, a coach, or a mentor. Someone should be there for you. If someone isn't, move along until you find someone who is.

Sometimes, what's holding you back is a situation you need to work through. Other times, it could be a person, and that might call for a candid conversation between you. Is this something you can fix today? Maybe not, but you'll know when you're ready.

Whatever the circumstance, you will take care of it, at the right moment—just don't wait forever. Clearing the "air" is essential. Think about what you may be missing.

When I think about my journey, it is a reminder that we all have the power to change the direction of our lives. It's not about what you do, it's about who you are becoming. Self-doubt and limiting beliefs are shadows that can be embraced and used as steppingstones to greatness. Believe in your uniqueness, have faith in yourself, and share your voice with the world.

As I embark on my own journey of self-empowerment, I have found that our own transformation extends beyond ourselves. We can use our newfound confidence and privilege to make a positive difference in the lives of others.

The privilege of pursuing what we love and becoming self-empowered comes with a responsibility to give back. Whether through mentorship, community involvement, or acts of kindness, we can amplify the ripple effect of positive change in our communities and the world.

Does everything "fit" all the time for me? No, and that's because I'm always evolving; and, of course, life happens.

When you get to know me, you'll notice that I always end my posts with the sign-off: "If you need help, simply ask." I always mean it and I am here for you. It wasn't always that way when I reached out for help, so I want my actions to support someone else's story.

As C.S. Lewis said, "You can't go back and change the beginning, but you can start where you are and change the ending."

If you need help, simply ask!

Chapter sixteen

A Journey of Resilience and Hope

by Homeira Izadi

IN THE HEART OF Tehran, Iran, I was born into a world where the air was perfumed with the scent of viola flowers, and the laughter of family filled our home. My parents, pillars of love and wisdom, fostered an environment where dreams flourished like the plants in our backyard garden. My father, especially, was a man of profound compassion and intellect. Every morning, as he prepared breakfast, his actions spoke of discipline and care, values he instilled in us.

Encouraged by my father, I aspired to be a doctor from a young age. "Help others," he would say, his words resonating deep within me. I remember playing with a medical kit, pretending to treat my family and friends. Little did I know, this childhood game would foreshadow a lifelong commitment to healing.

Then the peace and stability of my early life were shattered on February 11, 1979. The Iranian Revolution transformed our progressive nation into an anti-Western theocracy. The following Iran-Iraq War brought further devastation, marking my first encounter with the horrific consequences of conflict.

Amidst this turmoil, my father's wisdom remained a guiding light. His encouragement and open-mindedness shaped my worldview. Yet, fate dealt a cruel blow when he passed away from gastric cancer at the age of 61. His funeral was a revelation, uncovering his quiet acts of philanthropy. His humility and generosity profoundly influenced my path in medicine.

The war years were a brutal backdrop to my medical education. Witnessing the suffering inflicted by chemical warfare solidified my resolve to combat illness and injury. Despite the challenges, I thrived in medical school, owing to Iran's policy of free training in exchange for government service. This opportunity allowed me to serve in remote areas, bringing care to those most in need.

Each day in war-torn Iran was a lesson in resilience and compassion. I learned about the fragility of life and the indomitable human spirit. These experiences molded me into a more empathetic healer, committed to alleviating suffering.

******

Seeking advanced knowledge and opportunities, I moved to the United States, a decision that marked a significant turning point. The transition was fraught with challenges—cultural adaptation, rigorous exams, and the emotional toll of a failing marriage. Yet, inspired by my father's legacy and driven by my passion for medicine, I persevered.

In the United States, my medical journey was eye-opening. I encountered a healthcare system focused more on profit than patient welfare. Disillusioned, I established my own practice, blending conventional and integrative medicine.

I focused on preventative care, understanding that true healing involves treating the whole person—mind, body, and spirit.

Throughout my career, I've witnessed the consequences of preventable diseases, especially in long-term care facilities. These experiences reaffirmed my commitment to preventative medicine and inspired me to advocate for a healthcare revolution focused on education and early intervention.

Today, my mission extends beyond individual patient care. I aim to establish a multi-modality clinic accessible to all, addressing every aspect of aging and providing preventative measures. My journey, marked by resilience, compassion, and an unwavering pursuit of a dream, is a testament to the impact one person can make.

As I continue to navigate the complexities of healthcare, I am guided by the lessons of my father, the experiences of war, and the challenges of adapting to a new country. My story, a tapestry of personal and professional triumphs and setbacks, is an inspiration to those facing adversity. It is a reminder that with determination, passion, and a commitment to service, one can overcome obstacles and make a lasting impact on the world.

In the end, my fight to heal is more than a personal narrative; it is a call to action. It's about transforming adversity into opportunity, pain into resilience, and dreams into reality. My journey illustrates the power of hope, the importance of compassion, and the unyielding strength of the human spirit. It is a story for

anyone who has faced challenges, reminding them that with belief
and perseverance, anything is possible.

Through the years, I have encountered many stories of pain
and despair, but also of hope and recovery. I remember one patient, a young girl caught in the crossfire of conflict, her body and
spirit scarred by the horrors of war. Her resilience and recovery
were a profound reminder of why I chose this path. It's patients
like her who reinforce my commitment to healing and drive me
to continue my fight against the ravages of disease and injury.

My journey has also been one of personal growth. The challenges I have faced, from the cultural shock of moving to a new
country to navigating the complex landscape of the American
healthcare system, have taught me about strength, adaptability,
and the importance of staying true to one's values and vision.

In my practice, I strive to create a space where healing is a
holistic process. I have learned that treating the body is only part
of the equation. True healing involves addressing the emotional
and spiritual needs of patients, an approach that was inspired by
the compassionate care my father exemplified.

******

Looking back, I realize my journey has been like the viola flowers
in our Tehran garden—a beautiful blend of growth, resilience,
and continuous blooming. The path has not been easy, but it has
been incredibly rewarding. Each patient I help, each life I touch,
adds another layer of meaning to my story.

Mine has been a path of both challenges and immense rewards.
Each patient I help, each life I touch, enriches my story. I share
my journey to inspire others to pursue their passions, overcome

obstacles, and positively impact the world. My fight to heal is not just my narrative but a shared story of countless individuals dedicated to helping others. It embodies the power of hope, compassion, and a life devoted to service.

As I look forward, I am filled with purpose and determination. The journey continues, with much work to be done, lives to touch, and lessons to learn. I am ready for the challenges ahead, armed with the wisdom of the past and hope for a brighter, healthier future.

My fight to heal continues, a journey of resilience and hope, and I invite you to join me.

Chapter seventeen

The Road to Mastering My Voice

by Nori Jabba

DURING A CHALLENGING TIME in my 28-year marriage, I grappled with a whirlwind of emotions. My husband's failure to appreciate my voice and his lack of respect for my role as a stay-at-home mom left me feeling profoundly undervalued for years. It was painful, mainly because this absence of appreciation was coming from the person to whom I was the closest. When he used his voice as a weapon, the hurt was intense. His words would cut me like a sword. Each careless remark pierced my heart, undermining my sense of self-worth and shaking the very foundation of my emotional well-being. It was a kind of turmoil that deeply scarred me, leaving me feeling betrayed.

The tension in our relationship was further compounded by my prioritization of our children's needs over his. This imbalance led to frustration and a disconnection between us. Our problems often stemmed from how we used our voices, leaving us both feeling estranged. It was a challenging phase, marked by a struggle to find balance and mutual understanding. This challenge of how to use my voice effectively has been a pattern in my life.

******

When I was in second grade, I made the mistake of talking back to my teacher. She was cold, strict, and unloving. I couldn't help myself the day she yelled at me to stop sitting on my knees in my chair. Sitting this way was comfortable for me and had never been a problem. "If God wanted you to sit like that, he wouldn't have given you legs," she yelled. "Well, I don't believe in God," I snapped back as my cheeks turned red. She was furious and told me to shut my mouth.

The rest of the class was shocked that this quiet little girl talked back. What the teacher didn't know was that my parents were raising me not to believe in God, so I pointed out her incorrect assumption. The incident led to exciting talks about religion with my friends, who were envious that I didn't have to attend church. The funny thing was, I felt left out. From this, I learned that my voice was a double-edged sword. It was powerful; it could protect me, but it could also hurt me. That teacher had it in for me for the entire year. I loved school and was an excellent student, but second grade was no fun.

About a year later, I learned the hard way that using one's voice requires an understanding of its power. My dad took my sisters and me to ride go-carts at a carnival. Excitedly, I jumped into the car first, grabbing the coveted front seat. My older sister ran after me and jerked me forcefully out of the car, telling me that the front seat was not for babies. "I hate you, you big, fat pig!" I screamed.

My dad heard me and angrily told me to return to the house. Sobbing, I tried hopelessly to defend my behavior. Off they went without me. I was reminded that my voice was a double-edged sword, and I had used it to my detriment. With these and other experiences in my childhood, I discovered early on that my voice could be a tool or a weapon, and that having a filter is essential. Never afraid to speak up, this has sometimes cost me. I now acknowledge that mastering my voice is still a work in progress.

Every woman is also expected to "find" her voice. Finding one's voice implies it's been lost. "Find your voice" is advice reserved for women. I wonder if "she found her voice" is chiseled on any woman's tombstone.

******

In my twenties, I was conscious about finding the right balance of power and deference with my voice. I wanted to demonstrate my value and self-worth as a young professional, but I had to be careful, know my place, not overstep, offend, or say the wrong thing.

Of course, we all know that having a strong sense of self-worth is crucial for emotional well-being and combatting depression and anxiety. And I know that I'm more likely to take better care of myself when I value myself. My twenties were about learning to value myself. For the most part, I did an excellent job, but the anxiety associated with always trying to say the right thing lingered as I engaged in the delicate dance of using my voice.

At times in my career, I even felt powerful. I was promoted, and after several years, I managed a team and was responsible for a real estate portfolio spanning nearly half the state and millions of square feet. But balancing my voice still took concerted effort. I looked young, and everyone who reported to me was significantly older than I was. It took trial and error to learn how to be influential and respected.

People with a healthy sense of self-worth are typically more resilient in facing challenges. They are better equipped to cope with failures, setbacks, and criticism, viewing them as part of the learning and growing process rather than as reflections of their worth.

And self-worth always positively impacts relationships. When you value yourself, you're more likely to have healthy relationships, set appropriate boundaries, and avoid staying in toxic or harmful situations.

With a strong sense of self-worth, individuals tend to have less self-doubt and are less likely to be swayed by peer pressure or need external validation. A healthy level of self-worth can drive motivation and ambition. Ultimately, I have learned that my sense of self-worth is directly related to my sense of happiness, and my voice is directly related to my self-worth.

******

Once, a consultant told me my voice was "too folksy." What did that even mean? Apparently, my "folksy" voice lacked the formality or sophistication that this person expected in our corporate headquarters office in the mid-1990s. I am comfortable when my voice is more casual and conversational, and I had become too comfortable.

It was hard feedback to hear, but I tried to learn from it. This woman explained that I was trying too hard to be casual and to connect with my team members; I needed to be more of an authority figure.

When I called my teammates "guys" or started meetings with conversations about our weekends, I came across as someone who was trying to be a friend, not a boss. I adjusted my voice to show I was in charge but lost a bit of myself in the process. I was thrilled when the consultant's contract ended, and I could relax my demeanor and tone a bit. My team liked me a lot more than the consultant, anyway!

At 36, I took time off to be a stay-at-home mom. I enthusiastically left my work voice at the office and quickly identified with my mom-voice. As a mother of three children under age 4, I had to learn how to use my voice to be strong, nurturing, controlling, loving, firm, fun, confident, protective, and safe, sometimes simultaneously: "No, you can't have dessert before dinner, love-love girl." "Watch where you are going; look ahead, Sweetie. I don't want you to trip and fall again."

For the most part, I used it well, and my kids responded positively. While they learned to talk back, and sometimes it hurt, often, I'd chuckle and be reminded of myself as a child learning to use my own voice. Sometimes, I cautioned them that using your voice can get you in trouble. More than anything, my voice was my primary medium for showing love. And I never had to worry about being "too folksy."

******

Six years had passed since I last donned my professional attire. Then, I swapped my comfortable flats for heels, and stepped into the world that had once defined my identity. As I rode up the elevator on the first day of my return to the workforce, excitement and apprehension swirled within me. My return was a whirlwind of reintroductions and new faces.

The office, with the buzz of meetings, strategy sessions, and coffee, was at once comforting, invigorating, and demanding. As weeks turned to months, a harsh reality began to unfold. Once confident and heard, my voice seemed to echo into a void. In meetings, I fought to be heard, and my ideas were often dismissed with a chuckle or a casual interruption especially by my male colleagues. My identity as a mother and community member, a cherished role that was important for my job in community relations and one of the reasons I was hired, had also become a veil obscuring my professional capabilities to some of my coworkers.

There were moments when I felt like a lone warrior on a battlefield, my only ally being my boss. His support was unwavering, a beacon of hope in an otherwise daunting environment. But in his absence, I felt unguarded, as if thrown to a pack of wolves. The struggle to reclaim my voice was arduous. Yet, in these moments of adversity, I tapped my inner strength. I refused to be silenced or overshadowed. Gradually, I learned to assert myself, my voice steady and unwavering. Refusing to be interrupted, my ideas demanded the respect they deserved.

A central part of my job was to understand my community and use that understanding to inform the company's development projects. In the community, where others saw me as a leader, my voice found its rhythm easily and authentically. Whether leading community discussions or meeting with other community leaders, I listened and I felt valued and heard.

My days were a symphony of roles—from the nurturing tones of a mother in the morning to the assertive cadence of a professional by day and the engaging, passionate voice of a community leader by night. My colleagues began to perceive me through a new lens, reflecting my contributions and leadership within the community. Their respect for me grew, mirroring the respect I had garnered outside the office walls.

This journey was more than a quest for professional recognition; it was a journey of self-discovery. I learned that my voice, in all its forms, was not just a communication tool but a vessel for respect, empowerment, and identity. My voice became my most powerful asset, a testament to my resilience, commitment, and multifaceted life. It was the key to feeling respected and valued, not just as a professional, a mother, or a community leader, but as a woman of strength and limitless potential.

******

I then became a consultant for 10 years and continued to understand the importance of my voice for promoting my business and landing and retaining clients. When I decided to go back to employment so I could reinstate benefits and have a regular income when my children were older, I knew it would be hard to find a job since I was over 50. I had a solid résumé boasting degrees, awards, and valuable experience. But I couldn't find a job.

After months of disappointments, the job search began depleting my self-esteem, so I stopped, went back to consulting, and decided to research ageism and write a book about my journey.

Writing my book gave me strength and a sense of liberation I hadn't anticipated. As I poured my thoughts onto the pages, a revelation dawned on me: writing my journey was not just a means of sharing my story to help others; it was a means to amplify and liberate my inner voice, which unleashed my belief in myself. This discovery was akin to finding a secret door leading to a new dimension of unexplored possibilities.

This new understanding of the power of my written voice was transformational as writing became a conduit for deeper self-love and self-worth. Despite enjoying writing my whole life, it was as if I had been speaking one language and suddenly discovered the joy and intricacy of another.

Writing became not just a method of communication but a form of artistic expression, rich and fulfilling. This transformation in my relationship with writing led to a profound shift in my engagement with all art forms. I began to see every piece of artwork, every note of music, every written word as a unique voice, each with its own story and message. My approach to art shifted from a binary perspective of like or dislike to an exploratory journey into the heart and soul of the creator. I learned to appreciate these creative works' diverse expressions of humanity.

Listening to music, I would now find myself immersed in the emotions and narratives woven into the melodies and lyrics, even if the genre was outside my usual preference. I could hear the voice of the artist, their joys, their struggles, their unspoken thoughts. In paintings and sculptures that I wouldn't choose for my own home, I discovered a spectrum of perspectives and emotions, each piece a window into the artist's mind.

Books, too, became more than just stories or information. They were intimate conversations with the authors, each page reflecting their inner world. Even when a book wasn't to my personal taste, I found value in the voice behind the words, the passion and purpose driving the narrative.

Writing my own book and embracing this new perspective made me feel more connected to the world. It was as if I had tuned into a frequency that connected me more deeply with the humanity around me, enhancing my empathy and understanding.

******

Connecting with others through voice led me to understand what I believe is the true meaning of mastering voice. Learning that my voice forged my identity took over half a century. Mastering my voice means bravely and vulnerably filtering VOICE—Volume, Opportunity, Intelligence, Content, and Emotion—through a chosen format to achieve an outcome.

Understanding my goal for the outcome helps me determine how to filter my VOICE. The goal can be to soothe, care, demonstrate, nurture, express, opine, convince, advocate, lead, achieve, motivate, share, convey, humor, articulate, emphasize, instruct, influence, calm, excite, or love; or, it can be to damage, inflict, manipulate, or hurt.

After publishing my book, I used my voice to record the audio version and learned that my voice is delicate and needs care and that using it effectively requires my entire body. I had to sit up straighter, engage my core more, and even use my hands to help me convey my points. I learned the importance of delivery and breathing and that each variable works together as a perfectly interwoven fabric. Through this process, I learned to accept and like my voice and, through doing so, love myself more.

I believe you must love your voice to master it and I am finally starting to do so. I know that my voice is my medium to add value and demonstrate power. I must use it with care and determination.

My voice is my tool, my weapon, my most significant asset, my superpower.

Chapter eighteen

Follow the Yellow Brick Road

by April Joy

DO YOU EVER FEEL like Dorothy in "The Wizard of Oz"? Have you had a cyclone or two come along in your life that has taken you to a faraway land and you have no idea how you got there? You probably met a few characters along the way, too; some who brought you more grief than fulfillment and others who showed more kindness and emotional protection than you expected.

As a young girl, I got swept up in a cyclone. I was 7 years old, just starting the second grade, and awoke to my brother throwing a garbage bag over my head saying, "Put all your clothes in here; we're leaving." I remember that night like it was yesterday; interestingly enough, I didn't question or hesitate ... I did what my older brother told me to do. I got out of bed and stuffed all my clothes in that black garbage bag. While still in my jammies, in the pitch darkness of night, I dragged that bag down the stairs and out to my mom's station wagon.

Unbeknownst to me until that very moment, my mother was leaving my father that night. For good.

Little did I know my mother had fallen victim to emotional abuse from my father for several years. Decades later, in an intimate conversation with my mother about leaving my husband, she told me that the last straw for her in both marriages was when each husband had chased her around the house with a gun.

Dear God, why do we wait so long to leave?

These are the stories often left untold; and as women, we are doing our daughters, girlfriends, and nieces a great disservice by not sharing them sooner. This is a call to re-establish sisterhood—to prepare our young girls for the life events that may transpire and to encourage them along the way and warn them of things to come. We must teach them how to navigate those waters should the tide come in too strong at any stage of their lives.

When my tide came, I was completely unprepared.

******

After completing my undergraduate studies, I started my career in the sales and marketing industry. After about seven years of that meat grinder, I found myself emotionally drained, unfulfilled, and downright unhappy professionally. The recession of 2008 was taking its toll not just on the housing industry, but it began to seep into my industry as well. Clients began pulling back, contracts were left on the table, and budgets were being cut. Everyone was holding on and sitting tight in anticipation of what might ensue in the coming months.

This was clearly a sign telling me to get out.

Then came a phone call from my chief financial officer saying, "April, effective last period, you're going to have to take a pay cut." Three additional pay cuts later, the writing was on the wall and this ship was sinking fast. Some chose to stay on the Titanic, but I knew there was a pivot coming in my life.

With the tide shifting, I knew I had to stay on my yellow brick road even though I had no idea where it was headed. By the way, there isn't just ONE yellow brick road. You have yours and I have mine; and everyone's yellow brick road looks a little, or a lot, different.

Whether you believe in God, Source, the Universe, or another spiritual being, this supreme, omnipresent power is on the job 24/7 directing us and guiding us to our highest good. Thankfully, the yellow brick road is always conspiring in our favor.

I was completely burned out after working in the advertising industry, but I didn't know what else I was good at. I know this is where I might lose some of you, especially when you look at some of the chaos that has ensued in your life, but even those traumatic events were conspiring for your ultimate good. Unfortunately, we can't learn all the lessons we need to learn in life if everything is always peaches and cream. It takes some bumps in the road and seeming challenges to help us become the master of our fate and the captain of our ship.

I love the quote by Theodore Roosevelt, which I have taken liberty to feminize just a bit:

> *It is not the critic who counts; not the woman who points out how the strong woman stumbles or where the doer of deeds could have done better. The credit belongs to the woman who is actually in the*

> *arena, whose face is marred by dust and sweat and*
> *blood, who strives valiantly, who errs and comes up*
> *short again and again, because there is no effort*
> *without error or shortcoming, but who knows the*
> *great enthusiasms, the great devotions, who*
> *spends herself in a worthy cause; who, at the best,*
> *knows, in the end, the triumph of high achieve-*
> *ment, and who, at the worst, if she fails, at least*
> *she fails while daring greatly, so that her place*
> *shall never be with those cold and timid souls who*
> *knew neither victory nor defeat.*

It takes courage and vulnerability to enter the arena. Most people would prefer to stay in the grandstands as an onlooker or a social media critic. It's safe there. Only in the arena do you get to see what you're really made of. All the lessons happen in the arena. The pain and challenges happen in the arena. But joy and triumph also occur in the arena.

Your yellow brick road has likely led you into a few arenas in your lifetime.

Our ability to stay the course, even after being pummeled a few times, makes us who we are. How would we ever know what we really want until we experience things that we don't want? The contrast is necessary for that yellow brick road to keep us on track.

******

Even though my instincts told me to take the lower salary at the company in a different city, I stayed in my hometown because it was safe and comfortable. In safety, I discovered how big of a fish I was in this small pond; and although I was doing well financially, my relationships sucked, and I wanted to surround myself with more movers and shakers.

I wanted to be challenged differently, but that meant giving up my emotional safety of knowing everybody and everybody knowing me. Then I met a guy in my town who broke my heart, and that experience attempted to shatter any remaining hope of meeting Mr. Right.

Not fully over that heartbreak, I then became a caregiver for my elderly father. Desperation and despair began to set in. I thought, "I should have moved when I had the chance. I'm glad I'm here for Dad but how in the heck am I going to get out of dodge now? I'm getting older and my clock is ticking. No viable male prospects in sight and I'm ready to settle down."

Little did I know that Dad's temporary setback would lead me to someone; in fact, while picking up his prescriptions, I grabbed a coffee at my favorite café and ran into a man I had met while traveling on business over a decade ago. There was an instant connection. He was in town for a business meeting with a potential client and invited me to lunch. Over lunch, I began to realize the conspiracy to do me good was always in play.

******

Every choice we make, whether it seems to take us further away or closer to our dreams, is always working for us in our favor. The yellow brick road is forever loving toward us even during our darkest hours.

My darkest hours came during the years leading up to the global pandemic when my life turned completely upside down in the span of less than four years:

- I became a full-time caregiver for my mom;
- I was subjected to some of the worst gaslighting and emotional abuse by my own brother;
- I began seeing a therapist to work through the trauma of being molested as a 5-year-old by a female neighbor;
- My marriage was in shambles, and I felt zero emotional, financial, or intimate safety with my husband;
- I lost two brothers ... one to COVID, the other to unknown causes; and
- I left my husband to regain my peace.

That's A LOT. But in retrospect, my yellow brick road was working silently on my behalf.

******

Resilience is a blessing, but it's also not fun when people say things like, "You're always fine, April. You always land on your feet." Please don't ever say things like this to your friends. Even though those words may be true, it's not an excuse to be treated like a doormat.

When I finally had the courage to leave my husband, this is what finally dropped in my heart: "Don't sacrifice your own well-being for someone else's comfort." I began to realize that many of the challenging circumstances I was experiencing were because I was so focused on people pleasing. I would allow myself to get swooped up into others' drama and sacrifice my own well-being in the process.

"Don't sacrifice your own well-being for someone else's comfort." This statement became my new mantra. It became my filter, my litmus test for all my interactions and relationships.

Now, if I compromise, it has to be because it's what I really want.

Along this path of overcoming my addiction to pleasing people, I discovered that just because someone has a title does not give that person carte blanche to treat you like crap. This was a big one for me. I was watching a replay of a webinar Oprah Winfrey was doing with her private Oprah Daily subscribers and she was interviewing Nedra Tawab. She explained that when someone in our lives carries a title, we often let them get away with murder. That title could be mother, father, wife, husband, brother, sister, best friend, etc.

Titles tend to blur the lines of what we will allow. We have likely let people with titles get away with things we wouldn't dare let a stranger do or say to us. This is ingrained in our society. How many times have you heard people say, "Well, she is your mother."

Nedra, I've never met you, but you freed me when you said, "A title does not equal a relationship."

Relationships must be nurtured and sustained. They are built on mutual trust, open and honest communication, and respect. When those elements are not there, you don't have a relationship. What you have is toxicity. I'm not going to lie. This was a tough lesson to learn. I had never realized before just how much I had allowed titles to dictate my life.

Under no circumstances should someone's title cause us to place ourselves on the backburner. We have to always be on the front burner. That's where we show up as our most authentic selves. The back burner is filled with stress, regret, worry, doubt, fear, and downright suffering.

As women, we are often the sacrificial lamb; this is learned be-havior. We witnessed our mothers do it and subconsciously we thought this was the way it is.

******

And what about value? The value we place on ourselves, the value others place on us? Value is defined as relative worth, utility, or importance. When you consider the context of the word "value", ask yourself how many people in your life offer true value. Are they useful? Are they givers or are they takers? A close girlfriend of mine calls the takers "energy vampires." They latch on to those who are shining bright and then they suck the life out of them. If you're lucky or wise enough to break away, you later realize how much energy they were sucking out of you.

After my marriage ended, I started dating a man who would talk about all the things he wanted us to do together; but none of it ever happened. After a few months of watching and praying, I saw that not only was he an energy vampire and a narcissist, he also never acted on any of the things he said he wanted to expe-rience with me. Meanwhile, I'm supporting his business, making connections for him, getting him speaking engagements, setting up meetings for him with investors, and receiving absolutely nothing in return except a bunch of future talk and "I love you's." Strange way of showing it, buddy.

That experience taught me that if something smells fishy, it probably is. In the words of Maya Angelou, "when someone shows you who they are the first time, believe them." I learned to listen to what people say, but more importantly pay attention to what they do or don't do.

Our yellow brick road will always be filled with twists and turns. Every single one of them harbors a growth opportunity, one that will advance our lives even more. When I look back at my yellow brick road, I've met some real characters that saw the value in being with me and tried to hitchhike a free ride on my success. But I learned that after a few miles, if they weren't trying to keep me awake on the road, I would let them out at the next rest stop.

My yellow brick road had some massive potholes along the way. I bent a rim or two, but I learned how to change a tire in the process. Every single challenge has a seed of greatness for our next adventure. Those experiences have meaning and purpose. Nothing is wasted. The universe has a way of tying all those life lessons together into a beautiful tapestry. We often cannot see the beauty in it while we are experiencing hurt, pain, and disappointment. Start documenting every success in a success journal and you'll begin to see the magical way in which life is always serving us and leading us into our highest good.

My wish for you is that you relish your yellow brick road, no matter how bumpy it gets. It's up to you to navigate that road, bountifully and beautifully, to design a life worth writing about.

Chapter nineteen

The Chariot, The Tower, and The Page

by Drew Isserlis Kramer

THE SCREEN BABYSITS THE children. I settle in my yard with my dog at my feet. I light a candle and breathe. This is what my soul guides me to do as I try to bust my writer's block. In the quiet of my slice of the earth, I listen. I hear the hum of cicadas and the twitter of birds. I overhear a little too much of my husband's work call. He senses my discontent and moves along. I am alone again. I note the wind in the trees, energy flowing from branch to branch. The sounds of nature mix with the hammering of workers and cars speeding in the distance, reminding me that everything connects.

I pull three cards from my tarot deck, a practice that has become my writer's ritual. As I grow as a writer and artist, I've become increasingly witchy. Like many creatives, I see the presence of divine inspiration in my work. The cards help me unlock the words. I describe the card and how it relates to where I am in this moment. It helps me to feel connected. It gets me into my flow. Today's cards are: The Chariot; The Page of Swords Reversed; and The Tower.

The Chariot, a figure in armor pauses to survey the road ahead as he rides away from his village. Pulled by two sphinxes, black and white, male and female, the figure is guided by intuition, but takes informed action. The Page of Swords Reversed. The sword is a message. The Page is a youthful messenger. Upright, the card signals to be curious and open to learning new information. Pay attention to the subtle messages around you. However, in reverse, the card cautions us to be careful with information. Be mindful of how you speak. The Tower, a jarring visual from this infamous deck. People jump out of a tower in flames. The effect can only mean something ominous. However, the message is more hopeful. The Tower represents a structural foundation of your life that is no longer serving you. You must burn it down to grow again.

Life is a journey of continuous self-discovery and reinvention. The experiences in our yard with nature, my husband, and the tarot cards are microcosms of this larger journey. These are moments where I listened to my inner voice and allowed it to guide me through changes, just as I have done throughout my life's larger transitions. Mine is a story of celebration of the idea that change, whether prompted by external circumstances or internal realizations, is essential for personal growth and creativity.

Like all of you reading, I am on a journey. On all our journeys, seasons will change. Forward motion will stop and start. Through our own active choices and divine luck, we reinvent ourselves. A lawyer turned ad woman turned boy mom turned artist and writer—in my bio I call myself a "master of transformation." In each of those phases of my life, I received the call to burn down what I built to start something new.

******

As a young, shy, arty tomboy, I struggled to answer what I wanted to be when I grew up. Raised in a messy divorce, the messaging in my household was "support yourself." In my well-meaning, neurotic Jewish family, this meant becoming a doctor or lawyer. The creative industries seemed open to only the very best artistic talents—and I never felt good enough.

Without knowing what else to do with my love of words, I did what many others do: I went to law school. Do you ever notice that nagging voice in your head that tells you when something is totally wrong for you? I've come to understand it as intuition. In law school, that voice never shut off, but was overpowered by the louder, more shrill ringing of fear. I wasn't raised to be brave. I was raised to feel safe.

As I approached graduation, I was in a bad relationship and chasing someone else's dream. The voice was yelling at the top of her lungs that this was all WRONG. Safe didn't feel so secure anymore. At 25, I burned down my foundation to change my life. In a new direction, I searched for a creative life. I found my way by connecting with creative people, listening to the mix of seren-dipity and hard work that made them who they are. I learned that nothing happens by accident. I learned that having faith and tak-ing steps forward every day will lead to a life with passion and hopefully purpose.

At a moment of technological disruption, I entered digital marketing through a combination of bold determination and luck. In creative digital agencies, I learned consumer marketing and helped major corporations like Target and Unilever create community through content. I took risks, moving into roles at the intersection of technology and media to think about how businesses evolve for a modern cross-platform lifestyle.

For a decade, I climbed the ladder, but I always felt like a square peg in a round hole. Heeding a call to go it alone, I hustled for my own creative work. As a brand consultant, I found the confidence to write the stories, but the stories were not my own. I had my own ideas. I knew that this wasn't my forever business, but I was content to follow the path, letting one step inform the other.

******

I continued on my path until I found myself clinging on the steep side of a mountain. At first, the slope of the incline was unspectacular. At first, I didn't even notice it. In my early thirties, the call to have children wasn't on my radar. Frankly, babies scared me. Noisy, drooling, and difficult to appease, I was intimidated. Their origin story required too much physical investment for my taste.

Gradually, but then suddenly, the childless of my generation became outnumbered by children. It felt lonely to be left behind. Stagnation felt scary, but I learned it is impossible to stand in one place. We cannot control our bodies and our lives no matter how hard we chase wellness. I watched family members grow frail and pass, some far too early. I began to feel the call for the future, for family. What might be on the other side of the mountain?

I answered the scary call to motherhood and noticed my focus shift. Inspired and fulfilled by the manual labor of raising children, I thrived in the creative challenge of caretaking. After six months of music, food play, and theatrical recitations of Green Eggs and Ham, I felt compelled to press pause, burning what I've built, to produce something new.

Faced with the decision to step off the ladder, I called my single mother for permission. After watching her struggle, I didn't want to disappoint her even more than myself. My old fears of financial ruin were compounded with worry that I'd become irrelevant. When we spoke, she told me that if I had the interest and the privilege of making this choice, that I should take the opportunity because this moment is fleeting. She reminded me that life is long, but childhood is not. This is just part of my story.

******

When I made the decision to pause, I promised myself that one day, when the time was right, I would start something of my own. I also made peace with the potential that I remain just an ordinary mom. I told myself, if all I accomplish is to raise two good humans and support my family and community, I am successful. My days were long and hard, but the joy of raising my floofy haired boys filled me up for a while.

But in the winter of 2022, two and a half years into the global pandemic, I found myself feeling isolated and one dimensional. Everything I was existed within the four walls of my house. My creative life was in the pursuit of their entertainment. I sang and danced. I made up stories. I painted. I baked. I crafted small animals out of pipe cleaners. I did the manual labor of raising two small boys with very few extra hands.

I am proud of my hard work, but I again heard that familiar voice calling for change. I dyed my hair blue and then flaming red. When that didn't work, I began to explore. In June 2022, I launched a creative experiment, Lady & the Floofs, with two personal challenges: (1) host one baby class; (2) write one baby book—and tell the story on Instagram!

I set out to discover what might happen if I stopped caring what other people thought and put it all out there on the field. I created the character of the Lady, a quirky and bohemian British caretaker of Floofs. A Floof is a creature with many needs. While it most often refers to children, the definition is intentionally broad. A Floof could be a child, a cockatoo or even your ailing grandmother. We all have needs.

In my print books, at in-person sensory storytimes, and online, the Lady teaches Floofs of all ages to discover this sometimes scary, wonderful world. My currently unpublished illustrated songbook, It's Hard to be a Baby, is a baby's lament that calls for compassion for the Floofs as they embark on the difficult journey of growing up. Sharing her own path from fearful Floof to bold Lady, the book encourages trial (especially of food) through joy and empathy.

And try things we did. In my classes, we threw spaghetti and flour from all corners of New York's Tristate area. We built cars out of cucumbers and planted enchanted dinosaur broccoli forests. We finger-painted with triggering ingredients like onions and mushrooms. We planted seedlings in the ground and ate leafy greens off the stalk. We learned where our food came from and ate without protest because it was all in good fun.

******

I'd like to say that this is the story of how I launched my business and built a new tower on the hill, but creative journeys are circuitous. Six months into the experiment, I realized that the Lady was not just the story of a caretaker and her Floofs. The Lady is also the story of a woman stepping into her own as an artist—and that Lady is me!

Lady & the Floofs began an intensive, guided encounter with my own creativity. I wrote. I illustrated. I sang. I told stories. I performed in a play as an entirely different character. I learned to listen to my creative intuition, letting go of ideas that don't work or light me up inside. I built many towers and knocked them down.

As I pass through my second year of Floof, my chariot pauses to reconsider the way forward. I struggle with the Lady. The character's chutzpah and boundless energy drains my inner house cat. This year, I put her in-person escapades on hold, embracing the call to be quieter. Today, I crave a quieter writer's life. I want to share what I have learned in setting myself free. I'm writing about the topics that keep me up at night. For local and niche publications, I muse on food, faith, and family life, spreading a message of empathy and boldness to keep evolving, to keep trying things. If you sit with your own ideas and big dreams, but feel too afraid to try, I am here, writing for you.

Like the page, I am the messenger. I write to bring inspiration and hope to those who read. I yearn to help people witness the magic in the universe, to see that they are a part of something much larger than themselves. Like the page, I have vices. I worry about my artists' impulsivity and lack of experience. Will anyone care what one ordinary stay-at-home mom who never quite made it big in the corporate world has to say about life?

Maybe I was right when I was a teenager. Maybe I will never be good enough. Maybe my writing will always be local and niche. Maybe I'll always be ordinary.

I don't worry so much about being ordinary anymore. I don't fear failure. I'm OK with being small. In a world that celebrates exceptionalism and achievement, it is important to remember that we are all a tiny piece of a much larger universe that goes on forever and ever.

Our time here on this planet, however short, creates a ripple effect. When I create, I remind myself that reaching one person is enough to make an impact. My purpose here may not be to win awards or reach masses with my message of hope and bravery. Perhaps I am here to inspire just one person.

Maybe that person is you.

Chapter twenty

Healing Out Loud

by Caroline Markel

"**YOUR LIFE CAN CHANGE** in an instant, that instant can last forever," is my favorite line from a book by Laura Kasischke entitled *The Life Before Your Eyes.*

I can remember the instant my life changed. It was March 15, 2016. I am filled with wild gratitude now for that beautiful spring day because it also allowed me to make moves and create moments toward healing. If there is one message to carry forward from any of life's messes, it is this: Healing out loud, even if your voice shakes, is a catalyst toward building a village to help on the journey; and by using your voice in any healing process, others heal, too. All you have to do is make one tiny move at a time.

******

In 2016, I was in love. Big. Bold. LOVE! I had known my fiancé since college. We became instant friends as freshmen in 1987. However, as college rolled by, we ended up in different social circles; finding each other and falling in love 20 years later following our divorces.

The morning started off like any other. My fiancé was my personal alarm clock. As the senior vice president of a Kansas City–based company, he was up and out the door of our 4,500 square-foot home in an affluent neighborhood about an hour before I would get out of bed. Every day, after getting dressed and ready to go, he would come back to our bed.

The man I loved would take my hand, lean down to my ear, and whisper, "It's time to get up, Sweet Pea. I love you, Caroline. Let's dream together forever, please." His words were the most beautiful thing to wake up to every morning. He'd nuzzle into my hair, continuing to kiss my ear and neck. It was Heaven.

The morning of March 15 found us just four weeks away from our planned and paid for wedding in New York. New York was one of "our cities." We had traveled there often and had our list of favorite places we would visit every time. Our post-wedding dinner was booked at our favorite restaurant just across from Rockefeller Center. We rented out the platform in Grand Central Station for the ceremony, and the minister had met with us several times to craft the ceremony.

My goodness! I loved this man with all my heart. Life was a dream.

In fact, it was more than a dream, it was a second chance at love and a "Golden Couple" status that friends commented on, and others envied. Our eight years together had been spent combining families, joining bank accounts, buying a home together, food, fun, travel, sex, and a genuine love I couldn't imagine living without.

Then the day came when I would hear the most ominous words I could ever imagine, and my life was forever altered. Only 13 words uttered in less than 6 seconds:

> *Love, I think I've done something that is going to make you mad.*

It was the beginning of discovering a level of deception and evil that had been simmering under the "Golden Couple" surface since day one of our relationship. Suddenly, the façade he had crafted came into focus and revealed something far different from my dream-fueled view.

(TRIGGER WARNING: The moment my life changed, includes sexual assault, so if this is something you can't bear to read, then I'm so very fine with you putting down my chapter and calling RAINN at 800-656-4673. Please see the previous chapter for additional resources.)

******

My fiancé told me he had been communicating with a couple on Craigslist®. He had promised this couple, without my knowledge and consent, that I was willing to have sex with both of them. He had sent them pictures of me, told them where I worked, let them know what part of town we lived in. He then told me he had set up an arrangement for us to meet.

Wait ... WHAT?

Wasn't it just this morning he was waking me up with such love and devotion? Hadn't I spent the day trying on my wedding dress and confirming reservations?

Wait ... WHAT?

I was livid. I was sad. I was scared. I was confused.

My mind was a white-hot anger, and my mouth began to shoot off a mix of rapid-fire questions. I would never consent or participate in what he had promised. How could he do this to me? What was he thinking? Who are these people and what if they weren't even who they said they were? Did they know exactly where we lived? How in the world was he going to make this happen? How long has this been going on? I had no idea where this was coming from.

I ordered him out of our bed and out of our house. Then his face turned an ugly shade of red, and he snarled at me:

> *Shut the fuck up, Caroline. I knew you were going to ruin this for me. Now I suppose we are going to have to stay up all night talking about how hurt and mad you are.*

His demeanor scared me. Eight years later, I can still feel the evil that existed within him ... a side of him I never knew existed.

I do believe God was with me that night. I heard a voice, clear as if someone were standing next to me.

"Be calm. Climb back into bed. I'm going to keep you safe."

I followed the voice and climbed back into bed next to the newfound evil that was my fiancé. And that evil had the audacity to snuggle up next to me, spoon his naked body up to mine, and tell me how much he loved me while I cried into my pillow.

But wait ... there's more. And the "more" I discovered at approximately 3:35 am on Wednesday, March 16, 2016, was far worse than I could have imagined. As he lay sleeping in our bed, I took his laptop to our kitchen and opened his email.

******

My fiancé, the man I had known for over 20 years, had presented himself to me as a monogamous heterosexual. The reality on his computer showed me his secret life, which included meeting men for sex in parks and parking lots. His most common male sex partner was his co-worker and our neighbor I considered to be a friend. I had even officiated the wedding of this man to his current wife.

I found evidence of multiple affairs with women every time he traveled as well as in our home and in our bed when I traveled for work.

Then I discovered the horrific details behind his clandestine meeting with the Craigslist® sex couple—I was to be drugged and raped by these strangers; all while being filmed.

My fiancé belonged to a group in Kansas City that teaches men how to use drugs to incapacitate their partners to help facilitate their rapes. He was a willing participant in a group of predators; and without my knowledge or consent, I was included as the prey.

Often during our life together, he would tell me to get dressed up and we would go to dinner at my favorite restaurants. While sifting through his computer, I discovered that our restaurant dates and times also included invitations to three or four men. These men agreed to be stationed around the restaurant to check me out. Each email began with, "My girlfriend has no idea I'm doing this," and ended with, "I will facilitate what would be done to her."

I couldn't process what I had discovered. I withdrew from family and friends. Fear consumed me. Silence became my friend and my enemy. Silence leads to shame; and shame can kill you.

******

Doctor appointments, police, FBI, lawyers, therapists, domestic violence shelters, restraining orders, court orders, more restraining orders, too much vodka, too many potato chips, living in my car, a third round of restraining orders!

They all seemed like pop-up fire flares threatening to burn me alive.

My cousin, Marie, left me voicemail messages every day telling me why she loved me saying, "Caroline, I see how smart you are and how kind you are to people. I know these same inherent parts of who you are as a person, are going to attract more and more people to help you. Never stop asking for help."

My friend, Judy, would remind me that I didn't need to drink the entire ocean in one gulp, but take every problem as one drink from the most beautiful cup of ice water.

The biggest show of support and affection only happened after I started sharing what I discovered. It took me about 10 days to craft an escape plan, and a full seven months to implement it. My high school girlfriends paid for a moving company because I couldn't figure out how to keep that kind of money a secret from him.

When moving day finally arrived, I had arranged my own clandestine rendezvous. The moving truck, along with several friends, family, co-workers, and kids waited patiently in the cul-de-sac behind our house. Upon his departure, everyone descended upon the house in a quick and orderly fashion. They helped me move out of the home I had created in love and that he had disparaged in every way. I even had his co-workers keep tabs on his whereabouts to ensure he wouldn't surprise us before we were done.

In all these beautiful moments, I found gratitude. There really was so much to be thankful for, like the time I was crying outside my doctor's office and a random stranger came up to me and said, "My Darling. You are loved without measure, and I know you will be safe and happy soon." Or the nurse practitioner who had to deliver some sad medical news (turns out all his unprotected sex could have had a disastrous effect on my own sexuality) and she cried with me and said, "I need you to believe in your own health, and I will hate him for you."

My friend, Amy, sent me gifts and flowers on random days, which arrived when I needed them most. My high school bestie, Gina, who would call me to cry in silence together. We didn't need to talk, just silent tears on the most horrific days.

Really! How the hell does all this happen? Tiny little miracles.

The village I started to create kept cheering my every mistake with encouragement and love, as well as the offers for new insights and assistance.

My life changed in an instant, but that instant allowed me to make moves and create moments toward healing. Healing out loud, even when my voice wavered, was a catalyst toward building a village to help me. All I had to do was make one tiny move at a time.

******

The more I began talking about what happened to me, the more people offered to help.

Every day, the more I spoke out loud about what was happening to me, the more tiny little miracles started to show up in my life. I started to write them in the Notes file on my phone every day. Plus, I put them as calendar reminders that went off all day and night, reminding me how I could heal from my "instant" if only I kept healing out loud and sharing my story.

Some days, I had 75 notifications. I am eight years out from escape, and these notifications still go off on my phone.

I never want to forget that my choice to create tiny moves toward moments of healing saved my life and the lives of my children and pets.

This extended pit crew of encouragement allowed me to create SafeInHarmsWay.org with values encompassing a sanctuary where feelings find validation, where emotions find expression, and where healing begins. Safe In Harm's Way is a nonprofit founded on all the ways I healed and how the people around me stepped up to help once I started using my voice.

What I didn't know then, as I navigated my own life altering moment, was just how often bystanding friends, family, and coworkers do and say nothing. I now know my 75 daily calendar notifications were like winning the life lottery.

At Safe In Harm's Way, I work with people who experience the abyss of trauma, and their family says things like, "He has always been so nice to me. I think you're making this all up."

I have had people receive mental, physical, psychological, and sexual abuse and have family tell them, "You need to stay, you are not smart enough to leave him."

Some friends or family leave behind their loved one experiencing abuse because they perceive within themselves a lack in skill or ability to assist. Worse yet, some bystanders cast blame and fault with a loud, "I told you so," hurled in the direction of the person trying to heal.

We helped a young woman who finally worked up the courage to leave her abuser, and her best friend said,

> *I told you to leave years ago. I'm not putting up with your bullshit now. Get over it, bitch.*

This type of behavior means any survivor will be silenced by shame. Shame leads to isolation, tragedy wins, and there is zero movement toward healing. This is why my experience matters to anyone experiencing abuse from the person who claims to love them.

It's why at Safe In Harm's Way, we use my tiny little miracles to create tools and resources so that friends, family, and co-workers can be the difference in their person's life. We have 15 (and counting) ways that anyone can help a survivor create their own movement toward healing, one moment at a time:

1. Speaking love to the person experiencing life's tragedies sounds like, "I know this is really hard for you. Please know I will always love you."

2. Being the low-key cheerleader sounds like, "I am not sure what to do here, but can I find you two resources that can help you navigate what is happening in your world right now?" (Please notice here the ask. Offering unsolicited advice can cause further harm.)

3. When you worry that you are intruding on someone's life sounds like, "Can you agree to keep me posted about one action you've decided to take. I'd like to support you in any way you're choosing to heal."

4. If it so happens that their tragedy is a little too close to your own tragedy sounds like, "Please know it's best to seek professional services to help you navigate this. The

complexities of your healing need more than I can provide as your friend. Always remember that as your friend, I care about your success."

5. If what is happening also triggers you as the friend, then saying, "There's a time and place for every discussion, and I am unable to chat about this today. But I know you can look online and search for resources that will help. Love you, my friend. Can we check in next week, and you can tell me about your progress."

6. Always winning comments should be specific to the person, "I was just thinking about you today, and I remember that time when we were at a work event where you were kind to the new person. I really admire the way you bring people into conversations and make them feel welcome."

7. When your gut tells you something is wrong, but you don't know what to do, action is simple as, "Hey! I thought of you today. I wanted to reach out and let you know I'm always here for you. You're someone I value, and hope all is well."

8. When you want to offer inspiration, but don't know what to say, just trust yourself that any funny meme will do.

9. Consistency helps, so setting a reminder in your phone to reach out means the receiver will get consistent inspiration.

10. Start by believing. Always. Every time. Everyone's experience is just that—individual. If you've experienced something similar, it's not the same. The easiest thing to say every time is, "Thank you for sharing this with me. I am ready to keep listening."

11. Stop yourself from ever saying, "I think it's time for you to get over this."

12. Don't expect any response. Trauma impacts your brain in unique ways of forgetfulness and becoming frozen from action. However, know down to your soul that your words and connection matter, and keep up the random texts, emails, or voice messages, so that you stay a source of inspiration.

13. ASK! ASK! ASK! My favorite go-to comment is, "I am always here to listen. Right now, would you like me to comment on what you're telling me, or should I just keep listening."

14. My second favorite comment is, "I do have an idea on what you just told me. Maybe it will fit you, maybe it won't. Can I share it with you?"

15. Default for any situation, "I'm sorry you're going through this. How can I best show up for you right now?'

All these suggestions can be mixed up and tailored to each individual. In fact, the more individualized you can make it for each person, the better. Call in every great moment that you love about them, and blast that on repeat.

******

My mentor, Al, once told me that my entire career in pharmaceutical sales would be the springboard for how I built my nonprofit, and as long as I kept making moves to heal, the most beautiful solutions would show up along the way.

In 2021, I left my pharmaceutical career to pursue my nonprofit work full time. And in what would be my biggest sales close (so far) of my sales career, I secured billboards in Times Square and across the country that created over one billion opportunities for people to find help by launching my Safe In Harm's Way brand on video screens around the country.

People believed so much in our mission that over $4 million in collateral was given to us for free. FREE!

Standing in Times Square and watching my brand and message cascade down the billboards was a surreal moment of complete joy. My canceled wedding venue was just blocks away, and here I was only five short years away from my escape, watching the brand and entity I built save lives.

What is your next move moment toward healing from your "instant?" Healing out loud, even if your voice shakes, is a catalyst toward building a village to help on the journey; and by using your voice in any healing process, others heal, too.

All you have to do is make one tiny move at a time.

Chapter twenty-one

The 3 Rs
of Resilience

by Lesley Marlin

HAVE YOU EVER BEEN in such a dark place that you thought, "Well, this is it—it's over—I just can't do this anymore? I can't live like this." Well, for me, that place was pitch black.

I spiraled into a deep dark hole after a cancer surgeon told me to fight for my life. Then the surgeon delivered another blow. "Don't worry about having children."

I wanted to live—to make my dreams come true. But I didn't want to live like that—with a suspected life-threatening recurrence and under the constant cloud of cancer. I remember closing my eyes—hoping to wake up from the nightmare or just disappear. Spoiler alert—neither of those happened.

Instead, I stumbled through the darkness. What I know from that journey is that each of us can find the light and be the light. That's the heart of resilience.

I am not a stranger to the darkness. Like many of us, I grew up with a mismatch between what could be seen on the outside and what was being experienced on the inside. The outside looked put together—well, as much as I could be as a shy but sassy teenager. On the inside, I felt alone and unloved—scared and sad. The affirmation and validation I received was about what I accomplished—not who I was. I longed to belong—to feel like I mattered. Have you ever felt like that?

When I got to college, I turned that mismatch into action. I volunteered on a crisis hotline and trained other volunteers on how to handle suicide calls.

Fast forward, less than a decade later, it was my own life on the line. Were the scans and doctors right or wrong? Did I really have a life-threatening cancer recurrence? Those questions weighed heavily on my heart. I agonized over what to do. Doctors urged pre-operative chemo and radiation even before tissue confirmation of recurrence. I couldn't do it. I first needed to know what it was. So I opted instead for a "take me apart and hopefully put me back together" surgery.

Making the decision did not bring me out of the darkness, as I so desperately wished it would. My despair still felt unbearable. Applying what I learned as a suicide prevention trainer, I knew I had to find a reason to get to that surgery. I kept thinking about a box of cards.

A box of cards, really? Yes, a box of cards.

You see, my cancer diagnosis and treatment happened before the explosion of social media. I received cards in the mail from people I knew and even people I didn't know. I put them in a box and kept them. I would pull them out and read them when I needed support or encouragement.

******

As the darkness got even darker, the cards kept coming. I heard that I was brave and courageous. I heard that I was strong and an inspiration of strength. I simply could not escape the impact my situation had on others—family, friends, and even strangers. Not wanting to worsen that impact is what kept me alive until my "humpty dumpty" surgery.

With a hand squeeze, I woke up from surgery and heard, "It's not a recurrence—they did not find any more cancer." Those words were a glimmer of light—a small gift of relief. But they did not magically erase the darkness. So the journey continued—down the daunting path of healing and rebuilding.

I was told I was resilient. They said I'd be okay. But I didn't want to just survive. I wanted to thrive. I didn't know what that looked like or how to do it. The definitions of resilience were no help to me. "Coping well." "Bouncing back." Or even "You've got this." They sounded like words just strung together without giving me directions on what to do.

I wanted to bounce back but struggled with the reality that there was no going back. Life was different now, and I had to work toward accepting that. What I know now is that resilience does not just happen when we survive adversity. Rather, resilience is a skill we have to build through practice in the midst of adversity. That is how we move from surviving to thriving.

The word "resilience" makes me think of a strong warrior woman. Back then, I certainly didn't feel like one and even to this day, there are times when I don't. But there are also times when I do. Finding our way to that very feeling is how we practice and grow our own resilience.

Healing was much harder than I expected—both physically and emotionally. My body rebelled quite a bit, probably because it had been through two major abdominal surgeries and eight cycles of chemotherapy in the span of a year. I struggled to find foods that my digestive system would tolerate. I was often exhausted and lacked the energy I used to have. I rode the emotion roller coaster, sometimes crying and sometimes laughing. I lived in small segments of time—sometimes a week, sometimes a day, and sometimes even a moment.

Eventually, as one author so aptly described it, I began living between office visits. Each day, I tried to focus on gratitude. As I slowly found light, my world became a little brighter. Ordinary moments like seeing the beauty of nature became extraordinary.

But it wasn't all sunshine and roses. I lived with a constant shadow—the fear of recurrence. I battled infertility and insomnia. I was surviving—just barely, and yet I had not given up on becoming a thriver.

******

I had not yet figured out how to find that "strong warrior woman within" kind of feeling. Eventually, over time, I found several signs that provided hope that I was moving in the right direction. I found 3Rs that became my roadmap to resilience.

The first R—Reflect. I am a thinker. So reflecting and even ruminating come naturally. I naively thought I could think my way through my darkness and that would give me all the answers I needed. As I reflected, I grappled with what happened and why. Why did I get cancer? Although I would probably never know the cause, I could find meaning in what happened. Some reasons were cliché—carpe diem; live fully. And some were not—an in-house lawyer job in the Senate was not meant to be for me because it didn't have the benefits I needed. But when I thought about the recurrence scare, I kept coming up empty. Nothing answered the why question. I could not make sense of it, and I had to accept that sometimes there isn't any meaning.

Or maybe the meaning doesn't appear until much later. In 2012, I nearly died from giving birth to my twin boys. They were born a little over five weeks early—miracles in many ways. As I held both of them in my arms in the Neonatal Intensive Care Unit, I started to cry. Were they tears of sorrow? Or tears of joy? It was actually both. What I realized at that time was that bad and good could co-exist as paradoxical as it seemed. That is what the recurrence scare had taught me. It taught me how to live in and with paradox. That was a lightbulb moment for me, as it allowed me to start seeing my survivorship journey as bitter and sweet.

That took me to the second R—Release. How could I release some of the bitterness to experience more of the sweetness? I tried self-care—exercise, bubble baths, massage. Lovely but not the answer. Why? Because I was still scared that every ache or pain was a recurrence, still sad about what I had lost, and still mad at the unfairness of it all. I felt stuck. Whenever that happens, I know have more to learn. So I began researching and reading. I discovered that our bodies can find ways to experience feelings and release them, often through movement. That movement can be shaking, walking, writing—just to name a few. I experimented and practiced, often by playing with my kids. We danced. We colored. We shook our sillies out. And what a difference it made. I felt lighter—less weighted down by bitterness. That didn't mean the bitterness was gone completely. It probably never will be. What I know now is that it can come and go, and when it does, it reminds me of the strength that comes from surviving.

With less and less bitterness, I then had to find a way to get and enjoy more sweetness. The hole in my heart needed healing. That's where the third R came in—Restore. I am a doer. So I turned to my bucket list. Travel. Adventure. It was amazing but draining. I eventually learned that doing for the sake of productivity—or checking things off a list—is different than doing for the sake of being. Being, not doing, is what restores me. It connects me to the world and those around me. Looking up at the sky, I can see the sun, the moon, the stars, and sometimes even planets, and I feel my small place in this huge universe. I then snuggle with my children at night, putting my head on their chest to hear their heartbeat, and I feel in awe of life. Restoring brings peace and joy.

******

Those 3Rs—Reflect, Release, and Restore—are far more than words. They are ways that help me find that strong warrior woman in me. When life gets hard, I use the 3Rs to practice and grow my own resilience. I have used them to get through difficult work situations. I have used them as I advocate for myself and others.

The steps—Reflect, Release, and Restore—are always the same. Even though the steps are the same, they may look different in various situations and for different people. Yet, the outcome is always the same, and for me, that's deeper resilience in my soul and my being.

The 3Rs are my roadmap to resilience, and they can be yours too. Reflect. What happened? What can I do about it? What does it mean or what can I make it mean? Release. What am I feeling? How can I let negative feelings go and release them from my body? Restore. How can I find peace and joy? How can I feel whole again?

I want to know and feel that everything will be ok. That's what I want for you too. I am here to tell you that we can find the light. We can do more than survive. We can thrive. And think about this—we can also be the light for others around us.

So go use the 3Rs and thrive, and then go share the 3Rs and make the world a brighter place.

Chapter twenty-two

The Power of Owning Your Story

by Serena Mastin

ONE OF THE EARLIEST memories from my childhood, when I was just 5 years old, remains etched vividly in my mind. It was a distressing moment that found me seeking refuge in the depths of a cluttered closet nestled amidst a sea of clothes. My greasy blonde hair hung disheveled, veiling my tear-streaked face as I trembled within, hidden from the tumultuous world outside.

Through the slender gap in the closet door, my wide, frightened eyes peeked out, revealing the fear etched on my small face. I clung to my legs, drawing them close to my chest, quivering with anxiety, my heart pounding loudly in my ears. The sounds of violence reverberated through the house, an unsettling symphony of crashing dishes and the anguished screams of my mother. Rocking back and forth in the darkness, I wished fervently for the power to turn invisible, to escape the horrors unfolding beyond that closet door.

My mother exerted every ounce of her strength to shield us. Still, my biological father employed manipulation, brainwashing tactics, and cult rituals to conceal the abuse he inflicted, preventing her from grasping the full extent of the deception. Unimaginable experiences unfolded before me like a cruel tapestry—sexual abuse, manipulation, violence, and emotional torture. It was as though my life was marked by tragedy, forcing me to view the world through a lens of shame and guilt.

We encountered ceaseless surveillance until the day we successfully escaped the living nightmare I once referred to as my home. Just when I believed we had finally gained our freedom, I was ripped from my mother's embrace. I lived in witness protection and foster homes for several years while she faced grueling court hearings, striving to regain her parental rights.

This marked the inception of my journey as I confronted the unfolding trauma. I found myself echoing the patterns before me, driven by an unwavering determination to liberate myself from this destructive cycle. The unrelenting legacy of childhood abuse continued to cast a haunting shadow over every traumatic event in my life.

******

As a teenager wandering the streets, I discovered myself nestled in a fetal position under the night sky on a park bench situated across from the high school I attended. I tossed and turned as the frigid breeze formed dewdrops glistening from the twilight moon while tracing intricate patterns on my face. I patiently counted the minutes until the familiar sound of the school gates scraping against the pavement signified the campus opening.

I raced through the halls with urgency, eventually locating my path to the locker room. There, I slipped into a brisk shower to draw the slightest heat from the tepid water, then quickly brushed the water from my body with the last few paper towels hanging from the dispenser, pulled my black velvet dress over my head, clumsily stepped into my fishnet stockings, while leaning forward to secure the two-tone laces of my tall leather boots, weaving them through the vivid yellow welt stitches with speed.

As I concealed myself behind the worn bathroom stall, the bell echoed through the halls like a piercing siren. Impulsively, I succumbed to my addiction before rejoining the bustling crowd of classmates. Life on the streets felt like an unending abyss of hopelessness, a constant escape from dangerous situations, seeking solace in destructive habits and using addiction to numb my emotions. This cycle persisted, an unrelenting pattern in my life.

With each life experience, it leaves an imprint upon us. For some, like myself, there is a tendency to conceal these experiences, finding safety in the shadows and shielding ourselves from the light.

As I transitioned into adulthood, my quest for acceptance and love led me into turbulent relationships, where I inadvertently measured my self-worth by seeking approval from others. I found myself naturally slipping into codependent behaviors, constantly striving to please others and channeling my energy into supporting, nurturing, and shielding them from the consequences of their actions. In doing so, I gradually lost sight of my own identity.

******

At the age of 29, I found myself a single mother after a failed marriage while also blessed with two beautiful children. Simultaneously, my career was steadily progressing as I climbed the corporate ladder. My heart became captivated by a profound love for the man who would soon become my husband. He possessed an irresistible charm, keen insight, and an engaging, magnetic personality. Our love was nothing short of electrifying, the kind that stirred the soul, setting our hearts ablaze while providing a profound sense of peace when we were together.

Over the next few years, we meticulously mapped out our future, culminating in our families blending and the harmonious unity of our lives as one. Shortly thereafter, I founded an advertising agency, drawing upon more than a decade of marketing experience to forge a new path.

However, the subsequent 10 years brought unforeseen challenges, as unresolved issues from our past began to cast a shadow over our marriage. Lies, betrayal, and growing resentment marked this gradual descent into a downward spiral. My husband grappled with undiagnosed mental health issues and multiple infidelities, burdening our relationship with pain and turmoil.

Determined to safeguard my marriage, my family, and the business we had built together, I carried the weight of this struggle on my shoulders. The longer I attempted to self-soothe, conceal my pain, and mask my hidden emotions while drawing strength from within, the more I experienced a decline in my physical and mental well-being. This deterioration permeated every facet of my life. I lived under the illusion that I could control and mend everything simply by introspection and identifying my role in fueling the problems. Yet, reality dawned in the quiet moments when I once again found myself concealed, but this time, in a different form, visible yet hidden in plain sight.

For far too long, I grappled with a profound sense of isolation, unsure of whom to confide in or where to seek solace. Consequently, I endured in silence, downplaying my pain, distancing myself from the love and support of those around me, and harboring my secrets deep within.

The man who once illuminated my world later engulfed it in flames. My love for him had been so all-consuming that it led me to neglect my well-being and lose sight of my identity in the process. After navigating through many tumultuous years, I eventually cultivated a heightened self-awareness, recognizing my tendency to conceal my true emotions.

It was then that I made a deliberate choice to summon the inner strength required to confront my fears of judgment, shame, criticism, and self-doubt. This newfound clarity gave me the courage to end my marriage despite the insurmountable risk of losing everything, as I finally prioritized my well-being and self-preservation.

However, in a heartbreaking turn of events, just a few months after leaving my husband, I faced the devastating truth: I couldn't rescue him from his own demons. On March 27, 2020, he chose to end his life. In all my efforts, I would have readily given up my own life to save him, but tragically, it was a battle beyond my control.

******

Today, I stand as a survivor, having confronted the harrowing shadows of isolation, devastation, and victimization that once entangled me. My children are healthy and thriving; I find the utmost joy in watching them pursue their dreams. After enduring three years of financial hardships, our agency has finally found stability.

This hard-earned achievement wouldn't have been possible without the unwavering dedication and sacrifice of my incredible team. I feel deeply honored and profoundly grateful for the outpour of kindness, encouragement, and love from all those who believed in me.

A significant part of an abuser's power lies in their ability to silence their victim's voice, and I adamantly refuse to remain silent any longer. Throughout this transformative journey, I found my true calling—to inspire those suffering, enduring, numbing their pain, masking their scars, or guarding their hearts, empowering them to discover their voices and reveal their authentic stories. This process serves as a means to release the weight of past experiences and pave the way for natural healing to take its course.

Until you heal the wounds of your past, they will bleed into every aspect of your life. You might attempt to conceal, isolate, numb, or repress these emotions, but ultimately, you must summon the courage to confront these wounds, revealing the root of the pain that impedes your progress. Confront the memories, reconcile with them, and, in doing so, find the ability to release them and gently move forward.

The truth about trauma is that it leaves a tangible imprint on your body. So, when you close your eyes and recall a painful memory, your body serves as a constant reminder that it's still there.

I recognized the need for healing, but discussing it was merely the initial step; the most agonizing part was writing the explicit details and revealing aspects of my life I had concealed for so long. As arduous as this process proved to be, it was also immensely healing. Page by page, chapter by chapter, I released the raw, vulnerable details of my life. I shattered old patterns, shed my shame, and finally took ownership of my narrative. It was my story and mine alone to recount. I had the option to keep it hidden or bravely expose my scars by sharing the most intimate experiences of my life, in hopes that someone, even just one person, would hear my story, feel less alone, let go of their shame and find the courage deep within themselves to reclaim their power and own their own story.

When we keep our stories locked away, they begin to rot and decay within us—revealing our inner emotions and affecting our actions, choices, health, and well-being. It stung, and every instinct urged me to conceal it again, but something unexpected happened: healing emerged. Exposing my story and bringing it into the light, vulnerably laying bare my soul, allowed those infected wounds to begin healing themselves.

Recounting these memories was heart-wrenching but also a source of Heart-Healing. I no longer viewed myself as burdened by shame; instead, I saw a different version of myself. I saw a young girl, a rebellious teenager, an inexperienced young woman, and a self-sacrificing mother. I saw someone who had been broken but was still deserving of love, happiness, and healing. I saw someone with the courage to survive, determined never to give up. I saw someone who had fought for her children, her family, and those she cherished most and, in some way, without even realizing it, fighting for herself.

I didn't paint myself as a victim of circumstances or demonize others. Instead, I embraced my journey, and in doing so, I developed a profound love for myself. I welcomed my mistakes, extended forgiveness, altered behavioral patterns, and authentically uncovered a new purpose. However, I didn't navigate these waters alone; I surrounded myself with those who inspired, challenged, and empowered me to continue growing despite obstacles.

I firmly believe that each of us possesses a unique story to tell—our story—waiting for us to grasp and embrace imperfections, broken promises, and mistakes, and all, with open, loving arms, offering ourselves the healing we deserve.

******

Upon reflection, I am deeply grateful for the incredible individuals who enveloped me in unconditional love and unwavering support when I couldn't see beyond my tears. They lifted me up when I couldn't stand on my own, investing their time and energy in supporting my vision as I navigated my journey through childhood, adolescence, young adulthood, motherhood, and entrepreneurship.

Amid numerous pivotal moments, one statement resonated profoundly during my journey: "You don't have to sacrifice yourself to earn the affection or approval of others."

These words resonate deep within my heart. So often, I sacrificed my needs for the sake of others, laboring under the self-limiting belief that my value and worth hinged on what I could give rather than who I am.

This simple yet profound statement has allowed me to understand that my value doesn't diminish based on someone's inability to recognize my worth.

In my closing thoughts, I reflect on how the stars rise after the darkness descends, the sun rises after the night falls, a flower emerges from the earth after its seeds are buried, and with every stumble in life, we grow with more extraordinary grace, patience, compassion, and wisdom than ever before.

As an advocate for healing and an Emphatic Leader, I have a wealth of post-traumatic wisdom to share, having navigated through the peaks and valleys of life and entrepreneurship, drawing inspiration from the most tenacious and influential women in the world. These formidable women have lived in the trenches, endured profound pain, made their share of mistakes, weathered numerous failures, and though they've been shattered, they remain relentless and fearless. Rather than succumbing to adversity, it ignites their spirit. They rise above, extend forgiveness, love deeply, and persistently pour their hearts into everything they undertake.

This transformation characterizes the woman I've become and has guided me toward my purpose: to empower others to take ownership of their stories, look inward, embrace healing, stop hiding, and boldly step into their power.

Throughout this journey, three fundamental steps have served as my guiding light: First, summon the courage to uncover your inner wounds by confronting your truth and nurturing self-awareness.

Next, confront the pain head-on. Then, liberate yourself from the shackles of the past by relinquishing your grip on experiences beyond your control. Embrace self-forgiveness wholeheartedly, extending forgiveness to others as well.

Lastly, cultivate unconditional self-love and self-acceptance. Honor your unique story, recognize your progress, and gently pave your way forward.

Obstacles and sorrow are inherent in the journey of life; we all encounter difficulties, and sometimes, life reveals an unfamiliar aspect of ourselves. Remember, what is causing you pain is also fostering your growth. What burdens you is imparting valuable lessons. When you eventually take a moment to contemplate your path, you might not even identify the individual you've transformed into. Instead, you'll start recognizing the person you were destined to be, armed with greater clarity, courage, strength, and resilience. This transformation could be the most precious gift you'll ever receive.

While my story has been woven by hands not my own, they have cradled me throughout this transformative and healing journey.

No matter how your story began, you hold the power to change the path and write a new ending.

Chapter twenty-three

From Silent Ostrich to Empowered Peacock

by Sheila Murphy

I CAN'T BELIEVE I am sharing my journey here. Not because I was so honored to be asked (and I was). But since I was presented with this opportunity, I have dreaded putting myself out there in such a personal way. In fact, I contemplated making a dozen excuses to say no to this opportunity.

My inner voice said, "Don't do it. Opening up, speaking, and writing about your personal story is not for you." And this is not the first time I have heard this from my saboteurs. They always tell me not to share the ugly details because people will judge me and know I am imperfect. I was that person who had learned over time to hide and suppress my voice and story.

And yet, that is why it is critical to share my story: by doing something uncomfortable, I foster growth within me. It is also critical that I share my story so I and others know and appreciate that we can choose to be different, act on what we want, and attain that desired life and career.

My realization journey started in what I thought was a career-ending moment, and that my belief that being an "ostrich" attorney—keeping my head down at my desk—was the pathway to success. I was wrong.

******

Have you ever seen a peer get promoted or get a plum assignment instead of you? And I am not talking about a peer who deserved it. I am talking about the person who lacked creativity and, to be honest, basic skills. But it changed my career positively even though it did not start that way. It felt like a sucker punch. Let me tell you what happened.

The company I worked for as in-house counsel promoted "Matt," a lousy lawyer who gave terrible advice. Matt, unlike me, spoke up no matter how off-base he was and built strong relationships. I had always focused on the work (which I did very well) and never liked speaking up, but now it became a sticking point as I watched Matt get the accolades and corner office that I knew I deserved.

First, the irony was that I had the power but didn't know I had any power. Matt knew I did. When I self-reflected, I realized Matt had asked me to partner with him by going to management and advocating for advancement together. And I turned him down. I thought they would recognize my value and expertise through my work product.

Second, I had conditioned myself to keep the spotlight off me. I realized that avoiding the spotlight had started in kindergarten and had become ingrained in me during elementary school.

******

Are you familiar with the old TV show "Wonder Rama"? It was a children's show in the 1960s and 1970s with Bob McAllister. It was very popular with kindergarteners.

One of my classmates, Jill—who, in retrospect, was a lot like Matt—somehow got tickets to be on the show. Before she went that week, we danced and played music in the classroom. Jill was in the middle of the classroom—making all the wild moves—getting all the attention. When she bumped me out of the way while doing the mashed potato, Jill turned to me and said that I sucked as a dancer, and I was not worth dancing with.

Jill went on to say that she was great, and not only would she appear on "Wonder Rama," but the show would also choose her to dance on one of these big blocks they had in the studio. Jill then shooed me away. Everyone laughed at me (or at least I felt they did). And I didn't want to be in the spotlight. Nor did I feel worthy of it.

Like Matt, Jill got what she wanted. And I was mad. My only comfort was that the camera caught just her lower half and zoomed in on her buttocks. Yes, I could be petty even back then.

Fast forward a year when I was learning to read. You see, learning to read, especially in reading circles, was a nightmare. Although undiagnosed at the time, I was dyslexic. And it is not what people think. I don't read backward. I need help decoding words—a fancy way of saying I cannot read phonetically and have difficulty pronouncing words and names.

I remember sitting in reading circles and the teachers having us read phonetically. Now, the teachers had developed this game to entice and reward us. It had to do with a frog's transformation from a tadpole. When you got a sound correct, you would leap from lily pad to lily pad, transforming from a tadpole to a frog.

I was a tadpole for a long time, and I remember the frustration and crying, watching others quickly pronounce words while I struggled. And I remember I wanted to refrain from taking my turn to speak.

Second grade was not much better. I made my first Communion, a most solemn rite. But when my official portrait pictures came in, my mother was heartbroken and unhappy because I kept my mouth shut when smiling. I was missing teeth and wanted to hide the gap. My mother refused to put the picture up. Again, I failed at being the center of attention.

Then, in third grade, we had a Thanksgiving play. I had a single line where I welcomed the Native Americans and offered them cranberry necklaces. Except I kept saying cranberry sauce necklaces. And my teacher was so frustrated that I could not keep that line straight.

In my house, the word cranberry was only followed by the word sauce. It wasn't a berry in my mind. After all, you slide it all jelled up out of a can. I had never seen or heard of this pure berry thing. Despite my teacher's warnings and coaching, you know what I said. Again, I learned that when I am in the limelight, I disappoint people and believe nothing good can come of it. I decided to fade into the shadows by the time I left elementary school.

******

In the junior high chorus, I became an expert mouther. I silenced my voice and hunched over so no one would see me. Then we moved from Long Island to Syracuse. The Syracuse high school had three cliques: jocks, dirtbags, and wingers. And you needed to dress a certain way. The dress code for wingers was preppy, preppy, and preppy. My Sears tough skins® did not fit in. Who knew what a blazer or duck boots were? But as soon as I figured out the wardrobe, we moved again to a school where the dress code was now designer jeans and Candies®.

My life's goal was to be quiet and blend into the background. But there was one exception to my story where I had to step up front. It happened when my college professor assigned us a group project. Have you ever been on a group project? Well, then, you know it is a nightmare. And this was especially so; I had a team of slackers. They did not want to do anything. They did not care. But I did. And this project included an oral presentation.

I had to do that presentation, or no one would (or at least I fell for that bluff). I hated it and did not sleep for weeks. And guess what? We did well. Yet even though I was happy about the result (as well as the fact I survived), the experience cemented my feelings about being the center of attention.

So, in law school, I knew the spotlight was not for me. I sat in the back row—and would have joined my friend, Frank, in taking notes outside the classroom in the hall if it had not made me stand out. I prayed each day that the professors would call on others, not me.

And while I was there, I dreamed of being an "ostrich" lawyer, one who sticks her head in the sand and just works. I wanted to keep my head down, churn out documents, and not speak publicly. When I graduated, I landed my dream job as a corporate lawyer who just documented deals—the perfect "ostrich" job, or so I thought. Unfortunately, my law firm blew that dream up.

On my first day, the managing partner told me I would be a litigator, not a corporate lawyer, because they needed more litigators. My heart sank. When the law firm put me in a job where I would need to speak in court, I thought about quitting on the spot. But my mother, who had paid for my education, would have killed me if I hadn't stuck it out. I spent years making a pale impression of a litigator—avoiding assignments most litigators wanted like arguing in court or deposing a witness.

This even melted into my personal life. I had a massive fight with my parents, trying to think of a way to avoid the spotlight at my wedding. I wanted to blend and avoid standing out. But I also didn't want to ruffle their non-ostrich feathers, so I wore the white gown and was the center of attention.

Around the same time, I also found myself paralyzed when I had to call the local Chinese restaurant to cancel a reservation, fearing they would be mad at me. Yes, I was a wreck.

******

I later found out that while it is true that ostriches can't fly, they can make some minor sounds. But only male ostriches can make a sound known as booming. Ostriches use boom and dance to attract a mate, defend territory, or warn the flock of a predator. During this process, the neck of the ostrich inflates up to three times its average size.

Like humans, male ostriches boom and dance while the females probably hang out with their heads down doing the work. Matt and me, right? Matt learned to boom while I taught myself to stick my head in the sand. I was a mess. But here's the thing: I was a mess by choice. I chose to silence myself.

I felt relaxed when I landed my first role in-house because I was on my way to becoming the ostrich I always wanted to be. And then the Matt promotion happened, which led to a choice—be a wafer and safer or crow and grow.

I decided I wanted more. Being an ostrich simply wasn't good enough, even a male one. I thought that if I was going to break out of my shell, I needed to strive toward a goal—a big, bold, and beautiful one. I set my sights on evolving into a peacock, strutting and singing my way to a better life. But I knew a mind shift this drastic would take time and effort. It started with becoming more comfortable with my voice and growing my leadership, branding, and relationship skills. I chose to open up and discuss my struggles with my manager, allies, mentors, and coach. They all provided advice, support, and cheerleading.

I went from not sleeping for days before a presentation to only being restless the night before to not worrying about speaking at all.

One of the moments from which I knew I had made progress was the night before a conference I was chairing. Being the chair was mainly ceremonial, but you make the opening remarks. So I used the previous chair's opening, which was very pro forma, and handed in my draft remarks.

The night before, while practicing aloud, I realized the words didn't suit me and that I could make them so much more impactful and memorable if I allowed my voice to fly. After several revisions, I gave the remarks and knocked it out of the ballpark while wearing my head-to-toe red suit (that I could not hide in if I wanted to). People cried and laughed. People told me it was like talking directly with me and that they had never seen me more effective. I found my voice, used it, and succeeded.

My general counsel then asked me to do a presentation in front of the entire C-suite. Our CEO was a great visionary but also known for being extremely direct and exceptionally blunt. I remember after one woman presented before him, he made it known to everyone that he was not a fan. For the next 10 years whenever someone mentioned her, he would say, "Haven't we fired her yet?" Presenting in front of him was daunting, to say the least.

As you can imagine, I was a wreck, knowing this talk could make or break my career. I sat on pins and needles while waiting to be called upon. Finally, the moment arrived. My general counsel gave me such a glowing introduction.

When I approached the front of the room, I took a deep breath, looked at the CEO, and began to speak. I embraced the moment and said, "Wow, so this is how it feels to be the bride."

The CEO chuckled, and I realized I had found a way of connecting with people and ideas. Someone who had seen me rehearse asked, "Did you say one thing like you rehearsed?" My answer was no. I had chosen a natural and more authoritative voice that worked for me.

******

Senior management selected me to speak in front of our women sales representatives about career success. I was more comfortable with my voice but still tied to my notes in case I fumbled. I also wanted to be safely behind and protected by a podium. Then, the person speaking before me went out without notes and just walked around the stage and talked. I was impressed.

I realized I would be more effective and engaging if I dropped the notes and podium. I had a choice. I chose to get rid of my safety net and dump the notes and the podium.

I was all nervous and jittery about leaving my comfort zone, and it got worse when I introduced my talk. Instead of saying I was there to discuss success, I said I was there to discuss sex. I stumbled, corrected myself, and said that was a different talk for later. People laughed, and we moved on.

And by being myself, people were with me, and it went great. Again, I learned that I only needed to be myself and that stumbling was okay. You admit the mistake, rectify it, and, if possible, humanize it through humor or what works for you. While you may think people are out there judging you, they want you to succeed and cheer you on.

This complex mind shift was an evolutionary, not revolutionary, change. I worked at making small changes and building on success. Just as you will not be successful if you try to go from sitting on a couch and downing fast food for every meal to working out two hours a day and eating only vegetables.

Management and outside organizations began to approach me with more speaking opportunities. And not always because I hit it out of the park but because I showed my authentic self, expertise, and willingness to come out from behind the curtain and try new approaches.

Yes, there were missteps along the way, like when I chaired a cross-functional taskforce and assigned all the speaking roles to others. Upon reflection, I realized I'd made a poor choice. But I could move on from it—and make better use of my voice.

Choosing to use my voice at work made me more comfortable using it personally. I became more honest in my relationships with friends and family, and those relationships took quantum leaps forward. The more open and vulnerable I became, the more people related to me on a more robust level. They felt more connected and understanding of my hopes and dreams. They also became more transparent with me. This led not only to deeper relationships but to my leading the life I always wanted.

Now, back to Matt. My career catapulted while Matt's stalled. He never worked on developing himself more, and his lack of skills started to show. By the time Matt left the company, he reported to me. I don't say this to gloat but for you to understand that you can change your circumstances and take control of your career and life.

Today, I am using my voice, taking center stage, and sharing my story with you because I chose to change my narrative and act. I know I am not alone in this struggle, and I don't want that for you. I want you to know that you can change and create the career and life you want.

Finding your voice and change is a choice.

Chapter twenty-four

Self-realization and Renewal

by Jenn Ocken

IN 2007, I DECIDED to move from Chicago's bustling, artistically vibrant environment to Baton Rouge, Louisiana. This city, often bypassed by creative minds searching for grander landscapes, posed an unusual allure for me, beckoning me to carve my niche within its folds.

The move wasn't just a change of scenery but a step into uncharted territories of self-discovery and growth. I left behind the comfortable and collaborative creative business I shared with my brothers, venturing into the unknown to explore what I could cultivate independently.

Baton Rouge unexpectedly emerged as a place of solace for me, a community I have grown to deeply appreciate and love. Here, I've forged lasting relationships, built a supportive network, and found a clientele that values my work and contribution to their lives. This community and the bonds I've nurtured have become integral to my journey and successes. I retrace my steps here to encourage others to live boldly as their authentic, creative selves, sharing their lives and talents to benefit the community around them.

******

Before embarking on this solo journey, my foundation for supporting myself as a career photographer was well-established. Since 2002, shortly after I finished college, I have worked alongside two of my brothers who are both adept photographers and who profoundly influenced my creativity. Their photography mentorship complemented my business degree, allowing me to intertwine artistic passion with structured processes, tailoring them to my creative endeavors.

Yet despite the comfort of this collaboration, discontent lingered within me. I craved autonomy, a realm where my instincts could flow uninhibited, where my unconventional solutions had the freedom to materialize. I understood the traditional pathways, but my intuition yearned for uncharted ones. I needed the liberty to diverge when my spirit felt the call, respecting my brothers' approaches but realizing the imperative of my independent exploration.

To this end, I moved south in July 2007, with all my possessions loaded in a small U-Haul and a mere $700 in the bank. I arrived, and I went all-in by purchasing a condo. My decisions were unorthodox, but my commitment was unwavering.

This might appear to be a leap into the void, but I knew I was equipped with the appropriate tools and a fortified mindset. I was poised to mirror the triumphs achieved with my brothers but under my individual banner.

Fascination with the vibrant culture and rhythmic heartbeat of Louisiana's music had drawn me to the state multiple times before I moved. A family I had met earlier in my career in Little Rock—even before my move to Chicago—knew about my frequent Louisiana visits and requested a photo session during one of my visits. This simple request became a gateway, connecting me with multiple families, particularly in the Baton Rouge area.

I discovered a unique and heartfelt appreciation for portrait photography within this community. Once I settled here, I encountered an affection and appreciation for photography throughout Baton Rouge that was different from other experiences in my professional journey.

******

As I was establishing my business in Baton Rouge, I quickly learned that while skills and a passion for creating are crucial, they still need to complete what I now call the "Creative Business Trinity." In the years that followed my move to Baton Rouge, I was missing something that would solidify me as a career photographer with both the security and stability that come with it. I had talent, experience, and a solid educational foundation. Still, I needed to have the inherent belief that I was fully prepared and could be successful at living the life I wanted: doing what I love for people I adore and being paid well for it.

My quest thus far had been focused on validation from my family, peers, friends, clients, and the outside world. Because of that, my self-worth was perpetually on trial, leading to continual self-doubt:

- Who was I, the youngest of my siblings, to try to eclipse my brothers in our shared profession?
- How dare I strive to create something monumental?

The journey to realizing I already possessed all I needed was fraught with self-loathing because my path didn't resonate with the conventional wisdom I had grown up with, nor with my previous conditioning to conform. My uniqueness became a source of contempt. My divergent approaches left me feeling alienated. These internal struggles with self-value and worth overshadowed my instinct, drive, and passion—the forces that had initiated my journey. I became drawn to self-help quick fixes, external validations, and superficial affirmations, losing sight of the ambition that had propelled my journey from Chicago to my solo career.

My physical appearance, marked by weight gain and adult acne, plagued my self-esteem, and I felt adrift in a sea of despair, anger, and confusion, struggling to find solid ground for my recognized professional skills. I perceived the concept of manifestation as a futile pursuit, a cruel joke played on the hopeful.

Then, in 2010, compounding my struggle with self-doubt and questioning, I experienced a profound loss—my father, a mentor, died after battling complications from heart surgery for several months. Amid the anger and frustration, there was now also profound sorrow and a vacuum left by his departure. At 34, almost a decade into my career, I was at a crossroads, unsure how to proceed. This painful juncture, however, unearthed my latent resilience and became an unexpected beacon, illuminating my true path.

Through the loss of my father, I was brought back to forgiveness and acceptance of self and a renewal of my inherent passion and the intuition that had spurred my journey initially. The realization was revolutionary—Dad was no longer here to be the voice of uplift. My cheerleader was silenced. Now, I was called to be that voice.

In this labyrinth of emotions and existential queries, I realized a pivot was essential, but it would require more than my professional tools and talent; it required rediscovering myself. I yearned to embrace my father's faith in me, to fill the void his absence had created, and to see the brighter side of situations without his comforting perspective. It was time for self-healing, self-love, and channeling the unconditional affection my father had bestowed on me.

Thus began a journey to reconnect with my intuition and rekindle the flame of self-belief that had once spurred my leaps of faith.

Reflecting on my 2007 relocation to Baton Rouge, I realize that the leap of faith was also an escape, a flight toward embracing the final piece of the "Creative Business Trinity": total self-trust. Part of me thought I had to "really prove I can be successful on my own," so I chose a city where many creative people live. This pivotal leap or escape showed me I couldn't leave my insecurities behind. I had to align them with self-trust. I had to embrace what it meant to be a self-leader.

******

Do I still believe I need to do things unconventionally? Absolutely! There is so much fun in it! I thrive on the challenge and on finding solutions. But whether I am in Chicago, Dallas, Little Rock, the Gulf Coast, or anywhere else, and with or without my brothers, success is always possible. I just had to trust myself. It took over a decade and a journey sparked by loss and fueled by self-love to understand that the key to a fulfilled life isn't a location or external validations or my father; it's unconditional self-love, self-forgiveness, and acceptance. I was beginning to intentionally embrace the essence of a true self-leader by cultivating the confidence my father had in me.

Since embarking on this odyssey of self-discovery, I've delved into myriad resources. As maturity and self-work through therapy and reflective journaling practices became a constant, I gradually unwound the tangles of my soul. Year by year, I dug down to my essence, embraced change, and realized the significance of authenticity and self-truth. I learned to release the desire to conform to external expectations and embrace a balanced existence, aligning my financial aspirations with my life goals and owning my journey with newfound zeal.

Every step I took brought a more profound realization of the need for change, the recognition of harmful patterns, and a commitment to authenticity. I reshaped my existence, letting go of others' expectations and projections of those expectations to find a new equilibrium. My life became a reflection of my love, a testament to the resilience of my spirit, and a beacon of authentic existence.

And then 2020 rolled around, like a disturbing replay of the turbulent period when my father fell ill and passed away. My burgeoning career stability was now threatened by global upheaval. But there was a fundamental difference: I was now fortified with self-love and had fully embraced the Trinity: creative talent, foundational skills and education, and staunch trust in myself. This equilibrium equipped me to face the challenges the pandemic hurled at everyone. It allowed me to identify the serendipitous symmetry of experiencing a pandemic and personal loss in the same months, just a decade apart.

While fear and uncertainty about the pandemic clouded my thoughts emotionally, I found solace in stability and focus. It was a time for problem-solving and leaning into the positive aspects of my character. So, when the opportunity knocked for a project that would defy Baton Rouge's stay-at-home ordinance yet adhere to safety protocols of maintaining more than six feet of distance, I embraced it without hesitation, motivated by the uncertainty and doubts of my entrepreneurial peers.

Questions that haunted all small business owners:

- "Will my business endure?"
- "What lies ahead for my community? My family? My business?"
- "Is pivoting an option? How can I adapt?"

Every entrepreneur's worst fear had materialized. But drawing on the experience, strategies, networks, and lessons I had accrued, I managed to pivot and, along the way, offer a beacon of support to other local businesses, encouraging them to leverage their unique resources to stay afloat.

******

We all possess the experience, knowledge, passion, and talents necessary to manifest our visions and adapt to adversity. How we cultivate these resources is crucial. It's our responsibility to master chaos, whether it's an internal struggle or a universal crisis.

The Front Porch Project vividly illustrated this principle, a testament to the power of harnessing one's inherent strengths and experiences to transform internal chaos into a harmonious dance of purpose and action. It served as a reminder that facing fears, leveraging strengths, and uniting in purpose enables seemingly impossible feats, even amidst unparalleled challenges.

The Front Porch Project was a beacon of hope, an initiative where photographers traversed neighborhoods, taking snapshots of families on their front porches. The families, in return, were encouraged to support local businesses and share their experiences on social platforms, acknowledging both the companies and the photographers involved. Inspiring more than 40 photographers to come together, we captured around 4,000 porch portraits during the three months of the stay-at-home ordinance, infusing an estimated $1.2 million back into our local economy.

The Front Porch Project was a symphony of streamlined processes, an unwavering focus on a unified vision, and a dedication to innovation, guidance, and production. It wasn't merely an expansion of my role as a photographer; it was a revelation, a transition from capturing moments for my clients to becoming a catalyst for change and empowerment for the community. This journey underscored that mutual support and communal resilience can usher in monumental positive transformations.

This venture was a reminder of the potential inherent in the community, our adaptability, and the power of constructive transformation. It reinforced my faith in the potency of creative endeavor, the seizing of opportunities, and the embrace of metamorphosis.

Cultivating self-love and evolving past ingrained patterns is an ongoing battle that requires my active energy. However, The

Front Porch Project was a poignant revelation, a mirror reflecting the truth that I possess all the necessary resources to transcend adversity. This endeavor never invoked feelings of overwhelm or fear. Instead, it became a vessel for my dedication, enabling me to guide other photographers to replicate this initiative within their communities.

My journey with The Front Porch Project in 2020 was about mastering the art of nurturing solutions, balancing energies, and learning when to pause, reflect, and recharge. It showed me how to be resolute in my decisions, even when they don't align with external expectations, especially when prioritizing actions that serve the collective well-being. Much like the project, my personal progression is intertwined with the rise of the community around me; it's a dance of empowerment and mutual growth, where employing one's innate strengths and passions becomes a catalyst for communal elevation.

Yes, I still find myself shedding old habits and learning to delineate boundaries without the shadow of resentment. I'm still practicing letting go of the burdens of blame and choosing self-harmony over preconditioned responses. It's been a journey with occasional setbacks, the unpacking, and repacking of old baggage, yet also continual growth and an unwavering commitment to moving toward more complete self-love and trust.

The moments of joy and realization make it all worthwhile, serving a purpose larger than myself. Every hardship is a steppingstone toward loving more profoundly and emerging more robustly. Through all this, my father's spirit continues to be my companion, a reminder of the power of unwavering self-belief and resilience.

This narrative isn't just a recounting of my personal transformations and realized projects. It's living proof of the unyielding human spirit and the boundless possibilities that come with collective effort, resilience, and self-trust. It's a reminder that the quest for self-love and empowerment is always worth taking up, as it is intertwined with our shared journey to mutual uplift and community transformation.

In seeking joy and fulfillment, we can inadvertently contribute to a collective metamorphosis, a legacy far transcending individual existence. And this is what gives life meaning.

******

My journey from Chicago to Baton Rouge was a transition that marked the beginning of a profound personal and professional metamorphosis. This move was more than a geographical shift; it was a leap into self-discovery and autonomy. In Baton Rouge, I found a nurturing community and a deeper connection with my craft and identity.

Leaving the comfort of a collaborative business with my brothers to pursue an independent path was initially daunting. However, it became evident that this choice was necessary for my growth. Baton Rouge offered an unexpected haven where I established meaningful relationships and found clients who deeply valued my work. This experience taught me the importance of embracing change and the power of community in fostering personal and professional growth.

My journey was challenging. Struggles with self-doubt and the need for external validation often overshadowed my accomplishments. The loss of my father was a harrowing period that forced me to confront my inner turmoil. However, it also sparked a pivotal moment of self-realization and renewal. I learned to replace the quest for external approval with self-love, forgiveness, and acceptance.

The Front Porch Project, initiated during the pandemic, exemplified these lessons. As I guided other photographers in capturing portraits while supporting local businesses, I realized the impact of mutual support and resilience. This project involved photography, empowering a community, and harnessing collective strength in challenging times.

This part of my journey has taught me flow within these impactful lessons:

Welcoming Change: Those daunting shifts in life? They're actually hidden doors to growth and discovering who you really are. Learning to roll with these changes is critical to evolving.

Community Is Key: Connecting with others and giving back doesn't just feel good; it's a game-changer for both personal joy and professional wins.

Finding "You" in the Chaos: The road to embracing who you are is bumpy, filled with self-doubt and outside noise. It's all about seeing your story's worth within the lived experiences and skills.

Loving Yourself First: Here's the real deal: fulfillment starts from within. Loving who you are and trusting in your strength is crucial to tackling life's hurdles and genuinely being happy.

Strength in Numbers: The magic happens when we band together, especially in tough times. Together, we're capable of making big waves of change.

Boldly chase what feels right to you, even off the beaten path. Invest in your relationships and make your mark on the community. But above all, remember that self-acceptance and love aren't just lovely to have in your back pocket to pull out if needed; they're the foundation for a life well-lived.

By doing this, you're not just upping your game, you're part of a more significant growth and positive change movement.

Chapter twenty-five

When Others Can't Handle the Shine

by Sameena Safdar

YOU MUST TAKE CHANCES, bet on yourself, and not be afraid to amplify who you are to the world. Six years ago, I was too afraid to live that way. I constantly shut down the things I wanted to do because others didn't expect those things of me, and it made them uncomfortable.

I grew up among a lot of chaos, dysfunction, and abandonment, so I focused from a young age on trying to meet and exceed my loved ones' expectations, just to ensure they would stick around. That led me to an intense focus on accomplishments and achievements—not a bad thing, but not great when I realized six years ago that I wasn't truly enjoying how I was spending my time. I had a great and successful life, but I found I wasn't spending enough time doing the things that made my heart sing. I limited myself to only doing the things I loved late at night or on the weekends.

I realized I had gone through this journey once before, about 16 years prior. I started as a filing clerk at a small law firm while in high school and worked nights in a restaurant to support my family while I was in law school. After sacrificing so much time and money to become a lawyer, I landed an amazing role upon graduation—a non-chambers (staff attorney) clerkship for a U.S. Court of Appeals judge. Following that, I started as an associate at a small civil litigation boutique in my hometown of St. Louis, Missouri.

Having been so focused on achievements and accomplishments, I self-identified with being "A Lawyer," but quickly realized I hated the isolation of practicing law. While I enjoyed researching and writing appellate briefs, I found I was happiest when talking with clients or focusing on innovation or marketing. In short, I found the business of law far more interesting than the practice of it.

At the age of 30, after a lot of soul-searching to determine what I could do with my training and skills that might make me happiest, I leaped into legal technology, taking a job as a trainer for Thomson Reuters. I was thrilled to find a role where I could focus on working with clients, educating, and helping them while leveraging and marketing innovative technology. I thought it was the perfect job for me, and I always felt my worst day at work exceeded even my best day in legal practice.

For 10 years, I flourished in my career and my personal life, with Thomson Reuters promoting me to account manager, giving me responsibility for renewing the largest Washington, D.C. and Atlanta law firms' accounts and upgrading them.

I hit my numbers every year and deftly navigated my role over the years from one focused on customer support and education to one completely integrated into the sales cycle, strategizing with my sales representatives on how to exceed our sales and revenue quotas each year.

By the time I had reached my 30s, I had accumulated various life experiences and responsibilities. I was living in D.C. with my man and my family, which included our two delightful children. Soul searching at this stage led me to gain a clearer understanding of who I was as an individual. It was an opportunity to reflect on my values, beliefs, and priorities, allowing me to align my life with my authentic self. It was a natural time to evaluate my goals and aspirations after realizing my priorities had shifted.

******

Life inevitably brings challenges and setbacks. Soul searching gave me the emotional and psychological tools to better cope with these challenges, ensuring I was resilient and had a deeper understanding of my own strengths and weaknesses. This self-awareness led to a better understanding of my own values and boundaries and allowed me to communicate more effectively with others, forming healthier connections.

My 30s were not just about achieving existing goals but also about setting new ones. I identified fresh goals and aspirations that aligned with my evolving sense of self. Continuous self-examination and reflection are essential for personal growth. As I moved through my 30s, I became more aware—of everything!

But at the same time, I struggled with feeling authentically seen—by my clients or my employers. My clients typically saw me in a few ways, none of which was accurate.

I wanted them to see that I understood the problems they were facing and might have some solutions for them. But they just saw somebody who worked hard, which was great, but not indicative of what I truly brought to the table—what I am passionate and knowledgeable about and what drives me. That's how I felt the leadership of my company saw me, too—a very hard and consistent worker hitting my quotas each year, but not someone with "executive presence" (as many women before me have heard.)

I also felt as if something was missing in my home life. I had always focused on being physically and emotionally present for my kids. I may not have always gotten organic and home-cooked meals on the table or kept the house clean, but I always made sure to celebrate birthday week with the kids, sign them up for camps and afterschool programs, and keep a steady stream of playdates, festivals, and outings in their schedules—all the things I didn't always get as a child. It often took lots of juggling, late nights, and mental gymnastics to do all this.

I ensured we had a patchwork of camps lined up every summer so there were no gaps in childcare. If ever the kids were sick or had a day off, I was the one who took off work because I had a more flexible job. I balanced all this with work, often taking same-day trains to other cities to meet with clients so my husband didn't have to handle bedtime alone.

I didn't always get to do the things I wanted, but I felt that was part of being a parent and raising children. I started realizing that I didn't know whether I was truly happy. I knew I was great at all the things I was doing—my kids, husband, and bosses were happy—but I wondered if I was happy. If I wasn't, I questioned whether my happiness (or lack thereof) was a good enough reason to disrupt everything, especially when everyone else seemed happy with the status quo.

As I started having these nagging doubts about whether I was really living my best life, my boss "voluntold" me into a social selling pilot at Thomson Reuters. The initiative focused on connecting with clients and prospects through social media. I begrudgingly participated, but as I started creating the required social media accounts and posts, I found I suddenly had a forum to share what I thought about how technology and innovation could transform not just attorneys' and legal professionals' lives, but also drive their job satisfaction and well-being.

I could also post about the changing demographics I saw in the legal industry, how we were lagging as a society, and how to ensure people had equal opportunities. These were great topics because they were at the forefront of the minds of my clients (specifically, the managing partners and C-suite leaders at my client firms who I needed to see me in a different light than printer fixer or sales rep.)

Soon I was creating authentic posts, sharing my thoughts and ideas, and using my social media to amplify posts by others I admired. I realized I had more to say, and I started writing articles and speaking at conferences. I started cultivating my personal brand, thinking about what I wanted to put out in the world now that I had a forum to do so. My clients, prospective clients, and connections started to see me in a different light, a more accurate depiction of my joy, enthusiasm, and expertise.

Clients started asking me to help them prepare for upcoming client sessions on how artificial intelligence might transform the legal industry, to moderate a diversity, equity, and inclusion discussion, introduce them to someone in my growing network, or just help them build a community. I realized that beyond helping me reach my professional goals, I enjoyed what I was doing. When I presented tips on sharing your brand online to coworkers or clients, people would say, "Wow, you come alive differently when presenting this than when describing legal technology products."

The problem was that the leadership of my Fortune 500 company didn't really see how that was tied to my main performance metrics of meeting my sales and revenue quotas. They tolerated my social media and writing activities but didn't encourage them. So I carved out time (like many parents) after my kids went to bed (between 9:30 pm and midnight) to write articles and plan social media sharing. That's when I allowed myself to do all these things that brought me joy, not during the day because my job was too busy.

All too often in my life, I had known entertainment—but not joy, true joy. Now, I was finding joy, feeling true joy. I gladly added more onto my plate because posting on social media, writing articles, and speaking at conferences made me happiest.

******

At the end of 2018, Thomson Reuters held a round of big layoffs. I was not getting laid off per se, but the position I and others held was going to split into three distinct positions. I was interviewing for all of them, and since I exceeded my quotas every year, it seemed likely I'd get one of the roles.

But I started thinking, "Is this really what I want to do? Is this really what's going to bring me joy?" I knew sharing my expertise and personal brand on social media, empowering people to own who they are, and connecting people was what I truly loved. But I was afraid.

I have come to know that I do have a choice: love or fear. So I took a leap of faith with zest and love for life, which redirected my journey and truly transformed who I am.

This was the year I turned 46. I don't know why I started thinking about what the next 46 years of my life might bring, but I did and wondered if I wanted to do all this for 46 more years. For about seven or eight months, I'd been feeling unfulfilled in my marriage, but I didn't understand it because it didn't look like the same situation as any of our friends who had gotten divorced. Their unhappiness when together was palpable, they had started taking vacations separately and did not seem to enjoy each other anymore.

That was not the case for us, but I was feeling burned out and unfulfilled, and I was refraining from doing more things I wanted every day, just to keep the peace.

I started wondering, "Is there another life for me out there where I can be who I am and feel fulfilled and get the things I want in both my professional life and my personal life?" I was also slightly held back by imposter syndrome because I'd always been the perfect daughter, wife, parent, and employee who accomplished things and the one whom people could depend on to make things happen. It seemed much safer to stay where I was in all respects—in my big Fortune 500 job, in my seemingly fine marriage.

It seemed terrifying to go out and step out on my own. What if I failed?

******

I realized that I was more tired of dimming down my shine because other people couldn't handle the glare. I decided to bet on myself. On December 31, 2018, I shipped my laptop of 16 years back to Thomson Reuters, then drove to get moving boxes and started packing up my things to move out of the family home. It felt a little crazy to do it all at once, but I couldn't imagine any other way. I just let go of everything I'd been doing, all the burdens, everything people expected of me, and I just focused on what I wanted and needed.

I moved into a tiny rental house five blocks from our house so it would be easier for the kids. For the first time in my life, I didn't have a plan for what was next in my professional or personal life. I suddenly veered off my life path of meeting somebody, getting married and raising kids, getting a job, and continually seeking promotions. I didn't know what I was going to do.

Everybody urged me to use my severance to start my own company. But that felt like too much change. I instead focused on writing articles, speaking on podcasts, and helping build the She Breaks the Law community of women legal innovators in the United States.

The lesson in having no plan often revolves around the importance of flexibility, adaptability, and the ability to seize opportunities as they arise. Without a rigid plan, I found I was more open to unexpected opportunities and experiences, and this led to personal growth and discoveries that I might not have otherwise enjoyed.

When you don't have a set plan, you're forced to develop adaptability and problem-solving skills. This can be incredibly valuable in life, as it prepares you to manage unexpected challenges more effectively. Having no plan often meant I learned by doing, a powerful way to gain knowledge and skills.

For some lawyers, strict planning can lead to anxiety and stress, especially when things don't go as planned. Having a more relaxed approach led me to a more enjoyable and stress-free experience, encouraging creative thinking and innovative solutions.

Eventually, I started my own company, Amplify Your Voice LLC, but I started it as a side hustle while still gainfully employed by a legal tech company with a salary and a boss. I was too scared to branch out totally alone, though I shifted to much smaller legal tech startups.

I soon let go of any residual guilt I harbored over being the mom who moved out of the house and having broken up this seemingly happy family. It helped that I discovered my kids had a much better relationship with their dad once I wasn't there. He learned where our pediatrician was and how to cook and is a pretty great parent with whom I am happy to co-parent.

As for me, professionally and personally, I soared. I will say there were a couple of stumbles in there. That first legal tech job I took, I was in it for just 10 months. I don't think the market timing was right for that product then, but I also don't think I was the right person for the job. I chose to be honest with my kids about what happened because I wanted them to know that when you take risks, sometimes they work out, sometimes they don't; but either way, you'll be okay. Something else is always around the corner.

It was unfortunate timing with COVID lockdowns and job hiring freezes, but I ended up in another job until I dared to finally venture out on my own and invest all my time and energy into my business.

I realized that helping build a community of women legal innovators was what I was meant to do—to help others, especially other women, learn to embrace their whole selves and share that authentically with the world. Amplify Your Voice is the epitome of authenticity.

My biggest tip is to take the time to intentionally think about what you bring to the table that is unique, what your superpowers are, and what your "why" is that drives you. Build all that into your elevator pitch—and don't hesitate to share that with the world and amplify others who inspire you, too.

Bet on yourself. Invest the time in yourself, and don't be afraid to showcase who you are, even if it's not what people expect from you. You might stumble once or twice, but you'll be happier every day when you live true to yourself, your passions, and what you want to be doing.

Don't dim your brilliance because others can't handle the shine.

Chapter twenty-six

Innovate & Change to Succeed

by Nita Sanger

WE ARE LIVING IN a Volatile, Uncertain, Complex, and Ambiguous (VUCA) world. The only way to continue to be successful in this world is to be willing to innovate and change, to meet the increasing demands put on us, both personally and professionally.

I recently felt like a juggler trying to balance multiple plates and making sure nothing falls, when delivering on a recent project to a large demanding client. The project was in a constant flux as the client was not finalizing their work processes, and I had a team that was looking to me for guidance on the project while firm leadership eyed the work I was doing as this was our largest client, and the rise of Generative AI was causing panic among several of my clients who were looking for answers on how to deal with this new technology.

At the same time, I was trying to balance dealing with the health challenges of one child and the college applications of another. To handle this level of volatility, complexity, ambiguity, and uncertainty, I had to fall back to the six philosophies that guided my life over the years. I arrived at these philosophies through various events in my life that impacted me and helped me become the person I am today. They are:

1. Don't Let Others Define You
2. Open Your Mind
3. Have a Clear Vision for Your Life
4. Enable Evolution and Change
5. Support Others

******

Don't Let Others Define You: I was born in India and lived in Mumbai in a traditional family with a father who worked for a large global company and a stay-at-home mom and two older brothers. India is a deeply patriarchal society, and women are basically treated as second-class citizens.

I often heard from my father that my studies were not important as I was a girl, and that I was only going to be a housewife like my mother. My mother wanted me to help her with work in the kitchen. When I asked her why she expected me to help her and not my brothers, her comment was "because you are a girl. If you want to be equal to your brothers, then you need to study as much as them."

To me, that was an easy solution. I was going to study. Both my brothers earned their MBAs. Today, I have two MBAs, one from a university in India and the other from an Ivy League university in the United States. I have a 25+year career as a management consultant, focusing on business strategy and digital transformation, and have worked at one of the top consulting firms and with many of the leading global corporations. In a country where women were meant to be seen not heard, have little rights, and take care of the home and children, I bucked all the stereotypes and expectations laid out for me to define what I wanted for myself.

Open Your Mind: An open mind is critical and traveling and living internationally helps to achieve that. I was fortunate that my father was posted in Bangkok, Thailand, when I was in high school. I was the only child who went with my parents and was admitted into the International School in Bangkok and graduated high school there. The change that I experienced when I got there was a shock to my system. It, however, was the single most transformative experience that ended up shaping my entire life.

I went from an education in India, which is very traditional, where everyone conformed and learnt the same thing, to an American system where I could "choose my own adventure," on what I wanted to study. As a result, I got to study British literature, Chinese culture, Muslim culture, world geography, and many more fascinating topics.

Additionally, I went from being in a very ethnocentric Indian culture to being part of a society and school representing 80 different countries. Meeting and interacting with people from other cultures, I started to realize that each culture had so much to offer, there are so many different nuances to each culture and person that are so rich, and you can learn something from every person.

I have lived in India, Thailand, United Arab Emirates (UAE), and now the United States. Additionally, through work and personally, I have traveled to countries across the globe—Kenya,

Botswana, Zimbabwe, South Africa, Singapore, UAE, United Kingdom, France, Germany, Belgium, Netherlands, Canada, Mexico, Brazil, Japan, and many more.

My global perspective also translated into my work. I got involved in building and transforming businesses in the Americas and globally, and I got to work with people from various cultures. The skills that I developed because of my travels helped me succeed in my work. My children have inherited my love of travel and have lived and studied abroad. This has enabled them to have an open mindset, recognizing how much of a global world we live in, and addressing global issues and challenges. My daughter is studying world government and economic policy, and my son is studying international business.

Have a Clear Vision for Your Life: Once I finished high school in Thailand and returned to India, I knew I could not live the rest of my life in such an ethnocentric society; I wanted to settle abroad. The United States was my destination of choice and I wanted to come here as a single person. Additionally, I knew that to be successful in the United States, I would need to get a degree here, which can be very expensive.

Many Indians are not okay with sending their daughters abroad as a single person. They prefer marrying them to someone who lives abroad, often a near-total stranger. Knowing that there are stories of girls from India being abused and tortured at the hands of their husbands and in-laws, as they are so dependent on the person they are married to, these women receive little emotional and financial support.

I was totally opposed to that idea, and I faced stiff resistance from the family. I was eventually forced into an arranged marriage in India. We then moved to Dubai. My husband decided to study for the GMAT as he wanted to attend school in the United States. I went along with the idea and studied for the GMAT as well, and was eventually admitted to Columbia Business School, New York University, and a few other top business schools. He, however, did not complete his applications. I was able to divorce him and enter the United States as a single person.

I wish I could say that coming to the United States alone as a single divorced Indian woman was easy. It was not. I found the Indian community to be very judgmental and they completely ostracized me. I then decided to become friends with non-Indians who were more welcoming and accepting. I was soon able to make friends who were supportive of me and ended up with an active personal and social life; many of them are friends to date.

This experience taught me that if you have a clear vision of what you want for your life, you will get there. It may not be in a straight line, you may make detours along the way, but if you know your ultimate destination and are determined to get there, you will achieve your goal.

Enable Evolution and Change. We may have a clear vision in life for one part of our journey, but we need to be willing to continue to evolve and change that vision to meet the needs of the moment. This means being a lifelong learner. I had this interesting experience when I was working with a Big Four firm, trying to transform their Global Audit business.

I had very little knowledge about the audit business, the terminology used, etc., and at the same time had to work with leadership to transform it. We were also talking about using artificial intelligence, blockchain, robotics process automation, augmented reality/virtual reality to transform the business, which were still fairly unknown.

I needed to figure out a way to learn what I needed, find the people who could guide me, and then take the things I learnt and create a path to transform the business. As I was going through this experience, I followed the following approaches:

- I read up on everything I could get my hands on regarding the audit business and the various technologies.
- I became comfortable with not knowing everything.
- I worked with others, who were junior/younger to me, but had more knowledge and expertise in areas that I knew little about.
- I found the people who were the insiders and made them part of my advisory group. They gave me insights into what I needed to know based on their experience.

As a result of this approach, we were successfully able to transform the Global Audit business of the Big Four firm and even create a start-up within the firm to disrupt the business before an outside firm came and disrupted us. The start-up is still operating successfully.

Evolving and dealing with change also flowed into my personal life. During the time I was transforming the Global Audit business, we moved into the suburbs of New Jersey to provide my kids with a better school system. To ensure that they would assimilate into the town, I volunteered to coach my daughter for soccer and softball and my son for soccer. I had never played either sport before but wanted to be there for my kids.

When people asked me how I was going to coach, I told them, "I am a consultant. We often consult on things we know very little about. I am sure I can figure this out." Here again I followed the same approach:

- I read about the game, the various positions needed on the field, and exercises to run.
- I asked the kids who had been playing soccer a lot longer than I had been coaching on what exercises they wanted to work on, and I had them take the lead to make them feel more involved and take ownership.
- I worked with my assistant coaches and made them part of the leadership team on how to run the games.

Additionally, I asked some of the parents to provide feedback. We had a good team but lost the first few soccer games. One of the parents told us that we had good offense, but our defense was weak and hence goals were being scored on us. Both offense and defense are critical for the success of the team. Using that feedback, we adjusted how the team played and were able to win the championship. No one was more surprised than me when that happened.

This, however, validated the approach, and I have used it successfully several times after that to transform multiple global and local businesses. I continue to be an avid reader and am always looking to learn something new about the world, about the innovative technologies and how they are going to impact us, and how this is going to impact how we work and live.

Support Others: My Ikigai is to support other women and the next generation of leaders (our girls) to be successful. I think the only way for all women to succeed is to ask those women who have a seat-at-the-table to sponsor other women and pull them up. Men have been sponsoring other men for centuries. I often find women tend to be very insecure and want to shut out other women, as they believe that there can be limited "seats-at-the-table" for women. I believe we should operate from an abundance mindset and do exactly the opposite.

I have had people support me, both personally and professionally. When I came into the country, I had one friend who took me under her wing, taught me so many things, guided and supported me when I was struggling to assimilate, and was my guiding light. I would not be where I am if it had not been for her.

Professionally, I have had a few mentors, one of whom bears special mention—the Global Head of Audit, who gave me the authority and responsibility to transform the Global Audit business and continued to push me outside my comfort zone to be bolder, to not just make minor changes, but think about how to disrupt the business before someone else came and did this to us. My success in any of the work I have done can be directly attributed to the quality of the leaders I worked with, who would "have my back" while pushing me to be bolder and to stretch myself to learn and grow.

As women, we need to be role models so that others can see us succeed and believe they can do this as well. When my daughter's team won the soccer championship, one of the girls in the league asked her mother that if I could coach the team and win, why could her mother not coach her? The following year, a few of the other mothers volunteered to coach their girls' teams.

In my professional life, I continue to support the more junior members of my team, mainly women, to give them a seat at the table, take ownership of the work that they are doing, and then present it to the client and leadership. Additionally, I always make it a point to give them credit in front of other leaders.

The key to remember is that most people are not comfortable with change and want to keep things the way they were. This requires you to be more understanding, recognize that change is hard, understand where they are coming from, and bring them along on the journey. At the end of the day, it is about people and change management—and change is the only constant.

******

It is easy to be a follower. It is much harder to take the road less travelled. To be ready not just for today, but to be future-ready. There are likely to be naysayers who are here to disparage you and claim that "you do not understand." Remember the famous quote from Theodore Roosevelt (slightly amended):

> *It is not the critic who counts; not the man who points out how the strong woman stumbles ... The credit belongs to the woman who is actually in the arena, ... if she fails, at least fails while daring greatly, so that her place shall never be with those cold and timid souls who neither know victory nor defeat.*

Chapter twenty-seven

Great Expectations: A Love Letter to Women

by Lauren A. Tetenbaum

"I DIDN'T EXPECT THIS, but I'm thinking about starting my own business," I admitted to a girlfriend I had known for only a couple of years but who had become a close friend—a quaranteammate—during COVID. I didn't feel totally confident in confiding in her my innermost desires, or totally confident in my abilities as a businesswoman. But I felt ready to say aloud my hopes and needs. I felt ready to trust her. I felt ready to trust myself.

We were sitting on the floor while our babies played and their older siblings toddled in the backyard with their dads. We wore sweats, messy buns, and no make-up. We had gotten to know each other pre-pandemic when our first-borns struggled with separation anxiety while beginning their preschool program and we were both very pregnant and very emotional.

We'd seen each other cry more times than we'd had coffee before we moved to the same suburban town and found ourselves in the midst of a global crisis in which we could barely see our extended family. Throughout 2020, we had become like family to each other, going for stroller walks, celebrating Mother's Day and birthdays outdoors, exchanging Secret Santa gifts under thick blankets, heavy coats, and heat lamps in freezing weather because we knew it was worth it to be together and have some laughs.

My friend had a business degree from a top school and a former career in finance. She had left the corporate world upon becoming a mom. Like me, and like millions of women, she had tried different, seemingly more flexible roles within her industry, but ultimately felt pushed out because her bosses were unwilling to budge to meet her needs. She understood the expectations I was navigating while working at a law firm, including to be available on-demand to work—*i.e.*, to put aside other obligations I both wanted and needed to tend to, like my young kids. She asked me what kind of work I wanted to do, and I answered with simplicity: "I want to support women."

******

I didn't expect to have to carve out my own career. I was always more of a rule follower than an entrepreneur, a more qualitative than quantitative thinker, a person who liked to make pros and cons lists rather than take risks. But the professional path I had found myself on was not fulfilling.

After receiving graduate degrees in both law and social work, I pursued a career in immigration law, through which I thought I could earn a decent salary while also maintaining a robust pro bono practice focused on getting green cards and other forms of relief for survivors of domestic violence. Shortly after becoming a mom, I shifted to personnel roles without billable hours requirements, still making a difference by helping manage firmwide professional development and pro bono programs. But it didn't feel like I was doing enough for women. It didn't feel like I was doing enough for myself.

Since a young age, I felt compelled to advocate for women. I have always been a girly girl and I have been stereotypically feminine since childhood: long hair ready for styling with bows and other accessories, lots of pink, glitter, nail polish, dolls, dresses. I didn't enjoy engaging in athletics or getting messy. I was a good student and behaved in a manner considered proper. I loved listening to boybands and dressing up for costume parties.

As I approach 40, I'd still rather watch a rom com or read chick lit than attend a sporting event for entertainment. I've been described throughout my life as nurturing, organized, responsible, sensitive, and sweet.

******

I have also always been proud to be a feminist. I was a child in the 1980s and 1990s, when women were told they could have it all. I saw that women could marry later than their mothers (and by 2015 throughout the United States, marry other women if desired). I saw that women could be active in their children's lives while also having their own, become doctors, politicians, or executives with high heels and shoulder pads. They could get divorced and live their best lives afterward. They could be open about plastic surgery or denounce makeup altogether. They could be world leaders. They could be loud.

I believed in the power of women, and so, I didn't expect to feel cautious about trusting other women.

But for many years I did feel that way, beginning as a kid. When I was a teen, my friend groups shifted, the girls often taking their worst insecurities out on each other. I took comfort in my male friends, who didn't overtly stress about what they ate or insult each other's appearances to make themselves feel better about their own. "Guys are easier," I'd say, yet I felt like I was betraying my gender. I didn't engage in sorority rushing in college because groups of girls intimidated me. I didn't like feeling as though we were constantly being compared to each other. It's now clear we were made to feel like we were rivals.

Women who disparage other women because they are jealous of them or feel younger women must experience the same challenges they did in the name of fairness (or hazing) are reflections of patriarchal strategies I didn't expect to encounter as an adult. But I did.

I didn't expect internalized misogyny to be so pervasive among women; yet I've seen that it is. I regularly witness the deeply rooted, detrimental expectations of women, whether in the workplace or beyond. They are reflected everywhere in various settings.

I have been told by women managers (in flagrant disregard for laws and policies stating that employees have the right to communicate with others at their workplace about their wages): "Don't talk about salary with your colleagues, it's not a good look." I still see with too much frequency that women-led companies avoid putting salaries in their job postings, even though salary transparency is a proven strategy to combat the gender pay gap.

A woman boss whom I thought was a sponsor of mine once told me in response to good feedback I'd received from coworkers that it was her "worst nightmare" for colleagues to come to me as a point person on certain projects because she "wouldn't want others to think [she] was no longer in charge after all the hard work [she] put in." Far too many women colleagues (some of whom were mothers, themselves, or even my teammates on initiatives benefitting lawyer parents) were reluctant to sign on to firmwide letters advocating for changes in parental leave policies, because though they believed in my mission, they were afraid to make waves and felt more comfortable asking for individual benefits or just accepting the policy as it was.

Numerous times, I have been advised to avoid using the word "feminist" on my professional website, to appear more relatable to more people. When hired to present corporate workshops on women's rights for International Women's Day, I have been warned by women leaders at companies, "Just try not to make it too 'feminist.'"

The books I read with my kids feature the woman as the character packing the backpacks and doing school pick-up. "I'll ask your mom," I hear from school staff, the assumption so ingrained they don't notice their own words or feel their weight. "Dad is babysitting" is still a common phrase.

******

When I told my girlfriend, "I want to support women," I meant it. I wanted to learn from the mistakes the women around me, women including me, had made. I wanted to dispel feelings of competition and instead promote actions of collaboration. I wanted to loudly and proudly express that I was a mother with interests beyond my children and a professional with passions beyond my work, and I wanted to inspire other women to do the same. I wanted to share the message that if you open yourself up to other women, you can and will feel empowered.

Soon after this conversation, I launched my business as a solo entrepreneur. But I didn't do it alone. I did it—somewhat unexpectedly but also, so not—alongside other women.

I didn't expect to be supported by so many women while I set out to support women.

I am so fortunate to report that I have been. The women in my life, including the one to whom I initially disclosed my business idea, have literally and figuratively shown up for me. They have attended my fundraising and networking events, introduced me to individual and corporate clients for opportunities, read over and shared my work, and broadcast information on my business ventures. They take care of my children without being asked if dismissal policies change unexpectedly or a birthday party goes awry, drop off ice cream cakes in celebration of professional milestones or household illnesses, and spend time on the phone to let me vent, brainstorm, or chat about anything on my mind.

I didn't expect to ever have so many women friends whom I trust.

My mother used to advise me, "It's important to have girlfriends." She was right. I've been able to make so many in part because I've learned to manage my expectations. The women I know are nuanced and flawed yet fabulous and fierce. We may not always agree or totally align, but they do support me, and they support other women. Some of them I've met only via the internet, yet I rely on and respect them. I am emboldened by our friendships, our sisterhood.

And I now realize that women, myself included, are imperfect humans; the women I know may not always meet my needs in the exact moments I have them, but they can still serve a deep purpose. They can and do still add value to my life.

For example, a former middle school girlfriend responsible for cliques and gossip is now, or rather, still, a dear friend. We regularly discuss motherhood, money, mental health, and more. She's someone I laugh with about how challenging it was to be an adolescent, and also how challenging it is to be an adult.

My perspective has shifted with time in the professional context, too. A woman I'd admired but who didn't hire me for a job I desperately wanted more than a decade ago (I was warned she could be tough on other women) got in touch with me last year. Upon meeting, she said: "I'm your biggest fan. You are meant to be doing what you're doing now."

******

I learned the lesson of trusting other women not only because of maturity, but because of motherhood. I didn't expect that becoming a mother would make me feel so connected. I am so thankful that it has.

As a social worker focusing on women's rights advocacy and maternal mental health, I know—intellectually, emotionally, from research, from experience—that motherhood can be extremely isolating.

It is incredibly hard to let your guard down, to share what's making you feel scared or confused, especially when we are so used to comparing ourselves. And yet, "No one talks about this enough," the women in my postpartum support groups reflect with relief, about the pressures to breastfeed, the impact on libido, the tears, the rage, the guilt, the desperate need to be alone sometimes simply to reconnect with oneself. "I'm so glad we caught up," note my friends, upon carving out a few elusive minutes of their busy days to go for a walk, or chat on the phone, or sit with me while our children play or while I clean the kitchen—an endless task.

When I became a mother, as is the experience for many others, the early days blurred together. Even when I didn't leave the house, I felt drained. One day, a friend with a child one year older than mine invited me to go for a walk. I sent many frantic texts as the agreed-upon meeting time approached: "Still feeding... Can't figure out the stroller... Have to change my shirt... So sorry!"

I felt scattered and overwhelmed. My friend remained patient: "No worries. We'll walk whenever you're ready."

She greeted me with coffee, a hug, and knowledge of diaper bag packing tricks. She taught me it was okay to not have it together all the time. She taught me it was okay to ask for help. She taught me it was okay to lean on other women.

Women often understand things in a way that men don't because they haven't had to. I was recently walking in my native New York City, alone. It was a sunny morning in a residential neighborhood. I noticed out of the corner of my eye a man trailing me, too closely copying my random zigzag of crosswalks. A woman—a stranger—tapped me on the shoulder. "He's following you," she warned. "I know," I replied, feeling more angry than unsafe. She nodded. "I'll walk with you."

Women are stronger together, whether as a physical group protecting against forms of gendered assault and abuse we unfortunately know all too well, or on an emotional level. Women who know each other only through friends of friends or from social media will say, "Of course, I'd be happy to talk," about fertility issues, divorce lawyers, C-section scars, their kids' struggles, the loss of a parent, career goals, or identity shifts. Women may not always get along, but they get it. I am grateful for the many good men in my life, yet I am often overcome with appreciation for the women I know.

The women I know are physicians, finance experts, and artists. Some are in between professions, some are parents, and some have decided not to have children. The women I know can discuss, in the same group chat, the latest bestselling book they've read or how to contribute to a geopolitical humanitarian crisis. The women I know will lend each other outfits and share information on oncologists, each without hesitation. "How can I help you?" the women I know offer, and they mean it.

I didn't expect to write a love letter to women; yet, that is what I feel my story has become. I didn't expect to be the woman I am today, to have the career I have now. I have dedicated my life to empowering other women and each one I engage with—personally or professionally—leaves me feeling more powerful, too.

Together, we can push back against patriarchy, and we can have wine and watch reality TV in our loungewear. We can cuddle our kids and crave career growth. We can be vulnerable yet powerful. We can laugh and cry and be mad and sad and silly and joyful. We can do it all because we can do it together.

We must do it together.

Women of the world, will you walk with me? We'll walk whenever you're ready.

Chapter twenty-eight

When Life Throws You a Curve Ball ...

by Jennifer Marino Thibodaux

WHEN I TOOK THE stage at #EmpoweredWomen2022, I shared the lessons I learned when I lost the plan and found myself. I spoke about my nearly 20-year journey to achieve my dream of becoming a partner at a law firm, only to realize the disconnect between that dream and my true self. I shared that it took me over two-and-a-half years to find the strength and courage to walk away and take a path I never anticipated.

The theme of my talk was authenticity. I shared stories about getting to know myself, valuing vulnerability, and letting go of what others think. I'm a professional speaker and it's one of my favorite talks because it resonates with every audience, every time. So, imagine my excitement when I decided to put pen to paper to bring that story to you, dear reader.

Except, something felt off after my first draft. I couldn't put my finger on it until I had a eureka moment: This season in my life is defined by a different story and it felt inauthentic to share any other journey.

I know my story is not your story. But I also know these top four lessons I've learned will help you knock the next curveball life throws your way out of the park. When you're at bat, hit an authenticity grand slam! You can also use these lessons to help move past whatever limiting belief is holding you back.

Five days after the one-year anniversary of #Empowered-Women2022, I was diagnosed with a chronic medical condition called lymphedema. It is not life-threatening, but it is life-altering.

******

I stared at my foot and lower calf in disbelief. My foot was twice its normal size. There was little to no distinction between my ankle and calf. The podiatrist had just removed a cast I wore up to my knee to get rid of the fluid that had caused inexplicable swelling. Needless to say, it didn't work. Stumped, the podiatrist sent me to a vascular surgeon.

About a month later, the vascular surgeon ran a series of tests and stood across from me with his arms folded and a concerned yet apologetic look on his face. He said: "You have lymphedema."

Lympha-what? He explained my lymphatic system was congested like a traffic jam. This caused protein-rich fluid to pool in my foot and spread into my calf because it could not get back up to my heart. He prescribed manual lymphatic drainage and recommended a physical therapy team. He told me they'd "get the fluid out" and he sounded quite confident when he said, "You'll have your foot back."

I would later learn there is no cure for lymphedema. It can only be managed by wearing compression (bandages or custom garments) at least 22 hours a day. I would also come to accept that my foot will never look the way it used to. Instead, I live with a chronic condition—technically a disability—that requires extensive daily care. As an otherwise fit person in my early forties, staring down this curveball has been one of the most difficult periods in my life.

Yet I have learned so many lessons along the way—more than I can recount here. In many ways, writing this feels a bit like flying a plane while I'm building it. I'm still learning as I go, but here are my top three lessons.

******

Lesson #1: Feel all the feels.

I have been on an emotional rollercoaster since the onset of this condition. At first, I felt confused as to why I had lymphedema. I needed someone or something to blame. Is it because I don't drink enough water? Is it because I have a sedentary job? I was desperate for an explanation and determined to find one so I could fix the problem.

As I began to grasp that there is no "why," I got really angry. Everything about lymphedema made me mad: bandaging, garments, physical therapy, my shoes not fitting, the way my foot and leg looked—you name it. I felt overwhelmed as I tried to balance learning how to manage lymphedema, actually managing it, and still living the life I had become accustomed to.

All the while, the treatment modalities left me feeling insecure. Early on, when my foot was at its largest, I had to wear a black, orthopedic shoe with two Velcro straps because a regular shoe wouldn't fit. When people would ask me what happened to my foot, I was embarrassed to respond: "I suffer from chronic swelling, so I have to keep it bandaged." If I even uttered the word "lymphedema," I felt... ashamed. It was like there was something "wrong" with me or that I was inadequate.

As weeks passed, I felt frustrated and impatient by the peaks and valleys of treatment. My foot would look a lot better one day—albeit nothing like my right foot—then swell back up. What was taking so long to "get my foot back"?

This one is hard to admit, but I also felt envy. Everywhere I looked, women walked around with two same-size feet and calves, wearing cute shoes (my options are now extremely limited) or leggings (which act like a tourniquet and cause my leg to swell). Ugh.

When I learned my left foot will never look the way it did, I felt an enormous amount of grief. To be honest, I am still working through it because of the daily struggle to find shoes that fit and clothes that don't aggravate the swelling or draw attention to it. But that's another chapter for another book one day. (Flying the plane while I'm building it over here!)

You may have noticed that I haven't mentioned feeling sad yet. That's because I made the mistake of not allowing myself to feel sad for a very long time. While I was ok sitting with all the other emotions, sadness was unwelcome. I am a positive person and typically adopt a "mindset is everything" attitude. I reasoned that if I let myself cry, it would mean that lymphedema was managing me instead of the reverse. I refused to hold space for sadness or tears.

I didn't realize how wrong that was until my friend and business coach, Jen Grosso, called me out on it. She knew that deep down I was waiting for someone to say: "Here's your gold star for not crying! Here's your gold star for being so tough and stuffing down those emotions!" It was like a punch in the gut. Not long after that, an unrelated issue made me angry, and the floodgates opened. I was mad, sad, frustrated, and grieving. And I was finally—finally!—allowing myself to cry.

How cathartic! Surprisingly (perhaps to me only), it was not self-defeating. The tears stopped and I went back to managing my lymphedema rather than having it manage me, as I feared. I squared my shoulders and faced a new day. And I realized the import of feeling every single emotion associated with the unexpected.

Dear reader, mindset will only take you so far. There are no trophies for being tough and stoic when you're blindsided, dealing with tough stuff, or inside your own head. You don't need to start making lemonade the instant life hands you lemons. It's ok not to be ok. Allow yourself to feel it all. Because when you do, you will eventually welcome other emotions, too.

Today, more than anything else, I feel an immeasurable amount of gratitude because I am an otherwise fit and healthy person. Health is wealth. I feel proud when this body is at the gym—rocking cycle shorts and a long black compression stocking on my left leg—pushing myself, lifting weights, and not letting this so-called disability hold me back. I feel grateful for the people who have supported me along the way, including new friends in the lymphedema community whom I never would have met.

And you know what else? I feel brave in the face of my vulnerability.

******

Lesson #2: Let yourself laugh.

"It's my hot girl summer!"

That's what I would jokingly tell people who asked about my bandaging in summer 2023. I had graduated from the orthopedic shoe to a buckled sandal open as far as it could go. Every day, I wore a layer of foam across my foot, another layer of foam wrapped around my calf, and three long bandages holding everything in place. I also individually wrapped my toes in gauze because they were swollen like cocktail hot dogs.

Looking back, deflecting with humor was undoubtedly a defense mechanism. If I joked about the bandages, I could push away reality. I also like to make people laugh, so I got a nice dopamine hit when the joke landed. When I delivered the "hot girl summer" comment to an inquiring stranger, she quipped back: "Girl, you need to Bedazzle that shoe! Own it."

Humor got me through those early days and still does now. As that summer ended, I remember telling my husband that my closed-toe shoes don't fit, and I didn't know what I'd wear to upcoming professional events in the fall.

He looked at me and deadpanned: "So, you kind of have a reverse Cinderella thing going on?" I immediately burst out laughing. I also have never laughed as hard as when my then 6-year-old, challenged to imitate someone he knew, giggled and said in a high-pitched voice: "Oh! Look how good my foot looks!" Later, we decided I should be Mommy the Mummy for Halloween because I have multiple sets of bandages and could easily wrap my whole body any given day. I mean, it's all funny!!

You may be thinking, "Yeah, but my curveball isn't funny" or "I'm not ready to laugh at myself." I get it. I wasn't either for a long time. However, I speak from experience when I say that you'll know when the time is right for humor. Laughter allows me a respite from a chronic condition. Rest assured that laughter won't make what is going on any less serious, sad, frustrating, devastating, maddening—you name it. Instead, maintaining a sense of humor allows you to welcome comedic relief when you need it.

Especially when you're in on the joke.

******

Lesson #3: Keep an open mind—and try new things.

I had followed the unwritten rules. Conservative navy or black dresses. Blazers. Pumps. Mix and match. Rinse and repeat. After leaving private practice, I started to incorporate some color, but let's face it, old habits die hard. I stressed over wearing cobalt blue (gasp!) when I spoke at #EmpoweredWomen2022. Ha! A year later, I was rocking a jumpsuit at #EmpoweredWomen2023.

A black, sleeveless jumpsuit?! A vegan leather jacket? Open-toe, beige suede, stacked sandals? Never, ever, in a million years would this former law firm partner who wore pantyhose nearly every business day for nearly 11 years imagine she'd wear that ensemble to a professional event. But lymphedema broke me out of my mold.

It may sound small and insignificant, but this was a big move for me. If it weren't for the need to wear comfortable shoes and my insecurity about the size of my calf (which was yet to be diagnosed and appropriately treated), I would have worn my usual uniform.

As I got dressed that morning, I felt both panic and excitement. Was I really going so far out of my comfort zone? Doesn't this actually look ... kind of awesome? I've never received so many compliments on my attire at a professional event as I did that day. Go figure. I even rocked a pineapple brooch that my dear friend, Jing Wang (she's an author here, too!), gifted me. More on that in a bit.

After the diagnosis, a friend recommended I see a functional medicine doctor who had changed his life physically and spiritually. It sounded a bit woo-woo. I had never veered away from Western medicine. I had never even been to a chiropractor! But at that moment, I said yes. What did I have to lose?

Dr. Ken Davis changed my life. He taught me about the "Triune of Well-Being" connecting my mind, body, and spirit and the import of keeping the triune intact for optimal well-being. He taught me how my emotions, unconsciousness, and sense of self impact my physical health. I now understand how suppressed emotions influence lymphatic congestion. I saw a significant reduction in swelling after my initial visits. The lessons he taught me are ones I will forever carry.

I'm a rule follower and a creature of habit. I'm also a lawyer, so I like hard facts and rules. I'm trained to ask questions and poke holes. I'm risk averse by nature. I'm also an overthinker. (Gee, I'm not sounding very fun here!) But lymphedema taught me to try new things and keep an open mind.

Sometimes when we're at bat, an unexpected curveball forces us out of our comfort zone—and we find out we're better off for it.

******

Lesson #4: Look for the life lessons.

Dear reader, if you take nothing from this chapter, please take this: when life throws you a curveball, remember to look for the lessons. There's something to be said about finding the message in your mess.

When my incredible physical therapist, Ana Pozzoli, PT, CLT, told me, "It's time to start living life," I immediately imagined the words on a sign with blinking lights around it. We were talking about my plan to wear "real shoes" but with a compression sock to an upcoming social event. I was nervous about what my foot would do, and I doubted my decision. But Ana was right.

Smashing a curveball often knocks us off our feet. We all have something pushing or holding us back, whether it's a physical limitation, a limiting belief, or some other life event we never saw coming. Our reflex may be to take ourselves out of the game and sit on the bench.

My advice? Grip the bat with both hands and knock it out of the park. It may shake you to your core and you may lose your footing at the start, but it's going to change your life in more ways than one.

******

As for that pineapple brooch? I chose a pineapple as the logo of JMT Speaks because it represents authenticity. Pineapples stand tall, wear a crown, and have tough skin to protect the sweetness at their core. We, too, must stand tall with our chins up and shoulders back, confident in being our true selves.

So, why not pretend we're wearing a crown? Our tough exterior protects the sweetness at our core: our authentic self. How perfect I wore that brooch the day I stepped out of my comfort zone and, days later, into a life-changing diagnosis.

To follow my journey and learn more about living and learning with authenticity, visit me at www.jmtspeaks.com.

Chapter twenty-nine

Rising Up

by Courtney Thomas

THE "HMM," FOLLOWED BY the squinted eye and side head tilt usually trails my declaration that I remember exactly what our house looked like, I can describe the son of my babysitter to a "tee," and I vividly recollect the phone call to my grandmother where I begged with pleading tears for her to come get me. I wasn't quite 3 years old. And I remember it all with photographic precision.

Don't buy into the "there's no way you can remember things when you were that young" statement.

This is a story of rising up. It's about the emotional currency paid and the pain that birthed resiliency when the circumstances of reality could have much more easily blazed a path for caving to the radical disruption in my childhood and adult life.

It's about not shying away from the "hard stuff," but learning to lean into it, knowing that it's only through the cracks that the light gets in. And I believe each of us was meant to shine brightly.

And here's the thing... I don't want to erase any of my hardships. If I was given the choice to whiteout the hard things and rewrite them, I wouldn't. Because in them, beautiful things were born.

So with that, I sit in a place of gratitude, grace, and grit.

******

My mom was rebellious in high school. She ran with the wrong crowd, made poor decisions, and justified her actions (then and through adulthood) as though she was the victim of some insurmountable injustice. She convinced herself that change wasn't something she could create for herself. Don't get me wrong, I'm not saying her childhood was a bed of roses. With a father who had an explosive and violent temper, coupled with pattern of unfaithfulness, there were many things that likely scarred her heart.

Despite her desire to "shape up," the magnetic current into the wrong-way traffic lane was stronger than her will to fight against it.

At 19, my mom met my dad who was from the Outer Banks of North Carolina. It was young love that quickly moved to marriage. What comes after marriage? You guessed it... the baby carriage. At 20, my mom traded in her youth for becoming a parent. My dad didn't want a child, so they split up soon after I was born.

I have no memory of him, only a couple of pictures to underscore how much I look like him. He died when I was 3.

In the grocery store parking lot she said, "Courtney, I have something to tell you. Your dad died today." I wasn't even sure what that meant because I'd never had a "dad" and "died" hadn't even been introduced into my vocabulary.

My response was, "What is that?" She explained he died in a car wreck. He was driving too fast... That probably explains the hypersensitivity I have riding with people and why at age 6, I started panicking at night that I was going to die.

Not long after I was born, my mom's alcohol and drug use topped her priority list again. Frequently, my grandmother stepped in to ensure I was properly cared for. She was my angel on earth. If not for her, God only knows where I'd be.

In an effort to influence my mom to change, she'd say, "If you don't start taking care of Courtney, I'm going to have to call social services on you." My grandmomma would have NEVER turned me over to the state. She was simply willing change to happen. It didn't work.

Instead, my mom moved me to Daytona Beach, FL, where we lived on the top floor of a house on the beach. You had to climb the white wooden stairs from the sand to reach the swinging screen door. My mom worked night shift, so I spent nights with the babysitter. Her son would take me outside to the shed and scare the shit out of me with their baby alligator.

The ocean of tears I cried didn't bring understanding as to why my grandmomma was so far away. One afternoon, she called. I was sobbing on the phone—the kind of cry that literally takes your breath away—and begged her to come get me. For some reason, my mom gave way.

Being separated from my grandmomma was my first recollection of trauma. But there had been plenty before. Did you know trauma can leave an imprint before a child is even born?

After returning to North Carolina, my mom signed over legal guardianship to my granddaddy and his new wife; his secretary 30 years his junior. She ripped me away from the only person I could ever truly count on. It was devastating.

My mom gave my granddaddy strict instructions not to allow me to see my grandmomma. One day, she came to the door asking if she could just see me and take me for ice cream. They told her "no," and I whaled from behind the door, begging to just hug her. It felt like someone was ripping my heart from my chest. After a year, they released custody back to my mom because "having a toddler was just too disruptive for their new marriage."

Linda, the stepmom, hated me living with them. She would pinch me until I'd have blood blisters and forced me to eat all my food—including tomatoes, which I HATE. Kindness wasn't common. She'd put salt and pepper on the tomatoes, then sugar, then Sweet-And-Lo® until I'd finish them. It was horrible.

This is the first time I remember strategizing in my head, "I can't control what's happening to me right now, but maybe I can influence what happens next." Obviously between the ages of 3 and 4, my vocabulary wasn't quite that sophisticated, but it's when I remember the art of problem solving becoming my mode of survival. I believe it was the labor and delivery of becoming the entrepreneurially minded, complex problem solver I am today.

Situations we can't even register can have profound impact on us. Here I am, 47 years later. I made it.

******

I moved back in with my grandmomma—my safe place and the person I could count on. And even though the level of love and gratitude I had for her topped any skyscraper or the number of stars in the sky ... every child still longs for their mother. Every daughter whose mother chooses everything else in life but her wonders why—why doesn't she love me? What did I do? What can I do?

She'd tell me she was coming to visit, and I'd pull out my black metal folding chair and take it to the top of the driveway where I'd sit waiting for hours. But she never showed.

In kindergarten, we tried again. I'd spend some nights at her apartment with her new husband, Dexter. He was a gem. At night, I'd wake up to their bodies hitting the wall and the loud vibrations of yelling. The last night I remember with Dexter, the fighting was terrible. He left the apartment and cut the wires on my mom's car. There were so many blue lights.

And then the exhale came when my grandmomma took me away.

In elementary school, we tried again. But I'd wake up in the middle of the night and she'd be gone. When I was in middle school, age 13 to be exact, she'd take me to the bars with her. When it was time to go, I was her designated driver. On the weekends, she and her friends would snort cocaine and drink the bottles dry. I got used to fending for myself.

For my whole life, she's been in and out of rehab, the hospital, and jail. She lost her license permanently when I was in high school. My high school and college boyfriend, Chris, walked every path of being my mom's daughter with me. He knows me in ways others never could because he had a front row seat to it all. He and my grandmomma proved to be the only people I could truly count on.

******

Men came and went in my mom's life. There was Bill, Dexter, Arved, Frank, Jimmy, Bruce, Mike, Dennis ... and others whose names I don't even remember. She married five of them. Bruce was the best. He was truly the dad I'd never had. But her alcoholism cost her amazing jobs, and her greatest partner. When they divorced, it devastated me. After a few months, he told me it was too hard to stay connected to me and not be tied to my mom. It stung.

By this time, I was married. But not to Chris, to Tony. We met while I was managing a veterinary hospital. He was a K-9 officer, and his dog, Rico, was our patient. Chris and I were dating when Tony first came in, so I turned down his first offer for lunch.

A year later, Chris and I broke up because he wanted to move in together without putting a ring on my finger. While this southern girl was willing to break a Baptist cardinal rule, she wasn't willing to do it without a ring. Chris's parents' divorce had scarred him. Marriage was simply too overwhelming for him.

Tony came in for the take. Our first date was two days before Halloween in 1998. By Thanksgiving, we were living together, and in January he proposed. Yep—lightning fast. We were married in September 1999.

I didn't listen to my gut. I let what I thought others would think guide my decision for what was best for me. Tony lied to me three days before our wedding. Not a little lie—a big lie. I knew I would never trust him or ever look at him the same.

I thought I had to go through with it because "that's what I was supposed to do." My grandmomma said, "You do not have to go through with this ..." But I silenced the "don't do it" voice with "you will figure it out. You always do." By October 2021, we were separated. There are many pages to that story. A year later, I moved to Kansas City.

While I'd love to not have that "drive by" marriage on my track record, I know the situation further layered my sturdy foundation of resilience.

So how did I get to Kansas City? 1,110 miles away from the woman who was the air in my lungs to a place where I only knew two people—Chris and his mom. Yep, my high school and college love. He'd been a part of my life for half of my life. When Tony and I split up, Chris and I thought, "This is it. We are simply destined to be together." For several months, we had a long-distance thing. But then it happened. An opportunity of a lifetime.

For all my life, I've loved animals. My degree is in accounting, but I was drawn to animal welfare and veterinary medicine. In North Carolina, I was running a clinic and a nonprofit animal rescue. It was the magical blend of my passion and expertise. When I visited Chris in Kansas City, he took me to a shelter called Wayside Waifs. I immediately said, "I want to work here!" And they were hiring a VP of Operations! The job description felt like it was written just for me.

Then the self-doubt creeped in. Was I qualified? Would they consider me? The call came. I was their first interview and became a finalist for the position competing against a woman with 30 years of experience. They hired her but offered me the volunteer manager position to get me in the door.

When I returned to North Carolina, I was faced with a very difficult conversation I needed to have with my boss. He was mad. He didn't speak to me those last two weeks.

Telling my grandmomma was even harder. I thought she'd never support me moving away, and boy was I surprised! She told me, "Not having you here will be the hardest thing I've ever experienced, but this is the only way you'll ever escape the shadow of your mom to live your own life. I want you to go." Kansas City has now been my home for 22 years.

And remember that volunteer manager position I took? Less than 15 months later, I was offered the VP of Operations position I'd originally applied for.

Not everything went well, however; the first few months in Kansas City were hard. By Christmas, I was considering moving back home. In March, I met my husband, Jeff. I'll never forget calling my aunt the day after meeting him to say, "I don't know if I'll ever see him again, but I feel like he's changed my life forever."

******

I spent eight years at Wayside Waifs before leaving to lead the merger of our nation's first bi-state animal welfare campus. Following a successful six-year career as CEO, I left there to lead a turnaround for a women's leadership development organization.

Now, I have the privilege of leading a domestic violence shelter. Jeff has seen me through three significant career moves, one of which forced me to walk away from a job and industry I loved because I was asked to do something unethical. My personal ethics and integrity are never up for sale.

We are raising three amazing children. Jeff stood beside me and supported me during the loss of four people who meant so much to me within two months of each other. The most important of whom was my grandmomma who died April 26, 2021.

Two and a half months later, Jeff was diagnosed with a rare and aggressive nasal cancer. I didn't even have time to process the other losses before I was staring at the possibility of losing my husband.

Jeff was given six months to live without successful treatment. Three surgeries, 31 radiation treatments, and two high-dose chemo treatments later ... he's still my partner in life and doing great.

******

So what are the lessons I've learned?
1. Our experiences simply shape us—they don't define us.
2. Your intuition is a powerful gift. Listen to it.
3. Don't let your past cause you to miss out on living in the present.
4. Stop doubting yourself. You were built to do and overcome hard things.
5. Sometimes we have to walk away from the things we love most to see in full view what the world has to offer us.

For all my life, I've said my grandmomma was the woman who built me. And there is no denying that. But now I'm realizing that my mom did, too. Had I not had to learn how to overcome and survive at such a young age, I may not have been able to successfully navigate some of the other personal and professional challenges in my life.

And there have been plenty.

Today is the first day of the rest of your life. What will you do with that gift?

Chapter thirty

Life Is About the Journey

by Jing Wang

I HAVE A 7-YEAR-OLD daughter. The other day, she rushed into my room and announced that she would be a scientist to study molecules when she grew up. Before that, it was a gymnast; and before that, a flying fairy. There must have been four or five other "occupations" before that, which have now eluded me forever.

She is everything I was not at that age. It was not that I did not want to grow up to be a fairy, or a gymnast, or a scientist. The question never crossed my mind. For one, there always seemed to be only one path for me—hard work, good schools, and a stable job. And there was a time, not too distant in the past, when I would feel even undeserving of that. For years, I could not shake the feeling that I was not enough.

I am that girl no more. This story is about a girl who finds the courage to write her own story. Now, dear reader, please bear with me because to tell her story properly, I must start before all this began.

******

"Does she like me? I wish I were a boy, then she will like me."

My mom's parents have six children. The first and the last are sons. The four daughters have the same Chinese character 娣 in their names. The character 娣 is made of a symbolic component on the left 女 (meaning female), and a phonetic component on the right 弟 (meaning younger brother).

As if the character itself is not enough to carry their hope for another son, my grandparents named their first daughter 来娣 (meaning younger brother to come), second 龙娣 (meaning dragon brother), third 金娣 (meaning golden brother), and my mother 红娣 (meaning popular brother). My mother was indeed the popular daughter of the family, not because of anything she did, but because a son did come after her.

With that family legacy, my mother always wanted a son and never doubted she would be blessed with one. She did not leave that to "chance" either. I heard countless tales from various family members of how she tilted the scale to her favor: how she asked her 3-year-old nephew to sleep in her wedding bed the night before the wedding; how she visited temples regularly to make wish; and how she ate so-claimed "magic food" in preparation of the pregnancy of a boy.

You can probably imagine her disappointment after my birth. China implemented very strict One-child Policy from 1980. The policy was enforced through contraception, abortion, financial penalties, and ultimately the denial of "Hukou," the legal registration in the country to do anything. Unlike her parents, my mom knows I am her first, last, and only child in this lifetime.

She did not try very hard to hide her disappointment. I was wearing short hair all the way until I could do my own braids. She rarely came to my singing recitals or dance performances. Even feminine products my father had to get for me from time to time. Somehow, I felt my mother liked to pretend that I was a boy and resented every reminder that I am not. She had strict rules about how I would look and dress, how I should stand and sit, and everything else in between. The only thing that would make her happy was seeing me getting good grades, grades better than any boy in the neighborhood could get.

"Does she like me? I wish I were a boy, then she will like me."

Years later, when I was reading my teenage-year diaries, those remarks jumped at me and brought with them a flood of emotions. This doubt has haunted my entire childhood and young adulthood. I did not know my mother starved me of her love inadvertently because of her disappointment of not having a son, or deliberately to turn me into a machine that knows nothing except to study. I yearned for her attention and worked for it the only way I knew how—to plunge myself into academics and inundate myself with schoolwork so I could come home with grades everyone envied. I chased after scholarships, awards, and any recognition I could get my hands on, not because I wanted them—I did not even know what I wanted—but because that would make my mother proud.

For most Chinese, the ultimate test we must face is the College Entrance Exam. It dates back almost 1,500 years—a national exam to select the best and brightest among every student in the country. For my teenage self, the exam bore the additional significance of how my mother would see me for the rest of her life—with forever pride or eternal regret. I studied day and night, almost compulsively. Because whenever I stopped, it felt like riding an emotional roller-coaster. One moment I would be exhilarated by the prospect that my success would seal my mother's love forever; the next I would drop to the abysmal thought that she would never talk about me without disappointment and regret should I fail to impress on the exam.

The moment did come after 12 years of hard studying. I got admitted to the School of Journalism at Fudan University, the most prestigious journalism program in the country. My mother threw a huge party, inviting every family and friend, neighbors, and some old colleagues she had not seen for years. It was hard to tell if the party was for me or her. Everyone came to me with a brief congratulation and then went on to surround my mother, who was busy bragging about how to raise a good kid.

"No boy in the family can achieve what I have achieved. She must be so proud and shall finally start to give me the love I deserve."

I sat at the table, eating the cake in front of me quietly and thinking. I tried to make eye contact through the crowd with my mom, but I did not think she noticed me.

The summer after the exam was like a honeymoon for my relationship with my mother. She catered to all my requests every day before I even said a word. She would spend half a day in the kitchen preparing a single meal for me. She took me to the hair salon and let me choose any style and color. She even planned a trip for the two of us. I felt drowned in her attention. I wanted it so badly throughout my childhood and yet it felt so foreign when I finally got it. I had to fake a stomachache to cancel the trip.

Well, it might not have been completely fake. I felt nervous, anxious, and sick because I didn't know how to spend so much time with her, alone. We had never done that before.

The summer of 2006, I felt validated and was convinced it was the happy ending between me and my mother. "That must be what success is all about—you work to meet people's expectations of you. All you need to do is work hard for it." I thought to myself. I was living the story of many obedient girls in China and never doubted the life ahead of me: graduate university, stable job, marriage to a traditional man. Unbeknownst to me, something else had been gradually developing in my life and would completely knock me off this path.

******

"Maybe I need to focus on what I want, at least for once."

I met a boy.

He and I went to the same middle school but sat in different classrooms, so we never spoke to each other between sixth and ninth grades. However, I have always known his name from all the math competitions he won. Upon graduating middle school, I chose an easy route to continue at the upper school without additional tests. He, on the other hand, applied to another top but more liberal high school in the area. He was somewhat notorious for breaking the rules, and I had the "privilege" of hearing quite a lot of personal accounts from some of his middle-school friends.

I truly "met" him at a college preparation facility during my last year of high school. We were seated next to each other because we scored highest in the area. We became friends almost instantly because of our common background. He was much better in mathematics and I in literacy, so we ended up helping each other out from time to time. Conversation with him was always fun. He seemed to be a living encyclopedia of weird tales and unconventional stories. College preparation was monotonous most of the time; his company put some extra flavor on it, making it much more bearable.

"What are you going to study in university?" I asked him two months before the exam when we were about to submit our application.

"Mathematics, of course." He did not seem to hesitate for a bit.

"Why? What are you going to do with it?"

"Because I like it. I will figure out what to do with it after I learn more."

He did not even hesitate for a second. The answer was so simple that it was disappointing and yet gratifying at the same time. Disappointing because I never knew one could choose something as important as a university major so callously, just because they liked it. What about your parents? Are you not even concerned about what kind of job you can get? However, deep down in my heart, it felt quite gratifying to see someone make major decisions with such freedom. How I wish I could do that.

The summer of 2006, while I was swimming in my mother's belated attention, he got admitted to the same school and the mathematics program. This allowed us to keep in contact in university. We even took several General Education courses together.

Our feelings grew stronger for each other. Reason told me I should shut it down. He was not exactly husband material in my mother's mind. He was not taller than I. He did not come from a well-established family and did not have a plan for a well-paid job after graduation. He had already decided after one semester of university mathematics to pursue graduate school abroad after graduation. The best we could hope for was a fling followed by a seemingly unescapable break-up.

I did not know where I got the courage, or perhaps where I lost my reason. I let my heart take precedence for the first time in my life. We started dating in our second year at university. I was never happier. Our life was quite routine, but the time with him was never boring. We would go to class together and try out different types of food around the campus. Occasionally we would go to a movie; but most of the time, we just walked around campus and talked about anything and everything. It seemed we would never run out of topics for conversation.

However, the happier I was, the more anxious it made me at the inevitable prospect of our separation after graduation.

"Why do you have to study abroad? Many people studying math go on to do finance. You should, too. We can start saving for our family and our parents can help us out with buying a house here." Many times, I would ask him to reconsider.

"I have so much more I want to learn. You can come with me. There are many great journalism schools in the States."

"I don't know if I want to continue studying after graduation, I need to figure out what I will do but I know my parents want me to stay here and have a family." I was not lying. My whole life at that time was about making my mother proud. I never entertained the thought of what I wanted and never really wanted anything.

But the moment I finished the sentence, my heart raced to the other end. "Maybe I need to focus on what I want, at least for once." I looked into his eyes, confirming that our relationship was the first thing I really wanted for myself, and I was not ready to let it go.

The spring of 2010, he received a scholarship to pursue a Ph.D. in Applied Mathematics at the Johns Hopkins University in Baltimore, Maryland. I turned down the offer to continue a master's degree at Fudan University. Instead, I started as a management trainee at Johnson and Johnson Pharmaceuticals (J&J) in Shanghai. I competed with thousands of new grads for two roles in marketing and I got one of them; the other guy was a long-term intern there. I had no intention of "having a career" at J&J; I was secretly hoping I could leverage the experience to apply for an MBA program in the States and reunite with him some day.

My mother was not happy with the decision at all. She wanted me to be the first one in the family to be exempted from the graduate school exam and to continue my study at Fudan. Or she would settle on having me climb the career ladder at J&J and be a director in the company someday. I mustered all my courage to fight her off on that front and could not bring myself to tell her that my boyfriend was going to the States for at least five years and might or might not come back. She had already frowned upon our relationship for all the reasons I had imagined and more. I was not going to pour liquor on that fire.

I saw him off at the airport in August of 2010, thinking that must be the end. "We will figure something out," he told me, with the same unfounded confidence he'd expressed when he told me he would figure out what to do after studying math.

His name is Yikang. And he was right. Our story was just about to begin.

******

"I am enough, and I am ready to have a new beginning."

Half the people I knew told me long-distance relationships were hard; the other half said they were impossible. I started mine in the summer of 2010, with no light down the tunnel. Working as a management trainee was no breeze either. I got off work every day close to 9:00 pm and immediately jumped on a call with Yikang. Every morning, I woke up at 7:00 am to Yikang's call. That was our happiness, fighting for our life and dream, connected on the opposite ends of the earth.

I did not know how we made it work, but it only seemed natural as we both longed for each other's story and could not wait to share our emotions. The only thing we would argue about was the GMAT exam I needed to take for my MBA application.

"I think you should just go ahead and take it. Stop worrying about the preparation. You can always take it again."

"My work is just too busy. I have no time to prepare. I won't do well if I don't prepare! You don't understand because you always nailed the test without much studying, and you don't need to juggle between work, study, and life like I do."

Some people are born warriors; I was born a worrier. I lived my whole life worrying about my mother's approval, my grades, my relationship eventually coming to a demise. I worried about anything and everything. I did not know where I found the courage to eventually take the exam. I had to do it twice, double the pain.

Fortunately, I received a full scholarship from George Washington University. I was ecstatic. On the other hand, my mother was not happy with my decision. We did not talk much about this imminent change for months until she finally blew up the day of my flight.

"Why would you choose him and leave everything behind? How would you know he would marry you? What if he doesn't? You would be 'leftovers' if he does not marry you!" My mother bombarded me with rhetorical questions, which quickly escalated to scolding and insulting. I was covered in tears and could not bring myself to say anything in rebuke. I finished packing, with my head down, and not a word before we headed to the airport the next morning. I waved goodbye at the gate, and I saw tears in her eyes.

Growing up, it had been my worst nightmare how my mother would react when I defied her orders and wandered off the path that she planned for me. Bad as it hurt, I did not flinch. "I am enough, and I am ready to have a new beginning." I waved goodbye to her, but I noticed she covered her face. If this was the price that I had to pay to pursue my happiness, I would do it again, with sole control of my fate and nobody else dictating terms for my freedom. That day, I left behind the girl who wished to be a boy. Someone else got on the flight that night, someone with the courage to choose for herself and the composure to face any consequence.

I cannot say my life in the States has not been difficult, but it has certainly been eventful. Yikang and I continued our long-distance relationship for another three years. As an international student, I was extremely fortunate to secure a Leadership Program offer from Mars before graduation. While I have been with Mars, I have spent time on multiple different units across the country, performing a wide variety of functions.

Believe it or not, I also found my passion for bringing different people together—on the team, within the unit, and within the Mars group altogether. I had the opportunity to lead cross-regional teams in building new M&Ms® stores across the globe, streamlining many enterprise processes in conjunction with developing long-term strategies.

******

"Life is not about the destination, but the journey itself."

If I travelled back in time to tell my younger self about the future awaiting her, she would probably consider me crazy. I spent 18 years crouching into this well-protected shell my mother envisioned for me. It then took many years to climb out of it. The old Jing would be content to live someone else's story and dream. The new Jing will not let anyone dictate what she can or cannot achieve.

The fall of 2015, Yikang got a job offer in New York City, which finally put a definitive date to the end of our long-distance relationship. We decided to get married at the end of the year. One night, we were sitting on the couch and something suddenly occurred to me.

"Do you remember the first year we met you told me you are just going to study math and figure out what to do later? You said the same thing about our relationship that we would work something out. How did you know that?"

"I didn't know. It's also not me who worked out everything. You were the one studying while working, navigating the graduate school in a different country, and eventually finding a job that laid our foundation here. You are amazing and you should take credit for that."

"No, we did it together." I could not hide my smile.

We held our wedding on the last day of 2015 in Shanghai. That was the second time I witnessed my mother surrounded by family and friends, bathed in their congratulations. Only this time, she was not sharing experiences on how to raise a successful daughter. But just as I had learned to cope with her the only way I knew how, it was also her first time being a mother and she was loving me the only way she knew how. She was overly cautious because she lived under the same expectation and pressure her whole life. She was more scared of my failure than I ever was. And in the end, she was happier about my life choices than I ever imagined.

Yikang and I now live happily in New Jersey. Our 7-year-old already has lots of her own opinions. It seems futile to plan anything for her. Sometimes I imagine how she will grow up, other times I worry about when things may go wrong; but most times I am just grateful. I know she is enough for me, and it is enough for me to just love her. She is so different from what I expected and yet she is everything I could ask for, just like how my life has been unfolding.

"Mom, I want to be a scientist to study molecules." My 7-year-old rushed to the room and shouted after watching a YouTube® video.

"That's cool, I love that!" I responded immediately, not knowing what molecules were.

"What if I don't know everything, can I still be a scientist?" she started rambling.

"Of course! No one knows everything, it is all about what you find out along the way! Life is not about the destination, but the journey itself."

Chapter thirty-one

Words You Keep

by Becky Whatley

IF YOU GREW UP as a girl in California in the 1970s or 1980s, as I did, you may remember those notes in high school. The ones written on notepaper, folded into intricate shapes that rivaled origami, and slipped to your bestie between classes.

No texting for us; we communicated with pen on paper then. You asked your friends for advice on that boy you crushed on, whether to go to the football game, how to deal with your mom who is driving you crazy, what to say to your teacher because you were late with the paper due that day. The questions and answers to life at that time.

I amassed quite a lot of those creased and crimped missives. Shoeboxes full. Bags full.

Sometime in my twenties, faced with a move, and lots of packing boxes, I discarded all those notes along with other memorabilia from my youth.

Those notes chronicled the angst and turmoil during that decade of my life, but it didn't seem important to keep them.

Experiences I thought I would "never get over" and disappointments I was sure would scar me didn't really manifest.

Knowing I escaped fairly unscathed from those vulnerable
teenage days might be why I'm perplexed that I would be so
wounded by a single comment in my early professional life. Just a
joke by the Human Resources (HR) consultant in a follow-up conversation to a personality assessment I had taken. Her meant-to-
be-funny remark stayed with me for a long time, however, and
actually grew to become a judgment on how I show up in the
world.

******

Personality profiles were trending in the 1990s, marketed as a
resource to help with team-building to create more efficient production systems and provide better customer service. After fin-
ishing high school, I had begun working in the franchise print
shop that my father had recently opened. At an industry conference one year, an HR company had a booth offering a free assessment—something called the DISC® profile.

At the time, that particular product claimed there were four
personality profiles: Driver, Influencer, Steady, and Conscientiousness. Other versions of this assessment have listed these as
Decisive, Influence, Support, and Clarity.

The original DISC® profile (not the assessment), created by
American psychologist William Marston in the 1920s as a model
of human behavior, listed four basic personality types: Dominance, Inducement, Submission, and Compliance. The first letter
of these contributed to the name of both the model and the later

initial assessment created in 1956, when three of the types were renamed Influence, Steadiness, and Conscientiousness.

That day in July 1995, a female consultant I knew was working the booth. I wanted to support another woman in the industry, and I liked her quick wit accompanied by a brash Texan laugh. She and I were becoming friends the way that you do when you see each other at annual events. I agreed to spend a few minutes to take the test and the results were quickly returned.

"Well," she said, as she scanned my results, "Bec, I gotta say, this doesn't surprise me. You're one of the rare personality matches. You see, this personality type in less than 9% of the population. Look here, you're almost off-the-chart on D."

She pointed to the bright bar next to the D. Driver.

Didn't sound too bad.

I guess I should be grateful that I completed the assessment at a time when more friendly language was being used. But whether you ascribe Driver, Decisive, or Dominance to the D, the descriptive words tend to remain the same: self-confident, decisive, tough, competitive, aggressive, overbearing, demanding.

"You're pretty high on I, too," she added. "In fact, you are such a high D, that if you weren't such a high I, you'd be a big B." We both laughed, knowing what this letter stood for, as you do when you're strong women in a male-dominated field.

For months, that comment found its way into my thoughts. I mulled over the significance of this assessment of my personality. As I did, I embedded the description into my psyche. Not merely the harsh words, all those words with negative connotations, but also the B-word.

The unfortunate fact is, her off-hand comment made in jest, paired with the results of that assessment, genuinely influenced my opinion of myself. It also became a self-fulfilling prophecy. I attached that simple slur—one that we as women oftentimes toss around as a joke or sometimes claim as a badge of honor—to the attributes of self-confidence with a connection stronger than Krazy Glue®.

******

I continued to manage the family business. Over the years, I joined Junior League of Riverside, Chambers of Commerce, Kiwanis Club, American Marketing Association, and National Association of Women Business Owners. I served on boards, often as president, chaired committees, and led teams and groups. By now, I held stock in our small company that we had incorporated.

I was definitely a leader and a Driver.

I was confident, strong, influential, decisive … and often overbearing, demanding, and aggressive. For the most part, I was proud of my self-confidence, and I figured those descriptors just came with the territory.

Wasn't a woman business owner supposed to be strong and confident? After all, didn't comedian Tina Fey's popular 2008 Saturday Night Live "Weekend Update" declare that "bitches get stuff done?"

But by embracing the "bitch" tag alongside "confidence," I wasn't benefiting from a "grounded confidence" described by Brené Brown as "a powerful sense of self that comes from accurate analysis of what we've done and what we can do." For me, it was more a postured confidence, a façade, with a big helping of a hidden shame.

******

I am prone to hold myself to a higher standard than I hold others. To expect more of myself, and to be less forgiving of mistakes. I focus on my flaws and flubs rather than my achievements and successes.

Skills and abilities that came easy to me I just figured came easy to everyone. I didn't recognize particular gifts or special talent. Instead, I worried about what I didn't do well, and pushed myself to "figure it out." Working with family certainly didn't help. My father and brother, both working in the business, most frequently pointed out what I did wrong or different than they would have. A pat on the back was fleeting. Discussion of how I screwed up something was spoken of time and time again.

I was also recently divorced after a few years of marriage when we finally admitted that we didn't want the same things in life. Even though it was amicable, I filed it away as another failure.

In a subsequent relationship, I dated a charming, impulsive, manipulative, younger man. His rebel nature attracted me, but his out-of-control behavior scared me. That fear caused me to double down on regaining control of my life. Since we lived together, he saw this as controlling him. Maybe there was an element of that. By that time, I couldn't tell any more. I was always so determined to be in charge, thinking it was my responsibility to keep things from going off the rails.

While outwardly praising my drive—"oh how sexy a self-confident woman is!"—he also threw out remarks he knew would take me down a peg or two: veiled insults, pointed slights. A couple years of this, and we imploded, with hurt feelings and bitter invective. Never actually calling me a bitch. But I heard it anyway.

I was unhappy, confused, and lonely in a way that had nothing to do with not having a partner. But, as women often do, I kept myself going with determination and strong-but-shaky affirmations: "I've got this," "I can do this," "I'm okay." Until I wasn't.

Father, brother, ex-husband, now ex-boyfriend. In my psyche, it all piled up. Add in the other day-to-day defeats like a missed sales opportunity, an angry customer, an argument with a friend ... and a stuck toner cartridge.

One afternoon just before closing, printing out the day's reports, the printer jammed. I pulled and twisted, managed to get the cartridge out, and removed the paper stuck in the gears. Then I couldn't get the cartridge back in. I tried, I failed, I tried again and again, and that's when I started to sob. I broke down, crying, gasping, unable to catch my breath.

There I was, holding that damn cartridge and trying desperately to breathe. A full-blown panic attack. Over a jammed printer. Or maybe just my jammed up life.

******

For all those years, I carried a harmful self-image: I thought my confidence made me a bitch. The way my life was going, that judgment seemed to have been proven right: "This, this is what happens, this is what I deserve."

I had never been at such a low point, with a sick dread that anything could ever be better again.

I'm nothing if not driven, however. You can't hold back that high of a D. Once I calmed down and got my breath back, I knew I needed to get help. But what kind, exactly?

My ex-husband and I had visited a marriage and family therapist for a few sessions before we finally pulled the plug, so I thought maybe I should try that again. I pulled out the Yellow

Pages® and thumbed through to Therapists. Going down the page, I called three or four of those listed.

After 5:00 pm now, no answer; I left voice mails. That's when the Universe kicked into gear. Kate Kelley called me back, the only one who did; but as it turned out the only one who needed to because she was The One. Kate helped me through those shaky days. I had no idea what to expect but I was willing to open up to her, pour out everything—the good, the bad and the ugly—and see if she could help me come back from what felt like rock bottom.

In contrast to my self-confidence façade, I actually had a low opinion of myself; I remember describing my life as "smoke and mirrors." She listened patiently and assisted me in gaining perspective. She helped me curb my rush to negative self-judgment and recognize when I was being unjustly hard on myself. Most importantly, Kate gave me permission to really believe in my self-worth, not just pretend I did.

Choosing to go into therapy was one of the best decisions I've ever made. And finding Kate was a blessing. She has continued to offer support as I navigate my life.

Finding women who believe in you and help you believe in yourself—whether they are your therapist, mentor, life coach, mother, or best friend—can make all the difference. We can't always see ourselves clearly; the right person can gently open our eyes with love and kindness

******

In a bit of irony, that deeper level of clarity came to me from another personality assessment many years later. I attended another conference, this one geared toward women, where I was offered something called Your Talent Advantage™. This version was created by Lynda-Ross Vega and her partner, Gary Jordan, Ph.D. of Vega Behavioral Consulting based on their Perceptual Style Theory™. Naturally I couldn't resist, so I signed up and paid the $297 price to learn more about myself.

However, weeks went by, and then months; I avoided starting the assessment. I lost the link in the email. I decided not to pursue it.

Was there a correlation between my disappointing view of myself based on the previous DISC® assessment and my reluctance to follow through on this one? Probably. Most likely. Whatever the reason, I never completed the assessment.

A year later, at another conference, Lynda-Ross and her husband, Ricardo, were there. I skirted around the table, not about to sign up for something I didn't make use of before. Ricardo hailed me, "You didn't complete the assessment!" How in the world could he remember this? I demurred, telling him it's been too long, I understand things change, I don't expect him to honor my payment from a year ago. But he insisted, "Nonsense! Of course, we will. We will send you a link."

A link that changed my life.

I took the assessment, not expecting results much different from anything I've done before. But this was different. The description of me, my personality, different. The labels, different. Not judgmental words, but whole sentences, meaningful phrases describing skills, roles, natural abilities.

More than just a profile, it was a chronicle of my unique talents. Not a list of unhelpful adjectives, but a generous narrative of the why and how of ME. In almost every sentence, I recognized myself. This was so much more than mere labels. Uniquely me. My innate talents. My gifts. Additionally, I met with Lynda-Ross to go over my results. She went page-by-page, answering my questions, explaining my strengths.

Certainly, I had heard versions of this before. Maybe I had even acknowledged some of my talents in the past. This, however, was like a lightbulb illuminating. More, a floodlight shining down on me and chasing away all the shadow thoughts, the "I'm not good enough." "I haven't proven myself." "Who do you think you are?" thoughts.

The little manual about me, and the one-on-one with Lynda-Ross, made such an impact on me. Paired together, this experience helped root out the decades of distorted self-belief and filled that space with positive images that resonated.

Hello, me!

******

Self-knowledge is crucial; self-acceptance even better. My personality is my personality. That's it, there's no judgment there. No bad nor good, no right nor wrong. There are strengths and benefits in how I think—fast understanding, swift interpretation, rapid connection, quick decision. There are strengths and benefits in the way I communicate—energetic, colorful, persuasive— as well as some challenges, some things to be aware of, to modify as needed.

But me, uniquely me. Valuable as I am.

It was like a switch, or so it seemed at the time, from off to on, from lack of self-worth to "I'm enough, just as I am." There's no switch, really, because you rarely feel "on" all the time. Or, thankfully, off. There are days I rule my world, and rock it. And days when I feel like getting out of bed was a mistake; I cry, rage, and feel sorry for myself.

It turns out, however, that I really love this gloriously messy, fallible, brash, compassionate, fiercely loyal woman that I am. And oh, how I want the same for you.

If I could, I would tear out this page to highlight and underline passages. I would fold it up tightly in a small triangle and pass it over to you. To have it be a reminder to you to seek out and recognize your own talents, and to give yourself the gift of really loving and liking yourself.

Because that's what friends do for each other, right?

Chapter thirty-two

Learning to Thrive Not Just Survive

by Michelle Wimes

FOUR YEARS AGO, in the middle of a global health pandemic, I left a coveted position as the inaugural Chief Diversity and Professional Development Officer for one of the nation's largest labor and employment law firms in order to take a position as the inaugural Chief Equity and Inclusion Officer (CEIO) at my city's only pediatric hospital.

On the one hand I was elated, as COVID-19 had forced us all inside and remote work proliferated. It simply wasn't possible to travel to one of my firm's 50+ offices, where I was responsible for developing and implementing initiatives to ensure our 900+ lawyers had the professional skills to do their jobs effectively while learning to be culturally proficient leaders.

On the other hand, I was a bit terrified, as the healthcare disparities that had always disproportionately impacted BIPOC (Black, Indigenous, People of Color) communities were receiving much more press, and I knew part of my job would be to develop strategies to disrupt those disparities even though I had no experience in healthcare.

******

When I decided to leave the practice of law some 15+ years ago, many folks thought I was crazy. By then, I had worked my way up to equity partner in a small regional law firm where I practiced special education law, a niche practice I enjoyed. I was my firm's first Black part-time partner. Folks asked why I would leave an equity partnership to move into law firm administration. Well, I was unhappy.

As a Black female lawyer, I found myself uniquely positioned at the intersection of racial and gender biases, a crossroads that profoundly shaped my professional experience and personal well-being. My story, fraught with systemic challenges, often left me navigating a complex terrain that was both disheartening and exhausting.

In a profession that is predominantly white and male, my presence as a Black woman often felt like an anomaly. This sense of otherness is not just a perception; it manifested in tangible ways. The unhappiness that I experienced was rooted in a complex interplay of racial and gender biases. These challenges forged my path of resilience and advocacy. As I continued to break barriers and redefine norms, I contributed to a broader societal change toward equity through inclusion.

******

I was tired of arguing with other lawyers, and I had been recently diagnosed with lupus, a chronic illness that was exacerbated by stress (though no one outside my immediate family knew that, and it remained undisclosed until last year).

So, once again, I faced the same inquiry when I jumped from a world I knew (law firms) to the unknown (hospitals and medical systems). The decision was not an easy one—starting over at age 54, re-building my credibility in a different industry, and learning whether the principles of DEI homed in the legal sector would translate to a healthcare setting.

My professional journey as a practicing lawyer and later as a law firm and healthcare administration leader helped me uncover many lessons about leadership, career ownership, and resilience. I've learned that diverse professionals must share our stories so that attempts to marginalize our voices will lose their power and impact.

I know too many seasoned professionals who still carry the burden of being treated differently and have attempted to bury their pain and disillusionment by keeping silent and blending into the majority to assimilate. This is a problem.

Unless minorities and women start to tell our stories in our own voices and learn how to leverage our differences, a fundamental understanding and support for diversity programs, policies, and initiatives will remain elusive.

Somehow, we've all colluded to make stories of differential treatment unspeakable, and by doing so, we've given them more power. Their survival feeds off not talking about them.

By sharing our stories, we make them a necessary part of the conversation. It's time to peel back the painful layers and discuss the real stories behind the façade.

There is so much power in storytelling. Because as radical as it may seem, stories help us understand the realities people face and endure in their personal and professional lives. They can help us delve more deeply into the mindset needed to overcome barriers.

******

I graduated from law school 30 years ago. There were myriad challenges during the 14 years I practiced law, first as an associate, then as counsel, and later as an equity partner. One of my biggest challenges was the double whammy of being a racial minority as well as a woman in a field dominated by white men.

Thirty years ago, I was dissecting Kimberle Crenshaw's work on intersectionality because I felt left out of the discourse as a Black woman. The focus was on the impact of women entering the profession in more significant numbers. Then, the focus evolved around the lack of racial and ethnic minorities, especially in large law firms and Fortune 100 companies. There was rarely a discussion about the specific challenges faced by women of color or other minorities. Intersectionality has been defined as "the interplay of race, class, and gender, often resulting in multiple dimensions of disadvantage." Crenshaw's work in this area was the missing lens that I needed.

My first experience with these intersecting identities came early in my career. After completing the first semester of law school, I interviewed for a summer associate position with a Midwestern law firm and began that clerkship the summer after my first year. One of the most exciting things about being a summer associate at a law firm was being treated like a true lawyer regarding office size and salary. So, as superficial as it sounds, I was looking forward to this.

I grew up with both parents, neither of whom had a college degree but had very stable government jobs. I knew no one in my immediate family or circle who had their own office, was a lawyer, or made anything close to the lawyers' salaries in law firm practice.

On the first day of work, each of us was taken to our respective individual offices. As we dropped off each summer intern, we all "oohed" and "aahed" at each office. They were nice and spacious. I was the last person to be shown my office, and unlike my co-horts, all of whom were white and two of whom were also female, I was given a much smaller and less elegant paralegal's office with no fanfare or explanation.

It was a devastating blow to an inexperienced intern who expected the playing field to be level. Though dismayed, I set up my office and went to work. I did not know if I had been given a smaller office because I was the only Black, the only Black female, or because I was the only first-year law student. I assumed the latter and worked even harder that summer to demonstrate to myself and the lawyers at the firm that they did not make a mistake in hiring me.

Why, after 30 years should this matter to me? Why do I remember this situation so well all these years later? Because it was the first time in my professional career that I remember not feeling good enough. It was a subtle, devaluing message, a micro-inequity, which did not need to be verbally communicated but was in full view for everyone to see.

Whenever one of my fellow summer associates walked by my office or came in to chat with me, what must my physical surroundings have communicated to them? What about the attorneys for whom I worked? I was dogged all summer by the questions of whether I was good enough to be there, whether I deserved the job, whether I had what it took to be successful, whether I was an "affirmative action" hire. After all, I met two criteria: I am Black and I am a woman.

******

Kenji Yoshino defines covering as toning down a disfavored identity to fit into the mainstream. That summer, I toned down my "Blackness" as much as I could. I never told anyone I grew up on the east side of town. I never told anyone that my parents weren't professionals. I code-switched all day, every day. I had a different tone, demeanor, and language during the day as opposed to when I arrived at my parents' home weary after a long day of being my inauthentic self.

I lived in two worlds—the posh world where I was making a lawyer's salary, the equivalent of $1,000 a week, and the world where I would often awaken to the sounds of police sirens and gunfire in the wee hours of the morning.

Despite my environment, one thing my parents cultivated in me was a mindset of positivity and persistence. You simply did not quit; a victim mentality was not an option in our household. So, that summer, I chose to be engaged despite how I felt inside.

I went on the summer associate float trip, a first for me. I cheered my colleagues on in the summer baseball league. I wined and dined with clients, law firm partners, and peers. I worked hard, was given plum assignments, and much-needed critical feedback. My work was stellar; and at the end of the summer, I earned an offer to return for the summer following my second year of law school. That second summer resulted in another earned offer for permanent employment upon graduation.

During the first few years of my practice with the firm, I became active in the local civic and bar community. I helped start a nationally recognized charter school and became board vice president, fostering my leadership skills. I took on pro bono cases honing my writing, communication, and advocacy skills.

I helped the local Black Bar Association establish its inaugural minority scholarship program, nurturing a budding interest in legal diversity issues. I helped run student mediation programs in local high schools, improving my negotiation skills. I staffed "Ask a Lawyer Telethons," providing free community legal advice, refining my critical thinking and analytical skills.

In short order, I began to build a reputation for getting things done outside the law firm, which, in turn, increased my confidence and helped bolster my performance within the law firm.

******

I gave birth to two daughters during my third and fifth years of practice and automatically inherited another intersecting identity—that of a working mother. During my first pregnancy, I was asked more than once by male peers whether I intended to return to work full-time after the birth of my child. Frankly, this shocked me.

The working women in my life experiences, admittedly all Black, had all returned to work after birthing their babies. Why would I be any different? It never crossed my mind to not return to work full-time, so that's exactly what I did after the birth of all three of my daughters (my third daughter arrived five years later just before I was promoted to partner).

I was one of two Black partners in a small regional firm and the only reduced-hours partner. I helped to start the firm's first diversity committee and was an active member of the women's affinity group, which I joined when I realized that I was working more hours as a reduced-hours partner than many older white men allegedly working "full-time." After a while, this inequity was one of the reasons I decided to leave the practice of law altogether and embrace an opportunity to champion women's rights and diverse lawyers in a formal position.

******

I spent almost four years as the Director of Strategic Initiatives at an AmLaw 100 firm, where I was formally responsible for developing diversity programming in seven U.S. offices and two international offices and where my innovative professional development programs for diverse lawyers were emulated and ultimately impacted how all firm lawyers were recruited, hired, developed, and promoted.

I left that firm and later led the talent management, diversity, and inclusion departments at a much larger boutique labor and employment firm. I left both firms in better positions than when I joined them.

I now serve as the inaugural CEIO at Children's Mercy Hospital in Kansas City, Missouri. I create transformative programming and initiatives to support health equity for our patients and families while building a diverse workforce that is also an inclusive workplace. I know that I will continue to do my part to ensure that my unique personal and professional experiences and differences, as well as those of my under-represented colleagues, are brought to bear in this process. My past has undoubtedly prepared me.

As I navigate this welcomed responsibility of empowering underserved communities in my professional life, I do so while facing new uncharted territory in my personal life, inheriting yet another intersecting identity. As I write this, I have taken 60 days off from work. I have made the difficult decision to leave my marriage. The journey, laden with personal anguish, is further complicated by the weight of cultural expectations and professional pressures. I never once believed I'd be in this position, especially after 27 years of marriage; and the fear of professional repercussions for personal life events is a constant stressor.

Yet, as a Black professional woman, I must challenge myself, not only in my work endeavors, but also personally to elevate my self-awareness and heal myself as I actively manifest the life I deserve to live.

As I sit in the valley of this, what I know to be true is that marriage requires feeling seen and heard and equity of effort to do the work together and apart. It requires loyalty, trust, integrity, and a deep commitment to one's own healing and personal development—understanding the shadows that each person brings to the relationship without making the other person responsible for healing them

In truth, I abandoned myself long ago. Sadly, I adjusted to an alternative version of the deep emotional connection my soul truly craved while the unhealed inner child within me consistently chose safety—and the ever-alluring appeal of potential—over reality.

******

I am learning the importance of self-care and guidance from others. Reaching out to others in a global support group for married women experiencing the same or similar challenges has helped. This group has provided a safe space to unpack my feelings without fear of judgment. As I continue to navigate this difficult chapter of my life, I am learning to redefine my identity beyond the confines and societal expectations of student, lawyer, leader, wife, and mother.

In sharing my story, I hope to shed light on the unique challenges Black professional women face and to remind others in similar situations that they are not alone in their struggle.

For I will continue to get up, dress up, and show up ... as I try to thrive ... not just survive.

Afterword

Own Your Story

by Lesley Marlin & Jennifer Thibodaux

THANK YOU FOR READING this anthology. Whether you purchased the book for yourself or it was gifted to you, we hope that reading these stories has had a profound impact.

This book was inspired by the #EmpoweredWomen storytelling event because, simply put, speaking at and attending the event transformed us. We tried to capture the magic of that event in this anthology to continue to amplify women's voices, and we are grateful for your support.

But this book is also meant to teach.

As you read the stories, you may have cried and you may have laughed. You may have seen yourself in some of the stories.

Maybe these stories gave you a different perspective or new ideas. Maybe you realized we are a lot more alike than we are different.

Maybe these stories have inspired you and have given you hope. Maybe they empowered you to take action or create change.

And you might be asking yourself, "What now?" Well, it's your turn and time. Own Your Story! No one's storytelling journey is

the same. As you explore and embark on your own storytelling
journey, here are ideas to consider:

Understand That You Have a Story

We used to think, "I don't have a story" or "My story doesn't
matter." Let's debunk those myths right away. Each one of us has
a story. And each story matters. You don't need to have suffered
a tragedy, overcome an insurmountable obstacle, or be "special"
in some way. Yes, those stories matter—but so does yours.

Your story will resonate with someone who has a similar lived
experience, or it will resonate with someone who is nothing like
you. The person who is like you will realize they are not alone; the
person who is not like you will realize we are all more alike than
different.

Stories create connection, have impact, and effectuate
change—as long as we understand that our stories matter!

Be Curious & Learn About Storytelling

Start watching out for stories and storytelling as you go
through your daily life. As you do that, don't be surprised if you
start noticing stories in places and spaces you never expected.

Stories can be big or small. They can be about your career
change or health journey, but they can also be about that conversation with an elderly relative or an interaction with the stranger
in line behind you while you got a coffee. What did you take away
from the exchange? How did it make you feel? Pay attention and
allow yourself to be curious. What stories speak to you? What do
you find compelling—message, delivery, or both?

Learn about storytelling. There are so many resources out
there—from anthologies like ours to storytelling books to classes

to coaches and more. Knowing about the types of stories and the different ways to use them can help you start to see your own stories and how you might use them.

Find Your Message & Stories

Think about your life story and then think about the tapestry of stories that make up your life. What have you learned? What did you wish you knew then? What would you like others to know?

Think about your professional stories and think about your personal stories. Where are there similarities and where are there differences? Consider creating your own message and story "bank" that you can use when there are storytelling opportunities.

Consider what works for you: a journal where you can jot down stories or notes? An MSWord® document or Google Docs®? An email folder so you can email stories to yourself and save them? A note on your phone? Find what works. You might not be sure of how you will use a story one day—or even a quote—but if it speaks to you, memorialize it!

Know Your Audience

Who are you speaking with or to? What do they care about? What will help them? What do you want them to know, feel, and then do? Truly knowing your audience is critical to making sure your message and stories will be heard and well-received. Remember, your story is about you but your message or call to action is all about them.

Harness the Power of Storytelling – Content & Delivery

As you work to harness the power of storytelling, focus on both the content and the delivery. How can you show the listener and reader the content instead of just telling them it? Bring them on the journey with you. Use sensory details to engage the audience and create connection between you and them. What emotions do you want them to feel as they listen to or read your story?

For the delivery, how can you choose words to elicit those emotions? For spoken delivery, how are you embodying the emotions of your story as you tell it? Consider your tone, inflection, volume, and pacing. Can you use photographs or images? Maybe some props or mementos from your story?

When we experiment, play, and create, magic can happen. Own Your Story. When you do, you empower, connect, and create change.

Group Discussion Questions

Reflection on Personal Growth:

- How did each woman's journey reflect her personal growth and transformation? Can you identify specific turning points in their stories?
- In what ways did the challenges faced by these women shape their identities and life paths?

Understanding Diversity of Experience:

- How do these women's experiences reflect the diversity of women's experiences worldwide? Are there universal themes, or do their journeys highlight the importance of context and culture?
- How do the stories challenge or reinforce your perceptions of what it means to be a woman in today's society?

Themes of Resilience and Empowerment:

- What does resilience look like in the context of these narratives? How did each woman demonstrate resilience in the face of adversity?
- In what ways were these women empowered through their journeys? How did they find strength and confidence?

Impact of Social and Cultural Factors:

- How do social, cultural, and even political factors influence the shero journeys of these women? Can you draw connections between their personal stories and broader societal issues?
- How do the stories address themes of inequality, discrimination, or injustice, if at all? What lessons can be drawn about overcoming such barriers?

Personal Connection and Reflection:

- Which story resonated with you the most, and why? Are there aspects of any journey that you particularly identified with or were moved by?
- How have these stories influenced your understanding of your own life journey or challenges you've faced?

Action and Change:

- What actions or changes are inspired by reading these stories? How might you apply insights from these journeys to your own life or community?

- How do these stories contribute to the conversation about women's rights, equality, and empowerment in your society?

The Role of Support Systems:

- What role did support systems (family, friends, mentors, communities) play in these women's journeys? How did support, or the lack thereof, impact their paths?
- How can communities and societies better support women in their personal and professional shero journeys?

Freeman
MEANS BUSINESS
Amplifying women's voices
through storytelling.

SUSAN FREEMAN created Freeman Means Business (FMB) to empower women through storytelling, community, and connection. FMB amplifies women's voices through signature #EmpoweredWomen initiatives and events, including:

- Our annual **#EmpoweredWomen** storytelling event featuring live talks, workshops, and networking.
- The Wonder Women in Business podcast sharing stories from women entrepreneurs, lawyers, coaches, and professionals across various industries.
- **#EmpoweredWomenRead** book club focusing on women's autobiographies.
- **#EmpoweredWomen** wellness retreats taking a holistic approach to self-care.
- Wine, Women, and Wisdom small group events connecting local women in various cities.

And now, this list includes the **#EmpoweredWomenWrite** anthology!

These events and projects are designed to foster self-awareness, personal growth, and a network of mutual support among women. We hope that you will join us!

For more information, visit www.freemanmeansbusiness.com and connect with us on social media: @FreemanMeansBusiness on LinkedIn and Facebook.

Made in the USA
Monee, IL
16 June 2024

60013300R00203